MW01487695

One Stop West of Hinsdale

"What happens when great love fails; when the unimaginable comes to pass; when secrets replace trust, and anger becomes the new language? "One Stop West of Hinsdale" takes you on that journey—from a tight-knit loving family to one fractured by betrayal, failed dreams, and addiction. This coming-of-age memoir written by the middle adult child of three as a letter to her beloved but deceased father, asks some profound questions which have continued to plague her some fifty years after leaving home. Does she find answers? Yes, some. But no journey of self-discovery, if honest, answers them all. A beautiful, sometimes painful testament of someone brave enough to dig deep."

Susan Richards
New York Times Bestselling author of *Chosen by a Horse*

"Valerie Kuhn Reid has given her memoir an intriguing shape: it's a conversation, as if spoken directly to her dad, though he is no longer alive. Now in her sixties, Reid feels mature enough and well-equipped enough to grasp the complexities of her parents' divorce, her beloved dad's remarriage and seeming abandonment. In poignant scenes from childhood and more turbulent ones from adolescence, she insists that he see her and understand all he missed and all she lost. But this story is neither bleak nor despairing; in the end, it's a kind of testament to a writer's candor, enduring love, and bravery, as well as to the act of making peace with the past."

Kate Kennedy
Author of *Skin: A Memoir*

"*One Stop West of Hinsdale* is a book of longing. Shifting with eerie ease between herself as a young Nancy Drew and as an adult Agatha Christie, Valerie Kuhn Reid takes us on her sleuthing journey to uncover the astounding and confounding mystery of her original family's dissolution. Ms. Kuhn-Reid's alchemy renders her search for the truth both heart-rending and, with her gloriously persistent, stubborn optimism, somehow hopeful. The pages turn themselves as we plunge headlong into this case of family secrets and lies alongside both youthful and older Val as she uncovers clues, spots inconsistencies, chases red herrings and, ultimately, weaves a tale of deep, abiding love rich with the transcendent power of forgiveness.

Lisa Stathoplos
Author of *Make Me: A Memoir*

For Brent and Audrey

Hold on to what is good
    even if it is a handful of earth.
Hold on to what you believe
    even if it is a tree which stands by itself.
Hold on to what you must do
    even if it is a long way from here.
Hold on to life
    even when it is easier letting go.
Hold on to my hand
    even when I have gone away from you.

Pueblo Verse

Prologue

I've been alive for 65 years, Dad. You've been dead for thirty. For the past few years, I've been writing about you, but today I realized that it's *to* you I should write. That's the answer, isn't it? It's you who needs to hear this story. You, I need to tell. You may be dead in this world, but you are alive in the next, and I would not be surprised if you are saying to yourself, *"Finally."*

I started writing in the first place, because something happened that blew me back to the past. Meg's husband went missing. The people of Nantucket searched and prayed, and one prayer got answered—they found him. But he had ended his life. You probably knew all this before I did and I'm sure it broke your heart.

I prayed for Meg and their six children, and then I sat there wondering at the way life can keep such secrets from us. Keep them, then fling them at us years later, in ways we could never guess at years before.

From there my mind took off. It carried me back to the day I met Meg—a curly-haired girl in a pack of youngsters who appeared out of nowhere, calling you "Dad." Then further still, to the time before Meg, when we were happy, and you belonged to us and no one else.

I thought about how Meg grew up to stay with a suffering spouse, while others choose to leave. You, for instance, who chose to leave Mom. You, who chose to leave us.

When did we start to lose you? When you met Barbara, I suppose. Barbara, Meg's mother, with her red hair and freckles, and six kids of her own. But was that after you gave up on my mother or before? Was Mom crazy like you claimed and drove you to drink? Or did your drinking drive her mad? For fifty years I've wondered. Who really wrecked our home?

So, I've turned to the past for answers. I'm sifting through memories—mapping Mom's moods, searching your face—seeking the moment you decided we could live without you.

Do you remember that I loved you with all my heart? I mean *my whole, complete heart.* And you loved me with all your heart, too, I know you did, because that's how you made me feel. That a day could ever come when that might end, a day when you'd rather go live with other children, was inconceivable to me. The way there are no words for certain concepts in certain cultures, my soul hadn't the capacity to imagine it.

But it happened, didn't it? And I hate that I'm still not over it.

There. I've said it. I never got over it. Not once in all these long-gone years have I let myself tell you how much it hurt. I only pretended to cope because I knew how badly you wanted me to.

When I started writing about you—about you and Mom and Brent and me and Audrey—I wrote from all directions. But then my mind sharpened and tilted. Because one night on the Internet, I read the professional profile of Barbara's youngest child. There towards the end was this sentence: *My father was a storyteller.*

NO! I yelled in my head. MY *father was a storyteller! Not yours! MINE!*

Oh, Dad. How can I ever explain how that one innocent statement slayed me?

It's true, Dad, you were a storyteller. You told us magical tales, dreamed them up on the spot. But those were our stories, Dad. Mine and Brent's and Audrey's. Our stories—and our father—you gave to them.

Now that I am this old, I see you better. I see you the way black ground becomes a thousand separate flowers in the sun. And I ask myself— *If I were dead, what would I hope?* I would hope my children could someday understand me. And if it can't happen while I'm here on earth, they'll be left with one choice—go back to the past. See me—see *us*—and remember our story. And try with all their might to get it right.

That's what I'm doing here, Dad. Now I'm the storyteller.

Part I

We Sang in the Sunshine

Decisions

1965

I'll start with a day I'm sure you'll remember. I'm eleven going on twelve, so it's closer to our end than our beginning. But the memory is meaningful and should remind us both who we still were to each other in 1965.

It is summer in our fairy tale village of Clarendon Hills, Illinois. School is out and the best vacation of my life lays shimmering ahead. But first, I have a decision to make.

In a few weeks, we will head back to Nantucket, my very own heaven on earth. Nantucket, that sea swept island out there in the ocean, where we live in swimsuits and sweatshirts, and tumble in rolling waves till our salty lips turn blue. We first set foot on its enchanted soil last August, and returning this summer is a direct answer to prayer. This time, beyond my wildest dreams, you and Mom gave Brent and me each permission to invite one friend. Today I have to choose. Should I bring my new best friend, my cool best friend, Skylar? Or my old best friend, my true best friend, Sue?

You remember Susie. She lived two doors down, and we were inseparable. Had I known the term *soul mate* in those days I'd have known she was mine. But being a year older than me, Susie had left our beloved Walker School for junior high that year, leaving me to forge a fierce friendship with Skylar, who sat with me every day in our sixth-grade classroom. Sue and I still played together after school and on weekends, but Sky was luring me ever further away.

Do you remember Sky? She was a beautiful tomboy, a fetching

combination of spunk and femininity. Her eyes shined cobalt blue under frilly black lashes, and her small, impish nose topped a mouth crazily wide and sensuous for a sixth grader. Her cheeks and chin shaped an exact heart, and when she swirled her thick chestnut hair on top of her head, she exposed an exotic gray streak. (It appeared in first grade, she said, when her father died in a plane crash.) As if being beautiful wasn't enough, Sky was also the perfect size. I was that tall girl who stood with the boys in the last row for class pictures. Sky was the cute height, the right height, the height I yearned to be. She also had an irresistible bark of a laugh, a frolicsome spirit, and a spicy little smile that said, *"I know! This is me! Can you even believe it?"* Her darlingness surprised even her.

Susie and I played "Lost Orphans in the Snow" and "Malt Shop." We dressed up like Santa's elves to charm Audrey, who was still only four. We typed up a play to send to Walt Disney. We went caroling together, toting guitars, strumming two chords between us, singing our hearts out.

Sky and I were hipper than that. We still played kid games, but we also talked about boys, other girls, getting big breasts and periods. We sang into hairbrushes in front of the bathroom mirror, wearing Mom's ruby lipstick. We used the full-length mirror in the front hall to admire our tight new figures in our tight new Levi's. Oh, we'd make a mighty pair of allies when we entered seventh grade in the fall, no longer walking to school, but riding the bus to neighboring Hinsdale, where the children who lived in mansions outnumbered us ten to one.

Both friends had heard all about Nantucket. I couldn't stop talking about it. I couldn't stop thinking about it. I was caught in its spell. Over and over, I replayed the wonder of the previous year's vacation, when we piled into our Fawn Mist Buick and drove three days across six states, from Illinois to Massachusetts, where we rounded a bend and before us stretched a most spectacular sight—the Atlantic Ocean, vast and dazzling.

We wound our way through the town of Woods Hole with its

docks and seagulls, steered onto the ferryboat and set sail for "The Grey Lady of the Sea," thirty miles off the coast of Cape Cod. I fell forever in love. It even entered my young mind that maybe I'd lived there in a past life, so familiar to my soul the salt air smelled, the crashing surf sounded. When we packed up to go back to Illinois, the sense I had was not of going home, but of leaving it.

Which lucky girl would I bring to my special haven? I was seeing Susie less and less, and Skylar more and more. So, I couldn't help but gush to her about the upcoming trip and the possibility that she, Sky, might be part of the glorious picture. I could so easily see the two of us on the ferry, the cobble-stoned streets, the sandy beaches—a darling duo in our cut-offs and surfer shirts, stars of our own Disney movie.

Even though I'd talked it up, it wasn't firm; a formal invitation had to be issued. That last stage would involve parents. But I was still torn. The closer the time came for deciding, the more my conscience hounded me. Poor Sue. It pained my heart to imagine how crushed she'd be if I took Skylar instead of her. Yet on this balmy afternoon when you, Dad, declared the time had come, the choice must be made and parents officially asked, when I lifted the yellow phone in the hall to extend this remarkable offer, it was Skylar's number I dialed.

I don't recall the details. I know you were footing the bill for most of this dream trip, but a few expenses would fall to the other family. So, I had that information to relay, as well as travel dates. But other than that, the point was for me to ask Sky, and for Sky to ask her mother.

And Sky's mother said, "No."

It was too far away, we'd be gone too long, and she wouldn't or couldn't pay the additional portion.

No.

I hung up the phone and felt the sweeping relief of a load magically lifted through no effort of my own. I'd asked. She couldn't go. It was a miracle.

My relief surprised me. I had wanted Sky to go, I honestly had. But when push came to shove, loyalty steered me. I loved both girls, but I'd loved Sue longer.

At any rate, it was out of my hands.

I hung up the phone, raced up the sidewalk, and burst through Susie's door.

Susie and her parents are watching television in their family room. They spring up when I run in hollering, "Susie! Susie! Can you come with me to Nantucket this summer? Can you? Can you go to Nantucket?"

Susie grins like I gave her a sack of gold, then turns wide eyes on her mom and dad. "Yes!" they say. "Yes! Yes! Of course, you can!"

Susie and I throw our arms around each other and jump up and down. Her parents throw their arms around us and all four of us jump up and down!

I am so happy! I am happy and relieved and once again certain that everything really does work out for the best. I run home to tell you and Mom, but I stop dead when I see you waiting for me at the bottom of our driveway. You only do that late at night, after a scary show like Twilight Zone, when I have to run home through the dark. But there you are. And you're not smiling.

"Val," you say, calmly, gently, "Skylar called back. Her mother changed her mind. She can go."

6

*

Now, other bad things had happened: the death of Grandma, Mom's mysterious troubles, tornadoes; all causing me sadness, worry, or fear. Yet up to that day, no catastrophe was ultimately mine to handle. But this awful mess, this was all me. The realization was brand-new and sickening. Before that last word left your lips, I knew there was no easy way out. No matter what I did, no tidy solution existed.

"Oh, Daddy! Daddy, what should I do?"

I want you to sit down on the sidewalk, explain the pros and cons, then deliver the answer. But you don't.

Instead, you say, "It's up to you Val. Do what you think is right."

What? This is not helpful!

But I stop and think. You are a mountain of wisdom. I have grown up watching you, noticing that your words and actions are one, that you treat everyone kindly and fairly. And though your answer leaves me rudderless, it also tells me something crucial: Ed Kuhn, the man I most admire and respect, admires and respects me in return. You consider me wise enough and kind enough that my almost-twelve-year-old judgment can be relied upon in a crisis of this magnitude. If an honorable man like you trusts me to make the right decision, then, by golly, I will. I accept your answer and press you no further.

As I relive it half a century later, I believe that my adult conscience and I first met at that moment. I'd always known right from wrong, but that day I understood in my bones that mistakes carry consequences, even when the error is unavoidable and unintentional. Someone will pay; this would always be true.

I walk into our house, pick up our yellow phone, and dial Sky's number.

"I'm sorry, Sky, but you said no, so I invited Susie, and she said yes. I can't un-invite her. I just can't. I am so, so sorry."

*

We went to Nantucket, and it was indeed the best vacation of my young life. But I've always felt bad about Sky. We tried to hold onto our friendship. I sent her postcards and letters from Nantucket, and she wrote back. But I suspect she never fully forgave me, and I can't say I blame her. I would have to pay, at least a little.

As I sensed, Sky became immensely popular in junior high. Some days we were pals, other days not so much. In Spanish class she sat with one of the haughtier Hinsdale girls and when the mood struck them, they'd lean their silky heads together and whisper, pointing at me and snickering, forcing me to wonder if it was my skin, my hair, my height, or my clothes they ridiculed.

Although she moved to Indiana her freshman year of high school, Susie and I remain friends to this day. So, I see my choice that summer afternoon was about as right as a hard choice can be.

But what I see even more clearly is you, Dad, and how in that summer of '65 you were still my hero, my good and loving father, the solid rock of my existence. As essential to me as my own beating heart.

It Will Be Okay, Right?

Atomic bombs, the Red Chinese, Ernie the dog up the street, these were a few of the things that scared me silly as a child. To ease my fears, I looked to you, Dad, not Mom. She, too, was wise, but you were a bulwark of confidence. Every gripping terror of mine, you took seriously.

I can't go to sleep because I can't stop thinking about these bad things, so you tuck me in, then stay by my bed, hashing through my worries until I feel safe enough to close my eyes.

"I give you my word of honor," you say, "the Red Chinese have no plans to march down Grant Avenue. They are very busy over there in China. Now, I grant you, Ernie is scary, but he's more afraid of you than you are of him. Keep showing him who's boss. And do not fret, my pet, atomic bombs will not be launched upon Illinois, not now, not ever. I have spoken! Now dearest, off to dreamland with you."

"Daddy," I say. "Keep my door open, okay?"

And you say, "Always."

You were the source of my security. All you had to speak were four little words— *It will be okay*— and I knew it would be.

But that didn't last.

Let's head back to a day in October of 1964, a good eight months before my Nantucket dilemma when I will choose Susie over Sky. I've just turned eleven.

Skylar came over to play and now it's dinnertime, so we stand at the end of the driveway, watching for her mom's station wagon. Sky holds a yellow leaf above her head, lets it go, then watching it twirl to the ground, she says, "Sharon Miller's mother said your mother is mentally retarded."

The blue sky turns gray then black.

The air has left my lungs, but I suck enough back in to bellow, "My mother is not retarded!" My mother is smart! My mother went to college! She got a scholarship! MY MOTHER IS NOT RETARDED!"

Sky shrugs a shoulder, twirls another leaf. "I'm just telling you what Sharon Miller's mother said."

Right then, her own mother pulls into our driveway. Sky opens the car door and climbs in. "Bye."

Oh, God, oh, God. What do I do now? Where can I put this outrage, this shame? Strangled by fury, I stand shaking and lost at the end of my own driveway.

She meant, of course, mentally ill, not retarded. In 1960, right before I turned seven, Mom suffered some sort of collapse when her own mother died and three weeks later, she gave birth to Audrey. You and Mom brought the new baby home, then Mom went back to stay in the hospital. She went there twice. I knew this. I knew Mom was a vegetarian and believed in UFOs. Unusual in the sixties, yes, but even at eleven I knew these things did not make a person mentally ill or retarded. So, what did Sharon's mother know?

A secret fear blooms in my stomach. Maybe it's The Noise. Maybe Mrs. Miller discovered that Mom once heard a noise that no one else heard.

Mom brought this problem to Dr. Dreyfuss. And whether the walls in his office were too thin and Mrs. Miller happened to overhear from the next examining room, or a loose-lipped nurse repeated the story over cocktails, or even Dr. Dreyfuss himself announced to his whole waiting room, "Verna Kuhn is plain nuts," somehow Sharon's mother got it into her hateful head that my mother was mentally retarded and was spreading the word.

I find my way up the driveway and into our house, past poor Mom peeling carrots in the kitchen, down the basement stairs, where you sit watching a ball game. You stand up when you see me limping towards you, weeping and trembling.

"Daddy," I cry, "Sky said Mrs. Miller said that Mom *is mentally retarded!* Why would she say that, Dad? Why would she say that?"

You wrap me in your arms, where I sob and sob, as you say over and over, "It will be okay. It will all be okay."

But it wasn't.

The Noise

Hearing Mom labeled mentally retarded—by another girl's mother in public, no less—felt utterly obscene. But there was more. For some time, I'd been nagged by a queasy apprehension that some people, including you, Dad, did not consider my mother completely normal. Mrs. Miller's careless gossip struck too close to home.

It was true; a few years back Mom had heard a noise, an incessant high-pitched humming. It worried me because I saw that it caused conflict between the two of you. I could tell by the way you grew silent whenever she mentioned it, the way you pinched your lips into a flat line.

I am eight. Mom is complaining about a noise she hears day and night. It comes from our house; she hears it nowhere else. This high-pitched tone plagues her like a mosquito trapped in her ear. She wonders how she can be the only one hearing it. To her it is so obvious, so loud. I want so much to hear it. I trail her around the house while she tries to figure out where it comes from. I stand beside her in each room straining my ears.

"Here! Listen! Do you hear it now? It's very audible in this room! Listen harder. Here, near this wall!"

I press my head against the redwood panels and try with all my might. Nothing.

"Hear it?" she asks, her gray blue eyes brimming with hope. "Listen!"

To help me along, she tries to match her voice to the exact tone of the humming sound. "There. Hum-m-m-m. Like that!"

Sometimes I say I hear it, hoping to make her happy. "Yes, Mommy! I think I hear it now!"

And sometimes I think I actually do; I want to so badly.

"I know," she says. "We'll do an experiment. We'll take one day and one night and shut off every bit of electricity in our house. If I still hear it, well, we will have eliminated all kinds of possibilities."

I am swept up in her enthusiasm. You are not. In fact, the look on your face frightens me. I've never seen it before, and it is not the way you should be looking at someone you love.

The day Mom chooses to disconnect the electricity is our hottest day all summer. Still, we unplug the refrigerator; we can't talk her out of it. All cold things, she hopefully places in the milkman's metal box by the front door thinking they'll stay cool. They don't. The milk curdles solid by morning.

In the evening, you come home from work wearing that same terrible look. Your mouth looks like it's filled with some bitter liquid you wish to spit out but can't. When you left for work in the morning, we were still connected to power. Now you are back in a sweat-soaked shirt in a house without fans. Without ice. Without TV. I try to lift your spirits, twirling around you like a pixie, beaming and smiling, talking up the night's experiment.

"It will be fun, right, Dad? It will be like camping out! Right?"

Your pinched lips look ready to spit, so I clam right up.

Camping out. I've no idea what I meant by that except I do have a memory of dragging my red flannel sleeping bag into the stifling living room that night. What for? More air? That's all I remember.

I assume the experiment failed. I recall no solved mystery. No elated celebration. I was glad we could turn everything back on—including the television, but mainly the refrigerator—and that the dreadful look on your face eventually faded.

The noise faded, too, but it took a couple more years. So, Mrs. Miller's gossip was doubly unfair, because by the time Sky repeated it, Mom had stopped hearing it.

Maybe it left with the shock treatments.

Everything Changed

Shock treatments. Maybe that's what Mrs. Miller knew. Mom had shock treatments the year before Sharon's mom started wagging her tongue. But I didn't know what that meant; no one explained it to me, and I'm glad they didn't. It's best I didn't know what they were doing to her.

All I knew was the week I started fifth grade, in September of 1963—three years after grandma died and Audrey was born—Mom went back into the hospital. Later she told me that she had been locked in the psychiatric ward and given shock treatments. She spared me the details, but it had clearly been horrendous. What I want to know now is, why?

I knew Mom was different—soon you'd be calling her "crazy"—but today, armed with wisdom and education, I want to revisit what happened to her. I even know where to go—those three years earlier, in 1960. This is when everything changed.

I can feel you telling me, "Yes."

It is August 10, 1960. One month from today I will turn seven. Mom is thirty-nine and about to have a baby. You are at work, and Brent is off playing. Mom is washing the lunch dishes when the phone rings.

She walks to the yellow telephone in the entrance hall, picks up the receiver, sits in the chair. "Hello?" she says. That's all she says. She listens. She weeps. When she hangs up the phone, she stays in the chair and weeps harder.

Then she says, "Grandma died. Poor Grandpa. He couldn't even talk he was crying so hard."

I climb into her lap and lean my head against her big belly and cry, too.

I've always believed that everything bad began at that moment.

Mom was close to her parents. They lived only a few blocks away and were part of our everyday lives. Grandma's death was a blow to us all, but it was worse for Mom. I think it was her undoing. She was never the same again.

Since she was mourning and about to give birth, it was decided our mother needed rest. So, one week later, ten-year-old Brent and I found ourselves in the backseat of Uncle Ned's red and white '58 Chrysler, en route to a campground in the Adirondacks, in Upstate New York.

I adored Uncle Ned and his wife, your sister, Aunt Kathie, but I wasn't so sure about this camping business. As a Baptist minister, Uncle Ned didn't make the money you made in advertising, so camping was an affordable vacation for them. But even if he'd won a million dollars, they still would've camped. Next to Jesus, it's what they lived for. Their kids, too—Donna and Daniel. They were a camping family. We were not. Brent and I loved to play outside, but not necessarily sleep there. We liked our comfy beds, our clean, fresh sheets. But our aunt and uncle had generously offered to take the two of us along on their trip to Lake George while our broken-hearted Mom prepared for the baby she would deliver two weeks later; so off we all drove to Roger's Rock — two adults, two teenagers, two kids, and Lassie, the brown and white Border Collie.

I share a leaky pup tent with Donna, my glamourous big-girl cousin. The boys have a bigger, better tent, and the adults sleep in a short silver trailer shaped like a sausage and smelling like an old soup can. Each morning we drag our soggy sleeping bags across a gravel road to air them out in a field. The long grass and morning light make me glad since our campsite is nothing but shade and dirt.

In our sunless site, Uncle Ned tacks a mirror to a tree trunk which stands where our campsite ends and a steep hill to the lake begins. A hill with lots of tree stumps. Below the mirror he nails a plank, which holds our toothbrushes and a bowl of water. Brushing my teeth in my new summer pajamas one morning after a downpour, I slide on the once-dirt-now-mud and tumble all the way down the hill to the lake, bashing against every stump, and caking my new pink toothbrush and me in mud. I only do that once, but every day of camping feels like that — a long fall down a muddy hill in pretty pajamas. If that's not bad enough, Brent and I are deprived of the only beverage we can't live without—milk— and in its place we are expected to drink, without gagging, a vile concoction called "Carnation Instant."

Brent and I made it through our plight, never speaking once to you or Mom, 800 hundred miles away. We spent our last days of exile at Uncle Ned's ranch house in Tonawanda, New York.

On September 4th, right before lunch, the phone rings. Aunt Kathie answers, listens, sheds tears of joy. "Praise the Lord!" she says.

"Your mother had a baby girl," she tells us. "Your daddy says her name is Audrey Vernette."

A little sister—exactly what I wished upon a star for. Finally—thank you, Jesus— we can go home!

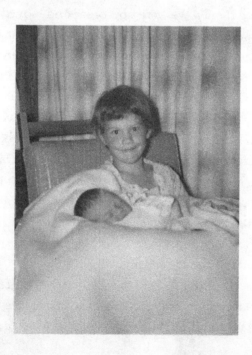

*

Brent and I flew back to Chicago the next day, on our first unaccompanied airplane trip, little silver wings pinned on our collars by our pretty stewardess, Sylvia. You met us at Midway Airport and the next afternoon, you brought Mom and our baby sister home from the hospital.

Mommy lays the tiny infant in her bassinet. Her scrawny chicken legs poke out of her big, droopy diaper. Your bedroom is now called a nursery, so your double bed sits under the bookshelf in the living room.

Mom lays down on that bed to rest, and I settle in on the couch with a library book about kittens. You and Brent head outdoors to play catch. Then Mom starts moaning. I rush to her bed and see that she is shaking.

"Val," she whimpers, "I'm s-s-s-so c-c-c-cold. P-p-please b-bring me more b-b-blankets."

I pile one, two, three heavy blankets on top of her shivering body. No good.

"Daddy!" I yell, running outside, "Daddy, Daddy, help!" In a flash, you and Brent are by her side. Your bodies look strong, but your faces look frightened. The next thing I know, the red and white ambulance is whisking Mom right back to the same hospital she came from only an hour earlier.

The next day, I started second grade and Brent began sixth. Mom didn't come home for three weeks. We were not allowed to visit her, and we were not given details.

I remember you, Dad, pacing the hall in the middle of the night, squalling newborn in your arms, mixing powdered formula with boiling water from the stove. I remember a parade of kind neighborhood mothers offering help and hot meals until your own mother from New York City arrived, with her echo-chamber hearing aid and her hovering ways. What a good woman; seventy years old, coming all that way to help us. I wish I'd gotten to know her better. At the time, she and her tinny voice embarrassed me. Scared me a little, too.

Finally, Mom came home. Thank goodness! Now life could go back to normal. But the mother the ambulance took away was not the mother they brought back.

My real mother smiled all day long. She wore a halo of positive energy as she waltzed through the house, as if heavenly music serenaded her being. Weeding her garden or rolling dough or driving the car, she looked like she heard a harp or an angel singing some sweet song. And even though she was fairly tone-deaf, she loved to sing; she just made up her own melodies. She taught me song after song — "Oh, Jolly Playmate" and "Cowboy Joe," and "I Gave My Love a Cherry," with my favorite words: "The story of my love, it has no end." That's how my real mom loved me. Back in those early sunlit years. I remember, Dad. I remember so well.

My mommy's love, it has no end. She loves having me for her little girl. I am her pal, her helper. Brent and you leave in the morning. Mommy and I stay home and tackle chores together. She teaches me to make beds, fold towels, roll socks into neat balls. Smiling at me, always smiling. We do our exercises with the lady on television, giggling together on our backs, riding pretend bicycles upside-down. We spread a blanket in the front yard and watch puffy clouds turn into dancing bears and castles. She calls me "Lambie Pie."

My smiling mommy sits on the floor with me and plays dolls. We dress them and make them talk. "Let's name this one Heather," she says. She sits beside me at the table and shows me how to draw queens in fancy ball gowns, how to add frills and bows to their dresses, and highlights to their hair. One day she drives me to the store and buys me a big, beautiful bride doll with pearl earrings, and it isn't even my birthday. When you two go to a wedding, she brings me back a slice of cake, wrapped in a napkin. "Put this under your pillow, Lambie, and you'll dream of your prince charming."

At night, when you walk in the door, Mommy and I run to kiss you. Brent is always off playing, so it's the three of us hugging in our hall. "Mommy, Daddy, and Valley!" Mommy says, smiling with all her love.

After dinner, you and Mommy play games with us. We act out nursery rhymes. You turn the orange chairs over to make a pumpkin for Peter, Peter Pumpkin Eater to keep his wife in. You chase us down the hall as we call back, "Run, run, as fast as you can, you can't catch me, I'm the Gingerbread Man!"

Mommy and you sing us to sleep at night. After our prayers, you stand by our beds singing, "Overhead the Moon is Beaming," or "There's a Long, Long Trail A Winding," or "Sleep, Kentucky Babe." While Mommy gets us cups of water, you sing us "Alexander's Ragtime Band." Our last song sounds like "Good-night Ladies" with different words. "Night, night, Brentie; Night, night, Valley..." And at the end, "Merrily we dream along, in our wee little beds," as you drift away down the hall, always leaving the door open, just enough.

But this new mother, the mother the ambulance brought back, she was not the same lady.

She looks the same, or almost, but I am not fooled—there's a different person inside that body. I know my mom. She is the pretty lady who smiles and hears music and loves me so. This new mother does not hear music. She is tired all the time. She hardly ever smiles. Instead, she looks sad or worried or disgusted. I don't delight her at all anymore, but I displease her plenty.

"Pipe down! Don't guzzle your milk! Don't sing at the table! Don't smack your gum! Don't bang so when you walk! Stop looking in the mirror!" I hear that all the time, now.

She uses the word "refrain" a lot and says Brent and I "sap her strength." She says "Oh, my shattered nerves." She never calls me Lambie.

This new mom acted sick and tired of everything. Like it was all too much for her. Like I was too much for her. She still took excellent care of us—I had the prettiest clothes of all my friends, and the kitchen stayed stocked with good food. But oh, how grueling it all seemed to be now that the music had left her.

I missed my smiley mother, and you and Brent must have missed her, too. I never gave that much thought as a child because Brent was perpetually cheerful. And you hid your worry well. You always wore a happy face for us. I realize now that you found that happy face more easily with a glass of gin in your hand and would need to keep one there more often.

If only I'd been an adult and not seven. Maybe we could have talked about it.

Mom Needs Help

That year after Audrey was born—fall of 1960 into the summer of 1961—you did everything you could to help your weary wife. On weekends, you made the whole house brighter and warmer, simply by being home.

Saturdays were best. The hours stretched out slow and sweet. You were ours all day long. You, in your Saturday clothes, no train to catch, no one but us to care about. Your presence wrapped me in a blanket of security I've never felt the likes of since.

Not only was our house warmer and brighter, it smelled good, too, because you took over the weekend cooking. Brent and I woke up smelling bacon and sausages. A platter of both waited for us on the table.

"Okay, you guys, what kind of eggs would you like, scrambled or sunny side up?" You'd ask this with the gusto of a camp counselor offering a choice of swimming or canoeing. You had already been to the village bakery two blocks away, so piled on a plate sat fresh Bismarck donuts, bursting with thick red jelly.

We came together as a family at lunchtime to eat the soup and sandwiches Mom prepared. But at night, Chef Dad was back in the kitchen whipping up his famous chili or beef stew, or my favorite, "juicy steak." Mom's new aversion to meat left us craving your cooking.

During the week, you went to work, of course, but you hired a team of women to lend Mom a hand. Loretta cleaned on Mondays, Edna ironed on Tuesdays, Betty sat with the baby when

Mom ran errands, and then came Maria from Chile, who spoke only Spanish, and soon reported to our chaotic home every day of the week. Maria looked perpetually perplexed, maybe because of the language barrier, but maybe too because Brent and I acted up a lot. We loved each other and played together, but we caused a ton of commotion. After bursting through the door for lunch, we'd spend the next hour laughing and chattering, but also teasing and name-calling and socking each other while we ate our summer sausage sandwiches and fruit cocktail. Then we'd charge back off to school again, still laughing, socking, and name-calling. Maria looked alarmed; Mom looked mortified.

Keeping house threw our newly altered mother for a loop. And our house, as you know, was not big. We had one floor, one bathroom, two bedrooms divided now into three, a living room, kitchen, and dining area. We did have a full basement, where we kept the washer and dryer, Lionel train set, ping pong table, and puppet theater. But that wasn't a cleaning priority.

I'm sorry to say it, but I longed for a different house—bigger, yes—but also just normal, like the two-story homes my friends lived in.

Even though it was small, I do recognize that our house distinguished itself from the typical homes of the era. Ours boasted floor-to-ceiling thermopane windows for a greenhouse effect, recessed lighting, a massive brick wall with built-in fireplace and television set, plus radiant heat in the floors. All pretty grand and unusual for its time, but to me it was conspicuously, even embarrassingly, modern.

Still, it was small. Before Grandma died and Audrey was born, Mom kept it immaculate. Now it looked like a mob of slobs lived there—coffee cups, glasses, ashtrays, magazines, coats, boots, toys, newspapers, coloring books cluttered every surface. The coffee cups were a real problem. They covered our kitchen counter, strewn from one end to the other. Mom drank coffee day and night and used a fresh cup and saucer each time. (When I was a teenager, I bought her an artsy hand-thrown mug for Christmas, thinking this would solve the problem. It became a pencil holder.) We kids were no help. We took our stay-at-home mother for granted. Yes, I had a particular penchant for scrubbing our bathroom sink. It was pink and shiny, and I hated to see it white and scummy, so I'd regularly grab the Ajax and scour till it gleamed. But, by and large, taking up the slack did not occur to us. And let's not forget, we foisted dogs on Mom, too. Dogs that ate shoes and draperies and coffee tables. She loved dogs, but we never lifted a finger to help with them either.

We needed those hired women. And you were good to get them for us. They got us through a serious hurdle, but they didn't stay indefinitely. By the time Audrey turned two, Mom was on her own again. Of course, Betty still babysat, but Mom resumed the chores, and what once was second nature, now seemed insurmountable. Completing an ordinary task became a major accomplishment. I can still picture her jubilant face on those rare days when she'd rush to the front door to meet me after school, announcing triumphantly, "*I washed the floors today!*"

I sure hope I acted impressed, but I doubt it.

Speaking of floors, it was around this time that we had our linoleum stripped out and new flooring installed — cork flooring. It wasn't particularly attractive, and it stained easily, but it was quiet. Mom needed quiet. The sound of shoes on the old linoleum was too much noise, and I have to hand it to you, Dad, for taking her requests seriously. She wanted cork, she got cork. Who knows how much more shattered her nerves would have been without it?

Although she looked miserable doing it, Mom still managed to tend to our physical needs. Materially, we wanted for nothing. But even if she had been otherwise robust, she continued to mourn her mother, and her scant supply of emotional energy, her limited tender attention, went to Baby Audrey.

I wonder if you knew that I felt invisible to Mom in those days. When she did see me, she delivered plenty of edification. But when she didn't see me, which was often, I figured I could dance on the kitchen counter in muddy boots with no interference. I'd gotten the impression I'd grown up overnight, or at least that Mom thought I had, and my need for her was a thing of the past.

But when it came time for my second-grade field trip to the Field Museum in Downtown Chicago, Mom, who cared very much about clothing, got involved. She wanted me to have a new outfit to wear. But instead of taking me herself as she would have before, she said, "Val, walk into town and try on some dresses at The Young Villager. Choose your favorite. Buy a couple if you want."

I picked out two—a lavender dress with a wide purple belt and lacy white bodice, and a dark green floral print with puffed sleeves and a green velvet sash.

"Charge it," I told the saleslady, and grinned all the way home, proudly toting my shopping bag like a proper Big Lady. Growing up overnight had some advantages.

Yes, life in our house had changed, but still, I remember those as good days, idyllic even. I was a cheerful, thriving second grader. Brent was a happy sixth grader. Even though he liked to tease me and pelt me with snowballs, we'd been pals from the start. All through elementary school, he came home and taught me every song, every fact, he'd learned that day in class. We played Davy Crockett and Daniel Boone, put on puppet shows, played cards and board games. He let me play basketball and flashlight tag with him and his friends. He couldn't have been a better big brother.

The two of us adjusted to our new mom. What choice did we have? Whatever worries we had, we kept to ourselves. And even if Mom had changed, you, Dad, had not. We clung to you all the more fiercely. Your love and affection were boundless. When you looked at me, I saw no end to the adoration in your twinkling brown eyes and making you proud became my life-long ambition. I swear no one has ever made me feel as valued and treasured, as *appreciated*, as you did while I was young. You disciplined me, but kindly and patiently, and always kept your sense of humor. Yours was the voice I trusted. Clearly nothing in life gave you more joy than being our father.

Why would I ever even imagine that might not last forever?

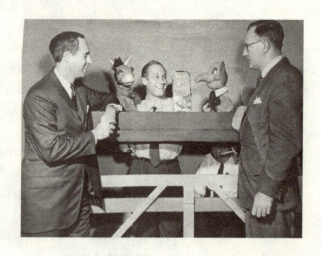

You Were a Jolly,
Good Fellow

In 1961 you still loved Mom. I'm sure of this. You loved her and wanted her well. But you were also what we now refer to as a "Mad Man," a bigwig in the advertising business, getting bigger, working harder, drinking more.

According to Aunt Kathie, "If your dad had come back from the war and been a gym teacher like he wanted, his whole life would have been different." No doubt. But television had arrived and brought with it the world of advertising. You were offered a job in this up-and-coming field, and you excelled at it. You would have excelled at anything, but your particular personality and creative intelligence were uniquely suited for the ad industry.

In 2006, I met an elderly woman who had worked with you in the fifties. It warmed my heart when she told me what you were known for at the agency.

"*Integrity*," she said. "Your dad had so much integrity."

I always knew that about you, but it was good to be told all those years later, that other people knew it, too. Nevertheless, those famous three-martini-lunches became a real thing. Over time, your drinking—you, when drunk— would damage us all.

Not when I was little. It was still under control and probably accentuated your jolliness. Later, it obliterated it. But in those carefree early days, you came through the door at night, set down your briefcase, stowed your hat and coat in the front hall closet, then turned your smiling face to me, your little girl who still ran to hug and kiss you. Snuggling in your arms, I tried to guess at the weird smell on your breath and settled on rotten pumpkins. (As a bartender years later, Audrey thought, *"Dad's aftershave!"* upon opening her first bottle of gin.)

As a girl, I equated that unique odor and the clear liquid you poured in your glass with heightened good spirits in our home. Late in the afternoon, after you'd finished your yard work on a sweltering Saturday, I loved to hop in the car with you and head to Hilltop Liquors in Westmont. It was dark and cool inside, and gleaming glass bottles lit up the dusky shelves, like some sort of jazzy jewelry store. I loved the breezy way you joked with the man behind the counter and how you bought me a bag of warm cashews for the ride home. The night ahead turned out all the merrier.

The liquor had not yet gotten the better of you. You were still my jolly, playful Dad, the man who turned everything into a poem or a song or a cheer: *"Are you ready? Well, I guess! Brentie, Valerie, yes, yes, YES!"* You coaxed me out of tantrums of frustration by disciplining my offending doll: *"Naughty Dolly! Sit still and let Val put on your little shoes!"* or telling me I was being a "daffy doodle" or "talking like a sausage" which always got a smile.

You brought home presents for no reason, things I loved like books and records. When I told you that my favorite song was "If I Had a Hammer," Peter, Paul, and Mary were spinning on the record player by the next evening. I declared my love of collies to you, and soon enough, *Lad, a Dog* by Albert Payson Terhune sat on my desk. You even bought us a real collie puppy when I turned nine, but when he outgrew our house and Mom's patience, it was sure fortuitous you had a friend on a farm who wanted a collie. You ran around the yard playing flag football with us, invented many a bedtime story (like "Sammy the Seahorse," my personal favorite), then sang us off to Dreamland. You were the best father on the planet.

You did not yet sit in the dark and glower.

Back to the Hospital

1963

I wish I knew what Mom said or did back in 1963 to make Dr. Dreyfuss send her to the psych ward for electroconvulsive therapy, and for you to give your consent. To me, sad or not, she was such a gentle soul, soft and serene, like pale pink petals on a still, blue pond. I'd seen a movie in which a thrashing, howling woman had to be restrained and hauled off to the loony bin. This was not Mom. Mom was the farthest thing from frenetic.

Her supreme composure and self-restraint befitted her Swedish heritage and we, her rowdy children, and my displays of temper, dismayed and disheartened her. The tranquil home in which she grew up left her completely unprepared for the havoc we wrought. She sounded so wistful when she compared her orderly childhood with our lamentable conduct.

"We had to keep our doors open," she'd say. "My parents wouldn't allow us to shut them. Shutting them meant we were doing something we needed to hide, so our doors stayed open at all times." And "All my father had to say was, 'Here now,' and my brother and I would behave instantly. He never even had to raise his voice."

This she would say in despair, after pleading with Brent and me for the umpteenth time to "pipe down" or "cease" whatever naughtiness we refused to cease. I did feel chastised, and I wished we could be as obedient as Mom and Uncle Roy, but, well, we weren't.

With Mom, self-control was guaranteed. She hurled no hair-brushes, smashed no dishes. She didn't even strike out with swats or smacks, unlike Mrs. Skillen, who lived in Sue's house before Sue moved in. That sharp-edged woman would slap each of her five little kids at least once whenever I played there. Slap them hard.

No, our mom was ladylike, refined, and unassumingly elegant, a model of self-discipline. How did she end up in a mental ward? Was it all on account of her grief?

What else happened?

Granted, hearing a noise no one else hears is alarming. But aversion to meat and medicine, an inability to keep up with the housework, a passion for UFOs, while surely a break from convention in 1963, are still flimsy grounds for insanity. Mom felt and looked unhappy, she didn't laugh and smile the way she used to, physical tasks depleted her, but were there worse secrets still bless-edly kept from me?

Her confinement my first week of fifth grade coincided with my 10th birthday party, which fell to you to facilitate. You did a fantastic job with that, Dad. First, you took us to see "Jason and the Argonauts" at the Hinsdale Movie Theatre, then home to the backyard for cake and games. I can still see you kneeling on the grass teaching a game you called "Poor Kitty" to a dozen giggling girls in party dresses.

When the hospital deemed Mom ready to release, they once again sent home a different person. I had inevitably adjusted to the one who returned to us in 1960, distant and despondent. But this time, the shift felt seismic.

She didn't remember things she'd said or done before the treatments.

I'd say, "Mom, remember you told me we'd go to Brookfield Zoo this summer?" or "Mom, remember that pie you made with the chocolate and peppermint?" and she'd cut her eyes at me, suspiciously. "I never said that," she'd insist. Or "I've never made such a pie."

I've since learned that memory loss is the most common side effect of shock treatments, but at the time it petrified me. *What has happened to my mother NOW?* She even looked different. Her amber hair had turned many shades of pale—champagne blond, snowy white, and everything in between. And it was not because she'd been coloring it before. But the most unnerving change of all was that she now seemed perpetually *stern.*

Maybe she was angry. Maybe she'd been committed without her consent, given shock treatment against her will. Laws to pre-vent that weren't passed until the 1970s. They had also locked her in her room and forbade her to call me on my birthday. She described how she had implored them, but they held firm.

"I cried and cried," she told me, "But they still said, 'No'."

Why Shock Treatments?

So, what led up to those shock treatments? What happened in 1962 and the summer of '63 to put Mom back in the hospital? Oh, how I wish you could answer me, Dad! How I wish we hadn't steered clear of the subject while we still had a chance to talk. I even called the hospital recently, on the off chance they might still have records, but of course they don't. It's up to me now to piece it together.

Searching for answers, I call Brent to ask his opinion.

"Brent," I say. "*Do you have any idea what Mom might have done in 1963 to warrant those shock treatments?*"

I wait through a long silence and then Brent says in a marveling way, "Val, I can't remember. I was busy being a kid. I honestly don't know."

We both wonder how this could be. But I'm not giving up.

"Brent, you were fourteen, don't you remember anything?"

"All I know is that they were fighting much earlier than you think. It made me anxious as early as third grade; that would be 1957 and 1958."

"Brent, please keep in mind that you have a low bar for what constitutes fighting. Heated disagreements aren't grounds for divorce."

I don't want him painting you unhappy a second too soon.

"Okay," I say, "Can you remember any particular argument from that long ago?"

He thinks for a moment, then his voice brightens with recollection.

"Yes! The day Dad hit you in the head with the shovel!"

I had not yet started kindergarten, but I remember that day, too. I'm sorry to have to remind you of it. But it bears inspection.

I am swinging on my swing set in my polka-dotted playsuit, singing "Jesus Loves the Little Children." You are digging a hole in our yard to plant a tree in. I want to watch, so I drift across the lawn and stand behind you for a better view. You don't see me or hear me. You dig down deep, then heave the shovelful of dirt over your shoulder. Crack! Right into my four-year-old skull.

My head hurts and bleeds. You and Mommy look terrified. She wraps a towel around my head, and we pile into our pink and white Buick and speed to the hospital. But you are not driving. You are crying. I have never seen you cry. It hurts me worse than my head.

I see your face before me now—the essence of guilt and remorse. Brent brings this incident up because of our mother's reaction. "*Mom didn't have a shred of sympathy for Dad,*" he tells me.

I do not want to believe this. Yet I do.

Why would she not reassure you, Dad? Why didn't she say, "It's all right, Ed, it was an accident. You must feel terrible. Please don't worry, dear. She'll be fine."

I cannot reconcile this type of coldness with our sweet mom.

Over twenty years later, you flashed back to this incident, grumbling that it was Mom's fault.

"*If your mother hadn't insisted that I plant that goddamned tree that very afternoon, it never would have happened.*"

I wanted you to stop talking. The contempt in your voice, the glass of gin in your fist, whipped up a slew of bad memories, and I quickly switched the subject. You were still angry twenty years later; what a dreadful day it must have been.

A small scar is still faintly visible on my forehead. I don't remember the stitches or feeling pain. I remember Mom making a doll for me out of washcloths. I remember your tears.

I wonder how Mom could have been so devoid of pity when you were so plainly guilt-ridden. The only way I'd be angry with my husband rather than sympathetic, would be if he had been drunk. But if you were drunk, why would she insist you go outside and plant a tree?

Yes, Mom had a breakdown in 1960 and changed in many ways. But this shovel in the head incident happened three years earlier. This forces me to accept that this unforgiving tendency was an odd part of her nature. It's not uncommon, but it's a bitter trait to reckon with. I'm thinking of you, Dad. I'm thinking of us. Audrey and I have discussed how it felt impossible to apologize to Mom. "*I'm sorry!*" we'd cry. "*I'm so sorry!*" And she would reply, "*Don't tell me you're sorry. Just don't do it again.*" I grant the logic to her words, but the reality was tough on anyone who loved her. We never felt absolved.

I did not see this stony side of Mom until after her breakdown. Then it was only a matter of months before I felt it firsthand and understood — her comfort and sympathy were now hit or miss.

Severe Disapproval

This chilling realization seized me on my last day of second grade.

We went to school for a mere fifteen minutes, long enough for our teacher to hand out report cards and tell us she'd miss us, and for some of us to give her parting gifts of flowers, perfume, or stationery. Then off we scampered to celebrate our liberation. Not me. I hobbled home swallowing tears. Once there, I crept into my room, closed the door, curled up on the floor, and wept.

Oh, Miss Lundgren, I love you so much! I love you and your classroom and I want to stay in second grade for the rest of my life! I cannot stand that my time with you is over. Next year you will have all new children to love. How can I bear it?"

Mommy must have heard me crying because she opens my door and looks down at me. I expect to see her face soft and sweet. I expect her to kneel down and put her arms around me. Instead, her face is hard and angry. She stands over me, glaring. Then, in the mean, crackly voice of a witch, she says, "Snap out of it! Go do something useful!"

She looks so disgusted, that I feel ashamed, like she caught me wetting my pants or something else bad and babyish. My heart shrivels up. Like I ran to her after getting punched in the stomach and instead of hugging me, she pulls my hair.

I am well aware that someone might hear that and scoff. "Oh, boo hoo. My mom talked to me that way every day of my life." But mine didn't. It was a shock.

Today, I wonder if something happened that morning,

something to offend or enrage her, and she misdirected her wrath at me. But the timing of this incident informs my thinking now— Audrey was not a year old, Grandma not a year dead. It was my personal introduction to Mom's new personality and still early enough for me to be properly shaken by the contrasts cropping up in her behavior. My other mom had been soft, not hard; kind, not cruel. But it wouldn't be long before these unsettling changes ceased to startle me, and the look of disapproval she so frequently directed at me became something I learned to live with.

Miss Lundgren looked at me the way Mom used to—with open affection. For the nine marvelous months I lived in her classroom, I loved Miss Lundgren as much as Mom. Maybe more. I couldn't help it—she seemed to love me more than Mom did.

In the spring of my second-grade year, Miss Lundgren got an engagement ring. The next year she got married. The year after that she stopped teaching. I was in fourth grade then and awoke one morning from a dream so vivid about Miss Lundgren, that it left me needing to see her. I used the telephone book to find her address and phone number under her married name—Carson— then called to ask if I could visit her. She said "yes."

I'm sure she thought I had Mom's permission. I did not. When I told Mom what I had done, she looked aghast. I remember wondering *Why does it bother her? Why does she care?*

Despite looking stricken, Mom didn't forbid me to go. She tried to dissuade me—this was clearly inappropriate behavior on my part. But I told her I had already made the date, I needed a ride, and— dripping disapproval—she drove me. Did you know about this, Dad? She must have told you. I'm guessing you saw no harm in my plan.

Finally! We are in the car heading to Miss Lundgren's house! I mean, Mrs. Carson. Oh, I can't wait, I can't wait! Mom sits behind the steering wheel looking gray. Her eyes, her skin, her coat. All gray. She doesn't say a word while we drive to Hinsdale. When we pull up to Miss Lundgren's house, she finally speaks, "I'll be back in an hour."

I ring the doorbell and there she is, my dear, soft-cheeked second-grade teacher. She smiles down at me as sweetly as ever; oh, how I have missed that smile! But something is different about her. Oh! She has a big round belly under her peach-colored blouse.

Miss Lundgren is pregnant! She will soon have her own little child to love. Oh, nooooo!

She shows me around her home. It is spick and span and smells like her, like roses and muffins. "And here is the baby's room," she says. It is sunny and bright, and I am sick with envy. I want so badly to be that baby.

When Mom came to pick me up, she looked like she had been chewing on her fingers the whole time I'd been enjoying milk and cookies. She also changed the story of why I called Miss Lundgren in the first place. Maybe the real story embarrassed her. I piped right up to correct her and humiliated her further, "No, *that's not right, Mom! I dreamed about you, Mrs. Carson! It made me need to see you!*"

Mom grew silent, grayer, and then we left.

*

I admit these things about Mom, Dad, in an effort to be honest. I pray that even the slightest negative detail is nothing but a straight fact. That's what I'm trying to do, face the facts. If the facts alter history in your favor, I confess, I'll not be displeased. But I'm not looking to take sides; I am looking for the truth.

So, here is one of my truths: on and off throughout my formative years I suffered Mom's severe disapproval. It wasn't so much a harangue of reproval as an air of distaste. Out of the blue, she'd grow cold and aloof and regard me with unmistakable displeasure. It could last a few hours, a few days, even a few weeks. When I was eighteen, it lasted almost a year. She didn't stop communicating with me or tending to my needs, it was the look on her face: closed and impenetrable. She'd come out of her bedroom one morning and I'd think: *She doesn't like me again.* Today I think: *Was it even about me?*

This frostiness swept over her randomly. Sometimes I could connect it to a cause, but usually I hadn't a clue what started it. I wish you could tell me—am I overstating this phenomenon or understating it? Or did she only act like this when you'd gone out of town and left her alone too long with us kids, and she maybe resented it? But I know eventually you saw it, too, and you, like us, had to learn to live with it. Or not.

With me, Mom's disapproval took the form of steely silence. With you, it came out in words, which she used artfully. I can safely say that Mom was the most articulate individual I have ever met. And when she objected to something, she spoke right up. Never in a biting or overbearing tone. She didn't even raise her voice. She merely stated her displeasure, quietly but emphatically. Within reason, it's an admirable trait. But maybe she objected to too much, and it made her a nitpicker in your eyes. Made you say, "*Lay off*". That's what you said when you couldn't take one more correction. *Aw, lay off.* Or "*I give. I give!*" Meaning, "I give up, I surrender." I heard these phrases out of your mouth often, but not until I was around twelve, so does that mean Mom's criticism worsened then? Or did it take you that long to stop tolerating it?

You were a successful advertising account executive. Other than a larger house (which we sorely needed) there was not much, in a practical sense, Mom went without. You earned good money, and she spent it on the household as she wished. Not only did you work hard and earn a good salary, but you were also a hands-on dad, playing with us whenever you were home. And let's not forget you cooked on the weekends. For a dad in the sixties, you were ahead of your time. So, in what way did you not measure up? What was it she found to object to?

Your temper would be my first guess, but to my knowledge, that didn't become a problem until I hit fifth grade or so. You gracefully put up with whatever rankled you for a long time, but you didn't grin and bear it forever. You were a sleeping giant of a foe, and when you awoke there was hell to pay. I said I grew up watching you and saw that you treated everyone kindly and fairly. Soon that would be everyone but Mom.

About your temper—which would indeed become legendary, and certainly objectionable—in the early days of my childhood I recall only a handful of examples.

Once you set a new fishing pole on the trunk of the car, then left it there and went back in the house. Playing in the yard, I watched you leave the house again, get in the car, and back down the driveway, forgetting about the fishing pole on the trunk, which fell off in time for you to roll over and crush. Your fury was awe-inspiring. You aimed it at yourself, not us, but you hollered obscenities heard round the block.

Another time we were on a plane heading from Los Angeles to San Francisco and your wallet got stolen. Stolen or lost. At any rate, it disappeared. This is before traveler's checks and credit cards, so all our vacation money was gone, something akin to several thousand dollars today. Understandably, you were beside yourself, and didn't care who knew it. We cowered in a coffee shop sipping soda pop while you reported the incident to the officials. My fondest wish was to fall asleep, then wake up and find out it was all a bad dream. I didn't and it wasn't.

Neither of these outbursts had anything to do with me, I simply watched and cringed.

In one instance, your anger thrilled me. I was seven or eight, because the fact that Mom's dad was mourning his wife figured into your actions. Grandpa had driven over to have dinner with us on Halloween night. Maybe to see us kids dressed up in our costumes, like it might lift his spirits. His silver Buick, of which he took excellent care, was parked near the sidewalk in front of our house. I'm not sure how we all happened to be watching when this occurred, maybe we were walking him to his car. But what I see in my mind's eye is a couple of big boys stopping to look at Grandpa's car, then pelting it with raw eggs, laughing loudly, and running away. This pushed you over the edge. You shot after them like a track star, sprinting all the way to the top of the block. They were either too fast for you, or had too much of a head start, because you didn't catch them and maybe that's a good thing. But boy, oh boy, was I ever proud of you. You weren't going to let those punks get away with abusing our grieving grandpa. I wanted to leap in the air and cheer as you ran up the block, awestruck at your speed and resolve. *That's my DAD, everybody! Look at him GO!!*

Anyway, the point I set out to make was that in my childhood, unlike my adolescence, you seldom gave way to unbridled temper. Those few memories serve as the only examples I have during the first nine years of my life. Before things went drastically wrong, you greeted each day by singing, "*Oh, What a Beautiful Morning*" or "*Zippety Doo Dah*" and were about as cheerful and free from moodiness as a man can be. At least when I was young. At least in front of me.

The anger I referred to as "legendary" was right around the corner though, and when it came, it stayed. How often did I hear

Mom say, "Temper, temper" to you? A thousand times? A million? Because your sporadic bursts of rage accelerated until you were angry every day.

One of those bursts shook our house in the middle of the night, when I awoke to your voice, top volume, hurling swears into the phone. It concerned a freakish situation we called "The Sewerage Problem."

The Sewerage Problem

Whenever it rained hard for more than an hour, we had to shut off our plumbing. This meant one of us had to dash out into the downpour, run to the back of the house, and there— in the deluge—crank a heavy metal wheel until our plumbing disconnected from the town sewer system. If we didn't, the laundry tub in the basement filled up with raw sewerage. Sometimes it got high enough to overflow onto the concrete floor where, during a fierce storm, more sewerage could gush up through the basement drain. If we managed to turn it off in time, the tub and floor stayed dry, but we still could not flush our one-and-only toilet or use the dishwasher or washing machine for as long as the rain lasted, which could be days.

I can remember instances when we didn't turn it off fast enough. Those were the times when the sewerage rose out of the laundry tub and flooded the basement only, but always ruining things, mainly toys, because that's where we played with them. Once the sewerage got so high it seeped into Mom's cedar chest and destroyed her wedding dress. Once we lost a whole collection of Madame Alexander dolls.

Then there was the worst flood of all. Oh, man—the shouting, the stench, your faces. The sewerage did not stay in the basement. It surged, impossibly, up through our bathtub, spilled out of the bathroom into the hall, onto our brand-new olive-green carpeting. We'd never had carpeting before; I thought it the most luxurious thing we owned. Now it was ruined; we had to rip it all out.

Most people go through something like this once or twice, then pull up stakes and scram. Not us. We stayed. To be fair, we were continually looking at houses, always planning to move, we just never did.

We endured this wretched condition and, on rare occasions, even made the most of it. I fondly remember our junior high principal appearing at the door of my seventh grade Social Studies class at the end of a Friday, asking for *Valerie Kuhn*, of all people! That had never happened before. I was told not to get on the bus, but to wait for you to retrieve me. You? Home from work early? Where were we going? To a hotel in Oakbrook with a ritzy restaurant and indoor pool, right next to a movie theater. For the whole weekend! The forecast was for non-stop rain and Brent and Mom both had the flu and needed a flushable toilet to throw up in. I took five-year-old Audrey to see a double feature – *Bambi* and *The Ghost and Mr. Chicken*. It remains one of our favorite shared memories.

But more and more, you weren't home when it rained, and it fell to Mom or Brent to scramble from their beds at the first flash of lightning, tear out into the storm and disable our plumbing.

For the next few days, we had to use a coffee can instead of our toilet. Or we could use the toilet, but we had to remember to obey the big sign that said DON'T FLUSH and keep bombing the air with Lysol. But now and then, force of habit, someone forgot and flushed. Up came the sewerage.

On the dreadful night in question, I awoke to your voice bellowing, "GET YOUR FUCKING SEWERAGE OUT OF MY FUCKING BASEMENT!!!" It was two in the morning, and you were on the yellow phone, blasting away at the Clarendon Hills Town Manager, Mr. Proctor, after deciding he was to blame for the slop in our basement.I pulled my quilt over my head and hoped I would not run into the man's daughter at school the next day.

Apparently, you and Mom tried constantly to bring this issue to the attention of the Town, but you got no results. Even after you left, Mom kept trying. I remember accompanying her to our local congressman the week before I turned eighteen. Another dead end.

It is positively appalling to think this was going on in our home, in our lives. We did not live in a hovel in the hills. Our small, but innovative house at 206 Grant Avenue sat on one of the nicer streets, in one of Chicago's better suburbs. We should have been able to use the plumbing when it rained.

Brent and I have discussed the sewerage problem inside and out and agree we have long underestimated the toll it took on each of us, but chiefly on you and Mom. This outrageous situation alone could make a person batty, or at the very least wear down a marriage.

We wonder endlessly why we never moved. We outgrew our house when Audrey was born, so we needed to move with or without the sewerage problem. It's a privileged slant, I know, but we had the means to do it. There was no excuse for you and Mom to sleep in the living room, or to cram two canopy beds into one small bedroom, or for Brent to sleep in the basement. All those fantastic houses we toured and never bought, why? Was it because no house ever satisfied Mom? No house was perfect enough? It's likely. This thought bothers us tremendously. We can't help but believe that if you and Mom had only managed to move to a bigger house with reliable plumbing, it would have altered the course of our lives.

But I sure did love looking at real estate with you two. Every house we toured promised a fresh start. I'd stand in a sunny bedroom or formal dining room or in the kitchen of my favorite house in Hinsdale, with its cozy fire burning in a stone hearth, and I'd think *If we move here, everything will be alright. We will be happy again. That's all we need—this house.* But we never moved. A failure with ever-lasting effects.

In 1964, you finally bought a piece of land with the intention of building our dream home. It was in Hinsdale on Madison, about a half a mile south of 55th. We drove by it all the time, me in reveries visualizing the joyful new beginning awaiting our family. Our lot even had a babbling brook out back! But we never built anything on that lot. So, we kept running out into storms, disconnecting the plumbing, bearing the insanity and all its grave consequences.

In the end, we sold the lot.

A Closer Look at Mom

Our sewerage problem cannot be over-emphasized. But back on track, it was your temper I was analyzing. So yes, you had one, but before I was ten or eleven on those rare occasions you lost it in front of me, I'd say you had good reason.

Really, I am still searching for what led to Mom's shock treatments. But now I'm also searching for what Mom had against you. How did you earn her severe disapproval? Most of the time you were a terrific guy. But, like all humans, you weren't perfect. And Mom believed in perfection. Literally. "*Strive for perfection. Try to be more Christ-like.*" These were Mom's common exhortations and excellent advice, if you recognize the acts of "striving" and "trying" as virtuous enough, and don't view perfection as an attainable goal. But I think Mom thought it was. She was so virtuous herself, that she seemed sincerely baffled that others might have to work at it.

High moral standards were impressed on us children by both of you, but she also stressed etiquette and posture.

"*Stand here against the wall, Val, and press the small of your back against the bricks. There now, that is correct posture. Stand and walk exactly like that.*"

"*Keep your elbows off the table ... Ask 'may I be excused' ... Use a slice of bread to push your food, not your fingers... Don't make disagreeable noises... The word is 'to' not 'ta.' Keep your knees closed when you sit in a skirt.*"

These are things mothers must say (and I am grateful for the guidance) but ours seemed to say them more than most. Her advice sounded constructive to my ears, never shrewish. But I did get the idea that I needed a lot of correction. I was the little girl who sang at the top of her lungs under the hair dryer in the beauty parlor, thinking—since I couldn't hear myself—no one else could hear me. The child who'd stumble into old ladies on the street to pet their fur coats.

I do know I was way too boisterous for her. While you relished my raucous ways, Mom shuddered around them. Do you remember the "Cathy's Clown" incident? When I was eight, we went out for dinner to a restaurant with a jukebox. Someone played "Cathy's Clown" and I went wild. Something about the song threw me into orgiastic contortions. I remember moaning and yowling and throwing myself around in the booth in uncontrolled ecstasy. I see Mom's horrified face before me now. Like I'd turned into a frothing werewolf right there in The Silver Dollar.

I talked too loud, I laughed too loud, I sang too loud, I even walked too loud for our quiet mother. When I took organ lessons, I practiced doggedly. I felt a need to practice the same line twenty or thirty times in a row to learn it. This was too much for her.

"Valerie, please! Stop! I can't listen to that over and over! *Please … it's shattering my nerves!*"

But it was you she seemed truly tough on, Dad. Why? Reading Mom's love letters to you from the 1940's I would never dream it possible. She absolutely worshipped you.

She wrote, "*Darling, people like you just aren't born every day. You are just everything I would ever want a man to be.*" And "*You are so thoughtful about so many things. Stay that way always, won't you darling? I want to learn to be more like you.*"

Yikes, Dad. What happened? Had you been putting on a front? I can't believe that. You were an NYU graduate, you spoke and wrote eloquently, so no act there. And "thoughtful" was a permanent trait of yours. So, what? Did she attribute some unrealistic moral superiority to you that became impossible to live up to?

For instance, Mom never swore. "God-awful" might be the closest she came. You, on the other hand, swore like a champ. That's what I mean. Had you tried to suppress the rougher tough-guy side of yourself, the side she might frown upon? Maybe you carried it off for a long time but couldn't keep it up. Maybe after a while you didn't even want to. Maybe she felt cheated when she found out you were a regular guy. A great guy, but not … perfect.

Sometimes your humor offended her. "Sarcasm is not for children," she would primly remind you. Other times, she would correct your choice of words. "Don't use the word 'mad' when you mean angry. Say 'angry;' mad means insane." These things mattered to her, and she had a right to say them. But over time, it could've sounded pretty pedantic to you.

A sloppy drinking episode can make a lasting impression. Is that something to consider? A twenty-one-year-old Verna described a *"horrible trip on the bus"* from Chicago to Champaign where, arriving after midnight, she waited for a cab. *"The place was just overflowing with soldiers who were so dead drunk they couldn't stand up. They were stumbling and falling, vomiting, and talking so loudly. It was a God-awful sight. It certainly wouldn't give anyone a good impression of the army to look upon them. I just couldn't think of them as being men at all."* People can be pretty offensive when they get a little too hammered. Were you ever "God-awful" like that in front of her? I'm leaning towards "yes."

Or did something even more serious occur between the two of you, something she could never forgive? Because she seemed to carry some secret sorrow from some sense of betrayal or bitterness that never went away. *What happened, Dad?*

As I think, a memory emerges. Buried for nearly sixty years, it leaps up and smites my heart. It is Mom, her long hair unpinned and spilling over her silky pink bathrobe, standing in the hall, crying. Without her customary heels, she looks surprisingly small next to your 6'3" frame. She is crying, and punching your arm, but there is no power behind her punches. It almost looks like that's why she's crying—she can't hit you hard enough. She tries again. Pathetic. She cries harder. You stand there and take it. What is that expression on her face? I couldn't name it then, but picturing it today, I'd call it outrage. Outrage mixed with defeat. Does that make betrayal?

When I got those stitches in my forehead, you two had already been married for fourteen years. Twenty, when she had shock treatments. During a marriage, plenty can happen between a man and a woman. Things not easily forgotten, let alone forgiven. This is all I can think of. Something happened between you— something of a private, maybe sexual nature—and it offended her sensibilities, sullied her opinion of you, and colored the remainder of your life together. Because it looked that way then, and it still does now. But what? Will I ever know?

Because I do remember the early days, those splendid days, and I cling to them.

And now, here I am, back on the phone with Brent. I want him to cling to them, too.

"Don't you remember? They sang us to sleep together and acted out nursery rhymes with us. We went on vacations. They hugged and kissed. I don't care what anyone says, those were happy parents who loved each other."

"I'm sorry, Val, I don't remember. But I'm glad you do so you can remind me."

"Believe me, Brent, those good days were real. Nothing will ever change that. Now, let's get back to those shock treatments. Let's figure this out. What was going on in 1963?"

We think for a while then something dawns on us: That was the year Mom kept seeing her mother all over the place. Grandma, who was dead and buried.

And Even Closer . . .

Mom came to believe that her dead mother walked the earth. You remember that, right? Or did she think twice about sharing that with you?

I happen to know she spotted her deceased mom among the living even earlier than 1963, because in August of 1961, she and I stood on a sidewalk in San Francisco where she pointed up to an old woman gazing out a hotel window. *"Look, Val! Doesn't that look like Grandma up there? Could that be Grandma?"*

Well, yes, she does look like Grandma. Only no, it cannot be her. I understand this at seven. Why don't you know this at forty?

This was not a passing phase. A year or so after spying that lady in the hotel window, a Salvation Army circular came in the mail right before Christmas, 1962, the photo of a needy old woman on its cover. Same reaction. Ultra-excited.

"Look, Val! This woman looks so much like Grandma! Maybe it is!"

I remember her trying to obtain contact information for the Salvation Army. She wanted to track down the woman they used for the pamphlet because possibly, it was Grandma, still alive.

That same December, I wrote a letter in my fourth-grade classroom that got published in our local newspaper, *The Doings*. Mom was thrilled; not because my letter made it into the paper, but because my salutation read, "Dear Grandma."

Miss Walks had asked us to write a letter describing what

Christmas meant to us. We could write to anybody. I wasn't actually writing to either one of my grandmothers—living or dead. I honestly think I chose "Grandma" because it sounded cozy. Mom, however, read big things into that small word. I can still see her radiant face, her hopeful eyes, the loving look, so rare in those days, directed at none other than me! I am sure that she considered it some cosmic sign that I was attuned to the truth: her mother never died.

She explained that doctors placed mirrors under the noses of corpses to make sure they weren't secretly breathing away in their coffins before they nailed them shut. This, she said, kept folks from being buried alive, implying that before they invented the mirror technique, it happened all too often. "*Did they forget to use the mirror on Grandma?*" she wondered aloud.

Today, Dad, I must tell you—this is not considered quite so wacky. I've read that millions of mourners have reported seeing their dead loved ones or feeling their presence. We have the internet now; we know so much more about human beings. But to us, at the time, it was scary.

Mom also told a story that was difficult to believe but I did, and I think I still must. She was out shopping and someone other than Betty was babysitting us. The phone rang.

"Kuhn residence," the sitter answered. "No, Verna isn't in right now, can I take a message?" When Mom came home, she read what the sitter had written: "*Your mother called. She said to tell you she is all right.*"

What in the world??

Sometimes I can't help but wonder if you were responsible for that, Dad. I know how far-fetched that sounds, but maybe you knew it would take something that fantastic to bring Mom peace. I just don't know what else to think.

Back on the phone I say to Brent, "Well, I think we've answered my original question. If Mom truly believed our dead grandma was alive, and shared that with Doctor Dreyfuss, he would have committed her before she left his office."

*

I've suddenly remembered that another significant event preceded Mom's shock treatments: Grandpa remarried.

After two years of visiting Grandma's grave daily, Mom's father met another mourner named Grace. Grandpa was seventy years old; Grace was twenty years younger. The graves Grace visited belonged to her parents, who had died in a car crash. She herself had never married.

Grandpa and Grace got chummy at the graveyard, and soon, shocking us all, up and got hitched. The person most upset was Mom's brother, Uncle Roy. No matter who had married Grandpa, Roy would have resented her, but Grace had some definite strikes against her. Most notably, was her refusal to let Grandpa talk. She either spoke over him or for him, and eventually he gave up speaking altogether. Uncle Roy simply banished Grace from his

life, which was easy because he and his family soon moved to Arizona. But Mom embraced Grandpa's new wife courteously, inviting the newlyweds over for dinner often and for holidays always. We were instructed to call her Grandma Grace.

How could I have forgotten? Before she got shock treatments, Mom got a stepmother.

Replacing even a dead mom can be upsetting.

*

I hung up the phone with Brent and thought: *All this was happening when I was nine. She went to the psych ward the week I turned ten. This all makes sense.*

Then another memory surfaces—my Hawaiian birthday party in 1962. It reminds me how much it mattered to Mom to make things perfect, how desperately she worked at it, and how hard it was on her and the people around her.

Today I am nine. It's the first week of school. I am hot and itchy in my party dress with its crinoline slip scratching my bare belly, watching the clock on our fourth-grade wall, inch its way to 3:30. Then my friends and I will burst through the school door, run across the playground, across the street, through the Gordons' backyard and onto on our patio where my Hawaiian Birthday Party is waiting.

This Luau party is Mom's idea, and she is going all out, as though kings and queens are attending, instead of nine-year-olds. She's spent a lot of money buying new things— a tropical tablecloth with matching cloth napkins, colored lanterns for our fence, and flower leis for each girl to wear. She promised she would have the record player plugged into the outdoor outlet, playing the brand-new album of Hawaiian music we bought last night at the record store.

There's the bell! We bolt out the door and run home, prancing onto the patio like giddy ponies. Only something's not right. The table is set, the lanterns are lit, the music is playing, but Mom looks...bad.

I glance around. The fancy fruit punch is cooling on ice in a crystal bowl, but the big fancy treats— the Pineapple Boats from Gourmet Magazine — are missing. Then I notice Mom's hands. They are scraped up and bleeding.

I get it now. She's taken this too far.

She has been madly carving up pineapples, racing the clock, hacking a sharp knife through the hard, thorny shell, and scooping out all the deeply attached pineapple, to make bowls for fruit and sherbet. She has finished three. Eight more to go.

54

She is panicked and in pain, but I know she will not relent. She will not say, "Screw this. It's too hard and I'm not doing it." That's not how Mom talks. And it's not in her power. She keeps slicing and bleeding and biting back tears. All this for a bunch of fourth graders. All I want her to do is GIVE UP.

Mom was a perfectionist, no doubt, but most likely obsessive-compulsive, too. Maybe it wasn't the primary problem, but it would surely aggravate any disorder. Her relentless pursuit of excellence put so much pressure on her, added such a woefully unnecessary strain to her life. And to those who are not burdened by it—like you, Dad—even perfectionist behavior, can appear irrational. It alone may have accounted for a considerable portion of what you called "crazy."

Some twenty years after Mom died, I learned that her brother, Uncle Roy, was considered bipolar by his family. Did you know that? Did Mom? Gosh, how I wished we had talked about these things. I learned this at Roy's funeral. He was a successful businessman and he and Aunt Ellen raised four fine children, yet according to his daughter, Marnie, he had such extreme mood swings that if he wasn't bipolar, multiple personality disorder was another strong possibility. Marnie said there was definitely something going on that was less than stable but that he was also quite brilliant most of the time. That applies to Mom, too. I wonder if they knew this about each other. Did they grapple with these problems as children, or did the loss of their mother trigger them both? Neither sibling agreed to medication or psychotherapy. Hardly unusual for the time.

That September of 1963, right after Mom came home from the psychiatric ward, I recall walking behind the two of you on a path in Morton Arboretum, Mom's favorite place. The leaves overhead were turning their autumn colors, and I watched you put your arm around Mom and draw her close to you. A soothing reassurance flooded my blood. That one ordinary gesture brought me infinite comfort. Which tells me how worried I must have been, worried for both of you—worried for *us*— a chronic, simmering fear.

But even after all this, from all appearances, in September of 1963, you still loved us.

A Christmas Dirge

Between her hospitalization in September of 1960 and her shock treatments in September of 1963, Mom had unquestionably changed. You, however, created the illusion that all was well, with your usual good-natured gusto. I suspect it required more and more gin to maintain that gusto, and it began to take its toll. One drink too many and your jolly face threatened to twist into that awful, pinched-lip expression I had early recognized as contempt. There is no denying it—disturbing moments were steadily creeping into our idyllic days. Take my ten-year-old Christmas for example, three months after Mom's shock treatments.

It is one week before Christmas. The trunk of our car is open, and it shouldn't be because I spy something I oughtn't.

I run straight to Brent's bedroom. "Brent!" Guess what! There's a pile of new toys inside our trunk!"

"Oh, yeah?" he says, "Well, maybe those are for our cousins."

"Well, I only saw a few but some of them were toys I asked Santa for!"

"Just forget you saw them, okay?" Brent turns back to his stamp collection.

I'm not buying the bit about the cousins, and I go straight to Mom who is in the kitchen with her hands, as usual, in the sink.

"Mom, I saw a bunch of new toys in the trunk. I saw a Little Miss Echo. That's what I asked Santa for. Are you giving that to me? Because if you are, I'm pretty sure he's bringing me one already."

Mom wipes her hands on her apron and sighs. She turns from the sink to face me.

"Val, you are old enough now to know that Santa is not a real person. He's a legend, a fairy tale for children, he is ... well, he's like a spirit, the Spirit of Christmas, of giving."

I am speechless. Does she know what she's saying? Santa a spirit? Where'd she get that idea? Santa is one of my favorite people. I have sat on his lap, looked into his eyes, for crying out loud. Not real?

"Well, then where do all those toys come from?"

"From us, your parents. We buy them. Please don't spoil it for Audrey, okay?"

She looks at me wistfully a moment longer, then turns back to the sink.

So that's that. Santa is dead and grown-ups are liars. There has to be something I can do about this.

I'll brainwash myself, that's what. Brent told me something called "brainwashing" can change people's minds, and they won't even remember what they thought before their brain got washed. You must repeat and repeat whatever it is you want them to think, and—presto! They will believe it.

I try it on myself that night. I fall asleep chanting, "Santa is real. Santa is real." Even if by some long shot he isn't, I will wake up not remembering. Only it doesn't work; I remember, all right. On Christmas Eve I crawl into bed with a hole in my heart.

But I awake at dawn with a positive attitude and scurry to the tree as usual. After all, what has changed? Only who gives us the gifts. You can't stop Christmas! But this one feels different from all the others and it has nothing to do with Santa.

That night, while sugar plums danced in our heads, you and Mom fought. I knew this immediately, because both of you still seethed in the morning, and neither of you spoke to the other. What on earth had you fought about?

I had heard the two of you head to the basement, as I lay in bed, still awake. I knew that was where you wrapped presents on top of the Ping-Pong table. Ordinarily, you'd have waited until I was asleep so as not to blow Santa's cover. It stung a little to know it no longer mattered. But you probably figured since the jig was up, and little Audrey was sound asleep, you could get a jump on things and for once head into Christmas Day with a decent night's sleep.

I imagine you began cheerfully enough. I imagine Mom smiled and said, "Let's go downstairs and get the toys ready!"

And I imagine you would have poured a drink, probably not your first. And your argument started early because it was evident the next morning that little wrapping took place.

I picture you both standing there, surveying the toys and clothes spread out over the Ping Pong table. You probably both sighed at the task ahead. So maybe Mom reasonably remarked on the need to stay awake.

Maybe she said, "*Ed, you shouldn't have another drink. Have a cup of coffee instead. This could take a while.*"

And maybe you ignored her suggestion and took another swig from your glass, and said, "*I'll wrap the Little Miss Echo. You wrap The Flintstones Play Village.*"

Maybe Mom frowned. "*I thought you were going to get Little Miss Echo for Audrey, too.*"

"*No, Vern. She's only three. That doesn't make sense.*"

"*But how will she feel when Val has one and she doesn't?*"

"*She's only three. She has Tiny Tears.*"

You regard the dolls in silence, then Mom can't help herself, "*I would have gotten her one.*"

You knock back half your drink and reach for the wrapping paper.

Mom says, "*Oh, dear. Did you notice Little Miss Echo has a stain on her skirt?*"

"*Where? Oh, you can hardly see that. Can't you sponge that off?*"

"*You shouldn't have bought one with a stain on the skirt.*"

"*It was the last one.*"

"*You should have gone to another store. I would never buy a doll with a stained skirt.*"

You drain your drink, pinch your lips, and mutter, "*Yes, Ma'am,*"

"*What did you say?*"

You are both still staring at the merchandise on the table. You don't answer her question. Instead, you say, "*Why did you get Brent a yellow mohair sweater? He won't wear it.*"

"*He has sensitive skin. Wool irritates him. You know that.*"

"*It looks like a girl's sweater.*"

"*It's the newest fashion. And it's too bad you think it looks feminine because I bought you one in red.*"

You turn and stomp up the stairs to the kitchen where you fill up your glass with gin.

Mom is right behind you. "*Ed, you're drunk. You shouldn't drink so much.*"

You squint and smile with mock deference.

"*Oh, yes, ma'am. I'm so sorry, ma'am.*"

"*You're acting like a nasty little boy.*" she says.

To which you growl, "*Aw, lay off, you louse.*"

Mom does not yell, call names, or throw things. In fact, she never will. "*You need to behave better than this,*" she informs you. "*You need to control your temper.*"

"*Nag, nag, nag!*"

"*Temper, temper.*"

"*Aw, drop dead!*"

By now, we children would be fast asleep. The two of you had to find a way to sleep, as well. You would have had no trouble in those years, given the gin in your system. Mom, on the other hand, would have poured another cup of coffee, lit a Pall Mall, and sat in the corner on her ironing board chair, staring into her bewilderment.

In the faint dawn of Christmas morning, we children stand before the Christmas tree, but the whole house feels frigid, as though the furnace snapped off in the night and the icy air seeped through our walls. Your gloomy silence on this happiest of mornings makes me scared and sort of sick.

There are presents under the tree, but even they look cold and angry. They are not spread out beneath the glittering boughs but stacked up like building blocks in three columns. Not one is wrapped. I can picture you and Mom, slamming down each toy on top the other, while the rest of the world sang Christmas carols.

The morning became the afternoon, we played with our toys, the two of you warmed up, but something menacing had moved in. This might have been the first time I genuinely understood that it lived with us now.

Like a rattlesnake under the bed, I tried not to disturb it.

Finding Nantucket, a Needle, and God

Sometime during fifth grade, poisonous phrases like "drop dead" and "you louse" had entered your vocabulary. Even so, Dad, you somehow managed to remain my hero and I still lived to make you proud.

I couldn't stand to disappoint you. Take the swim team, for instance. The summer before sixth grade you wanted me to swim on the Clarendon Hills swim team and I did. But I hated it. It turned my favorite pastime into a grinding punishment. Every morning I sat shivering on the wet cement, then swam lap after lap after lap, until I expected my lungs to burst, my arms to fall off, and my eyes to burn blind from chlorine. I wanted so badly to quit, but I couldn't. It made you proud.

After ten weeks of torment, swim team finally ended, and on August 18th, 1964, we arrived on Nantucket for the first time. The torture of swim team faded as the wonder of this newfound paradise grabbed hold of my soul. It grabbed hold of us all. Our troubles evaporated in that sparkling salt air. You were happy all day long, Mom was happier than she'd been in a long time, so we kids were ecstatic. *Life was good again!*

But our Nantucket happiness was short-lived. Returned to the real world by Labor Day, the mounting tension between the two of you bled back into our lives. Nevertheless, with the glory of Nantucket still in my system, I started sixth grade on top of the world.

Somehow, I had managed to maintain an essential detachment

when it came to the friction between you and Mom. At least for a while. I also believe the bad times were made less bad by how ultra-good the good times were. Like the nursery rhyme about the girl with the curl: when you were bad, Dad, you were horrid. But when you were good — man, you were awesome.

My solid self-esteem at school offset my worries at home. I found myself pleased with the person I'd grown into. I saw myself as smart, kind, and good at most things. Honestly: art, basketball, math, diagramming sentences, singing, making friends, I did it all with ease. And even the cutest boy in the class, had a crush, not on Sky, the adorable blue-eyed tomboy, but on me—the tall, brown-eyed competent girl.

Upsetting events like Sharon Miller's mother, Sky vs. Susie, the end of Nantucket, and worse, waited around the corner, only I didn't know it yet. At age eleven I had burst into being and felt capable and content.

And yet sixth grade was a pivotal year of contrasts, of personal highs and lows. One of those lows was missing my last Walker School Christmas program due to a needle in the foot.

Missing the Christmas Program was a bitter disappointment. Brent and I lived for our Christmas Programs. First, we got to sing for an audience. Then, of course, we got all that festive rehearsal time crammed into our normal school days, back when a real live fir tree stood decorated in every classroom. But the coolest part of all? Going to school at night! We girls in our velveteen dresses, the boys like little men in suits and ties. We stayed corralled in our classrooms; the gigantic windows thrillingly filled with cold black sky and sparkling stars. We played Seven Up and sucked on candy canes, until the messenger appeared at our door to say, "It's time!"

Oh, boy! Time to tiptoe through the hushed hallways, file through the secret door, which led us onto the old wooden stage, and stand in proud formation beneath the warm pink lights, which hung closer to our heads each passing year. Best of all was looking out over the sea of heads and twinkling eyeglasses of mothers, fathers, neighbors, and grandparents, all barely visible in the darkened gymnasium, until our eyes adjusted, then *Pow! Wow!* There you were—my very own mom and dad!

The fact that sixth grade would be the last of these events was tough enough. But worse yet— after being awarded the coveted leading role of Santa Claus in "The Year Without a Santa Claus," a poem by Phyllis McGinley requiring epic line memorization, I had to miss the program entirely. The night of the program, I snuck off to the one place in our house where I could keep my eye on the warm, lighted windows of Walker School—our pink bathroom countertop. I hoisted myself up onto the tiles, and with the door locked and the light switch off, I huddled there, peering out the window at the packed parking lot and lit up gymnasium, feeling sorry for myself. All because of what happened the Sunday before.

It snowed last night! This is so exciting because our Christmas program is this coming Thursday night, and the deep snow makes it look so Christmasy! After Sunday School, Anne Larson called a bunch of us to come over and go sledding. Afterwards, we went back to Anne's house for hot chocolate and cookies.

Mrs. Larson calls to us, "Take your boots off at the door!" as we pile into her hallway. "And put your coats and hats in the first bedroom!"

I yank my boots off, and oops—off come my socks. I take one barefooted step toward the bedroom and YOW! OW! I drop to the floor to inspect my foot. A needle's sticking out of it! A sewing needle must have been caught in the braided rug, standing straight up! I stepped down so hard and it plunged in so deep that it looks like only half a needle sticking out. I pull on it, but it won't budge. I tug and tug until it finally comes out. But here's something strange ... there's no tip. I know what needles look like and the sharp pointed top of this one is missing. The tiny hole in my foot bleeds only a little and doesn't hurt too much, so I pull my sock back on and join my friends in the kitchen.

The next morning, I climb out of bed and faint. Mom hurries me and Audrey into the car and drives straight to the emergency room at Hinsdale Hospital where I tell them about the needle. They take an x-ray and see that the pointy end of the needle is still inside my foot. The doctor gives me a shot of "local anesthetic" and starts digging around. A few hours later, he still has not located it, so he calls in a second doctor, who straps a "tourniquet" to my thigh. Through all this digging, I lay on my stomach, practicing my Santa Claus lines.

At last, they find the piece of metal, buried not inside the tissue, but inside my bone! When the doctors finally pulled it out, they cheered and clapped each other's backs.

I went home on crutches and when the anesthetic wore off, my foot combusted. As our family ate dinner, I lay in my bed, my eyes bulging out of their sockets, stupefied by the fiery pain. I could not even summon the breath to scream. Nothing so tortuous had ever ravaged my nerve endings. Now and then, Mom appeared to check on me. I could do nothing but grip her hand and crush it for all I was worth for the few moments she stood by my bedside. After an hour or so, the flames abated, and I conked out.

Were you even home, Dad? I don't remember you being there. If you had been, you would have given me aspirin, no matter what Mom said. You would have stayed in my room and let me crush your hand for hours. You just couldn't have been home.

I went back to school two days later, yet I was unable to walk home at lunchtime with the other kids, so for that next week, I stayed in the empty classroom. Mom dropped off my lunch at 11:50, and I ate it alone at my desk.

The Christmas program fell only a few days after my surgery; standing on one leg and crutches for that duration was out of the question. So, I huddled on the bathroom counter, peering out the window, pretending I was there, broken-hearted that I wasn't.

They gave my Santa part to Marilyn Dorn.

*

One of my finest moments during sixth grade came when the town crowned me "Snow Queen." Wasn't that exciting? Clarendon Hills decides to hold its first ever "Ice Carnival" complete with crowning one sixth-grade girl from each of the three elementary schools "Snow Queen," and I'm it for Walker!

What an honor. The whole school voted—all the kids in all the grades— and I felt both humbled and awed to emerge the winner. Even the title thrilled me: "*Snow Queen.*" No better queen to be, in my opinion.

It also happened to be the title of my all-time favorite fairy tale by Hans Christian Andersen. You know the one. Kai and Gerda, two best friends, wrestled with good and evil. Kai is captured by the Snow Queen after shards of glass from a demon's mirror lodge in his heart and eye, distorting everything into ugliness. When, after searching high and low, Gerda finds him, her warm tears wash the shard from his frozen heart, prompting his own tears which flush out the shard in his eye. He can finally see the world clearly again and turns back into himself. Gerda's love, "Her own purity and innocence of heart," saved her beloved friend. Fabulous!

Anyway, we three little Snow Queens of Clarendon Hills got our grinning faces in The Doings, a choice of anything we wanted from Young's Five and Dime— a plaid overnight case for me— and a small charm, shaped like Illinois, with a star up near Chicagoland, engraved in back with the name of our school and "Snow Queen, Ice Carnival, 1965."

We also presided over the Winter Carnival activities, crowns replacing our stocking caps. An event any mom could be proud of. But while I sailed along high on sixth-grade life, Mom had been shifting in and out of sullenness. She didn't act proud in the least.

Someone called to give her the glad Snow Queen tidings, and also asked that she keep it secret until the public announcement. She didn't. She told me then and there, not with shining eyes in a rush of pleasure, but with a face stern and tight with some silent reproach. For the life of me, I could not reconcile her manner to the situation. You traveled out of town more than usual now, leaving our house feeling dark and drafty when you were gone, and Mom, drained and distant. It had to have been about you, not me.

One more moment made this a pivotal year in the privacy of my own soul.

I am lying on my single bed, under my yellow canopy. Four-year-old Audrey is sound asleep in her crib four feet away. I sang her to sleep, like I do every night, and before I slide my transistor radio under my pillow to listen to the WLS Top Ten Countdown, I stare into the darkness for a moment and a tidal wave of awareness engulfs me. I see with stunning clarity that I am standing on the brink of the rest of my life. My childhood is about to end. Adulthood comes next and forever. I picture my so-far life as a slow climb up the steps of the high dive at the Clarendon Hills Pool. Clutching those firm metal railings, I could turn around and climb back down if I lost my nerve. Only at this top there is no turning back. I will walk to the edge of that narrow board and, like it or not, spring into space. Out in that vast unknown, for the rest of always, both good and bad will come hurtling at me. Even though I dread the bad, I have a strange sense of welcoming it, like I feel a hunger to experience every single second adult life will offer.

"Dear God," I pray. "Please let me experience everything. Come what may, I want to live it all and as fully as I can."

I am burning with some new courage, and I more or less tell God to "bring it on." But I also tell Him, "I'll need your help to handle it, to live it all well and bravely. I will do and be whatever you want of me in this world, only I know it will take stupendous strength and for that I will need you."

A *Divine assurance washes through me as I feel rather than hear God say, "I will come through on my end, but here's what I need from you: You must never lose faith. You must remember this conversation and doubt neither my power nor your purpose. You cannot tire of any of it, and you can never, under any circumstances, give up."*

Yet in between these events, so much more happened, and I am amazed to realize that so close to our ending, so much of it was so good. And because of those good times, I can't leave this year yet. It turned out to be our Golden Era. The last year we all loved each other.

Our Last Golden Era

1964-1965

That sixth-grade year, we learned about Ancient Greece and Rome, how they had Golden Ages of peace and prosperity right before they toppled. That is how our homelife felt to me in the fall of 1964 and on into1965; we were having our own Golden Era. You and Mom bickered yes, but I could still close my ears to it and honestly, I experienced more good times that year than bad. Like that rattlesnake under the bed sat trapped in a shoe box. The prosperity was exciting. But the periods of peace were the true blessings, as they gave me a much-needed sense of security.

You, Dad, acted rich. Rich and content and even jollier than usual.

Whatever it stemmed from, we all benefited, materially and emotionally. Part of this had to be because you legitimately came into money. Maybe this was the year that your maiden Aunt Lizzie died, and thousands of dollars were found under her mattress and left to you and your two siblings. We were doing things we hadn't done before, things that took money.

Best was the theatre. You took us to see the national touring production of *Oliver!* at the Shubert in downtown Chicago—my first live, professional theatre experience. I was besotted. Besotted with live theatre and besotted with the Artful Dodger, who in real life was Davy Jones. Every single song from that show knocked me out and you bought me the album, so I could learn every word. I even asked you for the songbook so I could learn all the songs on the organ, which I did.

I loved everything about that experience—the hush that fell over the darkened theater seconds before the orchestra burst into the Overture, the smell of hot stage lights, the synergy between the actors and the audience, the electric charge vibrating my very marrow when every voice —man, woman, and child—rose to a crescendo of heart-stopping harmony. My eyes filled with instant tears at the curtain call, when we clapped and cheered for the triumph we'd all been a part of. Nantucket and the theatre: both were like finding my twin.

And then there was Davy Jones. Of course, it was the character of the Artful Dodger who stole my heart, but he was played by a cute guy named Davy Jones from Manchester, England. Davy Jones became my first truly crazed, delirious crush. I guessed him to be about fourteen years old, which made him perfectly eligible boyfriend material. (He was in fact nineteen.) I think my love of the musical *Oliver!* made me even crazier over Davy, and my love for Davy made me even crazier about *Oliver!* I tell you about this so you might understand how clobbered I was by adolescence hormones and what uncontrollable passions permeated my pre-teen being. I mean, I considered it entirely possible that Davy would be on our ferry heading to Nantucket that summer, so I carefully planned what I'd wear—my beige corduroy Levi's, my olive-green Purdue sweatshirt, and Mom's beat up suede jacket. He would take one look at me and propose.

Anyway, you kept bringing us to plays and musicals that year and it made me feel like a princess. I'd don my pink mohair dress, grown-up nylon stockings and pink leather flats, and join the classiest group of people I had yet encountered: *theatregoers*. What a privilege!

Those trips to the Shubert or the Blackstone would have been exhilarating enough. But then came Christmas. That Christmas of sixth grade was as good as the dreary Christmas one year before had been bad. This year, you and Mom made a convivial team. Maybe because you knew how ecstatic we'd be with our gifts, and boy, were we ever!

Stockings first. I am stunned! Instead of the usual candy and trinkets, I find actual presents inside. Good ones! I get a "princess ring"—six separate bands of gem-colored rhinestones. A pink Baby Ben alarm clock, pink jewels encircling the face.

Best of all is my gold Monet charm bracelet. I know it is expensive and obviously Mom chose each charm with me in mind. Each one reflects an interest of mine: an artist palette, a tiny church through whose window I can read The Lord's Prayer, a Christmas tree, a telephone, a Bible, a tiny jug to hold a dab of perfume, and a gold disk with a cherub embossed which reads "You are an angel."

Mom picked this out! She picked out every single charm thinking of me and me alone. My heart soars. "You are an angel!"

And that's only my stocking! Under the tree, there is a Barbie Dream House; a grown-up, two-tiered pink jewelry box with a tiny gold key to lock it; a Kodak instamatic camera: an ID bracelet: and a book I still own and read (chosen by you, Dad): Favorite Poems, Old and New, and more! When we come to the end of our gifts, giddy and grateful, you and Mom disappear into the basement and come back up beaming, each of you carrying a black and white portable TV inside an enormous silver bow—one for Brent and one for me. That's like getting your own car!

It's no wonder I thought we'd struck it rich. That fall of 1964, you bought our house lot in Hinsdale, and Mom spent hours each day designing the home we would build there. She and I would pour through her sketches together, both of us blissful.

We did other cool things like spent a weekend at Pheasant Run Resort where we ate in a swanky restaurant, and, by diving under a glass wall, could swim from an indoor pool to an outdoor pool. They also had a golf course for you and Brent. Next to the pool, my favorite was the little replica of a New Orleans alley they called "Bourbon Street" lined with gift shops and white wrought iron tables and chairs for sipping Kiddie Cocktails while listening to a Dixieland band playing the snappiest music on earth.

We traveled to Lake Lawn Lodge in Wisconsin, too, for a weekend of swimming and dining and general living it up. You can see why I call that year a Golden Age; every time I turned around, we were on another family adventure.

These many delights culminated in our second Nantucket vacation, the one we brought friends to. Although it remains the best vacation of my childhood, I must admit, we hit some hurdles. Yes, we swam in rolling waves, ate quahog chowder and Indian Pudding, drifted to sleep to the hushing surf, but other things happened, too. Things that ushered in the fall of our splendid Golden Age.

It started the day we arrived, when Brent catapulted off the back of a motor scooter and landed in the hospital. As you recall, John, the friend Brent invited, had his driver's license, and rented a scooter as soon as we arrived. As the two boys rode it back to our cottage at Wauwinet (a quaint inn at the time, not today's posh place for the uber rich and famous), John overshot a bend in the road, swinging into the oncoming lane and an approaching truck. To avoid hitting it head on, he swerved into the scrub pines and crashed. John was unharmed, but Brent broke his collarbone. He wore a sling and could not swim, not once, our whole vacation. Eventually the doctor gave him permission to ride in our boat. Wearing his neatly pressed shorts and collared shirt, he took the wheel while John, who lived in his striped speedo, cavorted along behind us on water skis. I know you remember all of this vividly. Do you also remember how it grieved Mom even more than it did her son?

Another bit of misfortune befell us when that pesky menstrual period I'd begun six months earlier, came like clockwork to ruin the fun.

Oh, no! How can this be? I can't have my period now! How will I swim? How can I even wear a bathing suit?? People will see my Kotex pad. No, it's impossible. I can't swim!

"*They make something called a Tampon,*" Susie says, "*You push one up there and you don't need to wear a belt or a pad. It stays up there with a string for pulling it out.*"

"*I know, but my mom says I'm not old enough to use them. Do you use them?*"

"*No, my mom says that, too. Well, okay, what else could you do?*"

"*How about I wear the belt but I could cut the pad down as tiny as possible so it fits between my legs, and no one can see it?*"

I tried. I cut it in all sorts of formations but once in the ocean, the make-shift mini-pad got water-logged and instantly popped out the sides of my bottoms. It was no use.

It embarrassed me for anyone except Susie and Mom to know my problem, so I kept this secret from you and caused you days of exasperation, when your "swimming bug" daughter inexplicably refused to go in the ocean you had brought her over a thousand miles to enjoy. It was bad enough I couldn't swim, but even worse—I could not bring myself to confess my problem to you, not even to ease your frustration.

Next to Brent getting injured, the worst moment came on the last day of our trip. I could not bear to leave Nantucket and didn't care if I never went home again. The gray sky reflected my heavy heart and probably yours, too, releasing rain for the first time in three weeks. Then, right when we closed and locked the door to our cottage, Mom fell down the stairs and sprained her ankle.

Gloom enveloped us. You and Mom barely spoke to each other. She sat in the car in the hold of the ferry with nothing to do but be miserable. Why? Did you each blame the other for her fall? I think I brought her a cup of coffee. I hope I did. Beyond that, all I know is she vowed never to go back to Nantucket for the rest of her life, which meant we couldn't either. It felt like the end of the world to me.

You and I, unbeknownst to one another, each made our own private vow that we would go back, whatever it took, and some years later we each succeeded. But on that day, the tears I'd been holding back pushed to overflowing when, all because Mom fell down some stairs, a beautiful part of life had ended, and the gloom of that day never fully faded.

True, your drunken tirades had already begun, but most of the time you acted content, pleased with yourself and with your children. You bought our first boat that year, one of the best thrills of the summer. Not only did we bring our friends to Nantucket, but we also brought our own speedboat. At home, you docked it in the Fox River and taught us to water ski. You would soon join Medinah, our prestigious country club, where you and Mom attended fancy events and we ate Sunday dinner as a family.

When I was in sixth grade you still loved us. *Oh, you must have!* Because all of this strikes me as the actions of a man finding more to do with his wife and children, not less. A man planning to stay with his family, not leave them.

Unless you had a different family in mind.

Love is Blind but Now I See

It occurs to me that in describing you, I've used words like "integrity" and "honorable." I've said I admired and respected you, and that is true. Odd, perhaps, since you were already swearing at Mom and calling her names. How could you still be my hero? I say it is proof of my unshakeable love for you and so my willingness to block out these bouts and wipe the slate clean after each frightening episode. As long as you bounced back to normal, I could keep loving you.

A particular flashback from that summer of 1965, tells me that I was already desensitized to your name-calling by the time I was 11. Susie and I decided to camp out in the playhouse you built for me when I was six and would later become Brent's pigeon coop. We lay in the dark, head-to-head in our sleeping bags, eating Jiffy-Pop when Susie decided to share a grave secret with me.

"Val, you can't tell anyone what I am about to tell you. Not even your parents. My parents have sworn me to secrecy so you can't breathe a word."

"Okay," I promise, wondering what in the world she will say.

"You know how my brother Pete is in the Marines? Well, he's going on a secret mission. They're flying helicopters into a place called Laos. It's like a war and my parents are really afraid."

"Louse!" I shriek, like it is the punchline to a joke. "Louse? Oh, my gosh! That's what my father calls my mom when he's mad! There's really a country called LOUSE??"

Poor Sue. What a bizarre response to such a somber secret.

"Val, it's not funny! This is some sort of a war, and we're scared he could die!"

"Oh, gosh, Susie, I'm sorry. I mean, well, I can't believe Louse is a country! I won't tell anyone, I promise, and I will pray for Pete."

The point is that even though you were calling Mom a louse—which is awful in itself, and awful for a child to hear—also awful is the fact that I had no choice but to accept it, overlook it, refuse to let it affect me, if I was to keep loving you.

Another critical point is that even though you intermittently behaved abominably, the rest of the time you acted like my real dad, my champion. I want you to know that I know that.

And I want you to know how well I remember all the times you came to my rescue. Here's one. Do you remember? We were at that extremely rustic dude ranch in Colorado when I was almost nine. Our cabin sat on a hill about a quarter of a mile from the horse corral, where Brent and I hung out, admiring the horses and talking to them. On this occasion, I fed sugar cubes to my favorite horse, Pancho, and did not know to flatten the palm of my hand. I presented him my fingers first, which he promptly tried to eat. I shrieked, he let go, and I pulled my hand out of his mouth to find deep crimson teeth marks where he had chomped down hard. Brent went running for you. He shot up the hill to the cabin, and in a flash, you were out the door, running to my rescue. I can see you at this moment clear as day, tearing down the hill, ripping through the tall grass, leaping over the longest weeds, as I staggered up the hill to you, holding out my dented hand, wailing. Nothing in your life mattered to you in that moment as much as me.

You know, as I relive that moment now, I want to weep. As I see you running down that Colorado hill, I feel like I've swallowed pure regret. It hurts to see so vividly the magnitude of love I was destined to lose.

Anyway, my devotion to you in those days was unshakable. It would take a lot to undermine it. But there's another explanation for my blind loyalty, my refusal to let your reproachable behavior spoil my reverence for you: as long as one of my parents remained "normal," the ground stayed solid beneath my feet. I *needed* you to stay normal. And aside from your tirades at Mom, you stayed normal in every other respect. But when that normal parent slides off the deep end—then it's all sinking sand. That day was drawing closer as we approached 1966.

Eureka

After the gloomy finish to our Nantucket vacation in August of 1965, your hostility towards Mom was obvious. If you'd ever tried to hide it, you'd given up and now disparaged her openly and often. Audrey, who was only five that summer, told me recently that she clearly remembers thinking "My *father does not love my mother.*"

That abysmal end to our golden summer added an extra layer of turmoil in our house right in time for me to start junior high, which—ask any Walker School kid—was hard enough. Things at home grew murky during my seventh-grade year, and downright dismal during eighth.

No doubt about it, our Golden Age was over.

It's also when my health deteriorated. A sturdy girl from the start, I developed ailments. It began with mono the week sixth grade ended, and I'll refresh your memory, because starting around then, you were gone more than ever.

Sixth grade ended with an in-depth report on the country of our choice. I chose Sweden and went at it like prize money waited. Even Mom jumped in. Delighted that I chose her ancestral home to study, she bought a record album of Swedish folk songs for me to play during my presentation and made Limpa Bread and Swedish butter cookies for me to share with my class. Night after night, I sat up well beyond my bedtime working on my project. All this zealous effort and lack of sleep left me critically fatigued. In the middle of a music lesson, two days after school let out, I collapsed at the organ. A blood test revealed mononucleosis, and I lay in bed for two weeks, my head and neck covered with glands the size of golf balls. After I recovered, I still felt feeble and grew cold and tired easily, setting the scene for more illness to come.

The first day of seventh grade I developed a headache that lasted two years. I know now that I suffered classic tension headaches. Even Dr. Dreyfuss, when Mom, after months of my suffering, finally allowed me to see him, felt compelled to mention my "home environment."

My head started hurting first thing in the morning and abated only when I fell asleep at night. The pain waned and waxed during the day; sometimes manageable, sometimes crippling. What could I do other than live with it? I still maintained excellent grades and made tons of new friends. Eight other elementary schools poured their sixth graders into Hinsdale Junior High, meaning we kids from Walker had about 300 new boys and girls to meet. Pretty exciting, since every seventh-grade girl seemed at the height of her gleeful friendliness. I attended a different party every Friday night where the whole bunch of us spent the evening laughing our heads off and adoring one another. I still love each of those dear, irrepressible 12-year-old girls, myself included.

Despite what was going on at home to cause the pain in my head,

I remained—for the time being— my sunny, confident, well-adjusted self. Back then, I could still find ways to block out your brawls. Despite those infernal headaches, I loved seventh grade.

But here's where I freeze the film and pick up the microscope.

That summer of 1966, between seventh and eighth grade, we took a vacation to Upstate New York. Cousin Donna was getting married in

Interlocken, and Audrey and I had been asked to be flower girl and "junior" bridesmaid. Mom made our dresses and also sewed several nice outfits for herself, which was rare. Again, we hitched our boat to the back of our Buick and drove off, this time, to the Finger Lakes.

We have rented my dream house on a lake called Cayuga and Rod Serling from The Twilight Zone lives down the road! This house is straight out of Walt Disney's "Summer Magic." It's what is called a Victorian and has garrets and cupolas and a wrap-around porch. It's exactly the kind of house we need to live in! I have my own room on the second floor with a bay window that looks out over the lake. This room is three times larger than the one I share with Audrey back home. And it's yellow; I love yellow! The furniture is white wicker and I have a big double bed all to myself! There is only one thing wrong with this room and that is spiders. So many spiders live in my room that every night before bed, I spend a solid twenty minutes hunting them down and squishing them dead. I start the day like

that, too, as they all give birth to hundreds of spider babies all night long. One morning I open my eyes in time to watch a spindly black spider drop from its web directly above my face and dangle two inches from my nose. It almost stopped my heart!

I write in my diary at bedtime; I never skip a night. I pour out my innermost thoughts, and I write such volumes that it never fits on the small page allotted, so I tape sheet after sheet of extra paper into the small leather book to accommodate all I have to say about my life this summer.

We swim, we boat, we water-ski. But as usual, it's Brent and you and me. Mom and Audrey seem missing from this vacation. Where are they? Why do they do nothing with us? I feel like Mom never even speaks to me when I do see her, which might only be at dinner. Well, Audrey is still only five going on six. She can't do the things we do at almost thirteen and almost seventeen. Still, Mom is quieter, more serious than usual.

Something was unquestionably wrong between you and Mom that summer, certainly on our long and strangely hurried drive home. No one named it or explained it. But the air in the car grew so charged with acrimony that, for fear of adding one more ounce of angst to the situation, I kept from both of you my need for a Kotex pad. I kept wadding toilet paper into my underpants at every gas station restroom we came to during our two-day sprint back, so as not to stress you out any further.

(I also experienced crushing regret when I discovered about a hundred miles into our trip, that my precious diary, which I kept in the top right drawer of the antique white dresser, remained there when we left, lost to me forever.)

Your regular business trips had become even more frequent that year. You spent more time away than at home. I noticed also that although Mom acted exceptionally glum and distant, you acted exceptionally happy. Euphorically happy. *The happiest ever!*

Ah.

I am sixty-five years old, sitting with my laptop on my green velvet couch, getting pounded by a Maine blizzard. My husband is outside on the snow blower. The dog is upstairs on the bed. I am alone here, but my twelve-year-old self is in the room with me, at my shoulder, and I tell her: "You see? We had to grow up and grow old, to understand that the anger comes later. The anger comes when you are trapped. Find the angriest year and look a year or two before that."

We have answered one of my questions, my young self and me. Somewhere between 1965 and 1966. That's when we lost you.

It was the year you were the happiest.

Part II

Don't You Want
Somebody to Love?

The Storm Inside

1967

You had made up your mind to leave. You just didn't know when.

Reaching that first decision must have been tough enough; choosing the best time to go would be no less problematic. But you needed a breather. Am I right? There was no rush, not yet. I understand all this only now. Only let me tell you what was going on inside me, as you watched for your opportunity.

First, I got sick again. I got sick and I couldn't get well. My eighth-grade report card reveals that I was absent from school 45 days that year. An entire quarter. Something was up. Not only was I sick, but it is the one year of my life about which I remember virtually nothing. I attach great significance to that fact.

In March of 1967 my throat started hurting. Soon it got too sore to swallow. My temperature shot up to 102 and stayed there, along with the pain, day after day, week after week. I lay in my canopied bed in the small room Audrey and I would share for another year. Audrey was in first grade and Brent a senior in high school, so Mom and I were the only ones at home all day. I stayed in bed around the clock and slept and read and fevered. During one good stretch, I read *Gone with the Wind* in three days. If my head didn't hurt too badly in the evening, I turned on my little portable television set and watched one of four available channels. It felt like

Mom lived in the kitchen and you lived elsewhere, but you breezed in once a week and checked on me. Thursdays, maybe.

At this point, you and Mom fought constantly. You roared and rampaged while she spoke in calm, measured tones. When you raged and she didn't, it was easy to blame you for the mayhem and I did. Yet Brent insists that the words Mom spoke so evenly were artfully designed to goad you, that behind her composure she hid her own brand of passive-aggressive torment. Whatever I may think about that, it is Brent's truth. And now I wonder ... was it your truth, too, Dad? Did you feel antagonized? Did self-composed Mom instigate some of those nightly fights?

Seriously, why "louse?" That's what I would call someone who has done something disdainful, especially to me. "Heel" would be similar, or "cad." But a cad is a man who behaves dishonorably, in particular towards a woman. What did Mom *do* for you to choose "louse" above all other insults? All I can think is that Brent got it right—she was a passive-aggressive genius. She knew the exact buttons to push to send you into conniption fits. She pushed those buttons in retaliation for whatever crime she perceived in you. "Louse!" you shot back. Maybe instead of "Low blow!"

Brent felt sorry for you, while I felt sorry for Mom. Did that anger you further?

Whoever started it, everything Mom said caused you to swear and explode with such fury, I feared the top of your head might fly off and literally hit the roof. Thankfully you came home less and less. Still, you did come home—it was, after all, where you lived—and when you were there, you and Mom locked yourself in a ghastly pattern of endless recriminations, always the same. Mom, sober and didactic. You, liquored up and mad as hell, combining sarcastic snarling with blind rage. And profanity. Always profanity.

I've successfully suppressed most of these exchanges, but I

know you called her a "louse" over and over. A "son-of-a bitch," too, which confused as well as sickened me. She would calmly say, "Temper, temper," and you would bellow back "DROP DEAD YOU LOUSE! YOU SON OF A BITCH, DROP DEAD!"

Night after night after night, you played out the same nightmare, as if a spell had been cast upon you and you were powerless against it. No amount of crying from Audrey or pleading on my part broke the pattern. It was as if you could neither see nor hear us, as if we existed in separate dimensions. Only we were right there listening, wanting to scream.

One night I finally did.

The usual chaos is being unleashed in the kitchen while outside a rainstorm batters our house. Tonight, you are particularly malicious, using your nastiest voice, your most vulgar vocabulary, oozing, just oozing contempt. "Drop dead! Drop dead you miserable louse, you fucking son-of-a-bitch!" You shout this at Mom, while I am there in the kitchen, only a few feet away.

I cannot stand it anymore. I cannot take one more word of this. I fly up to your face and scream at the top of my lungs, with every ounce of blood in my body: SHUT UP!

Then louder and closer: I HATE YOU!

Never have I uttered these words to either of you. I might throw up.

Ferocious silence. No one moves. Not a human sound is heard until I run out the back door, howling into the downpour. Rain slashes my clothes, my skin, my face, and I fall against the tool shed, sobbing.

Through my tears and the pounding rain I hear a noise. A drum nearby. I freeze. Where does it come from? Who is beating a drum so close to me in a rainstorm? I stop weeping and listen, straining to make sense of it. Then I understand—it comes from me. The banging in my eardrums is the pounding of my own shattered heart.

*

I stayed sick. Why didn't I go to the doctor? Well, that's one of the things you and Mom fought about that spring of 1967. She feared doctors and medicine and, maddening as it was, I think we can agree she had her reasons. The year before, you had finally prevailed regarding my headaches, and Mom agreed to let me be examined. But she forbade me to take the pills the doctor prescribed and refused the head X-rays he'd ordered. Instead, she prayed that God would transfer my pain to her. He chose not to.

This time, after who knows how long, Mom again broke down and took me to the doctor, who said I had tonsillitis and needed a tonsillectomy. He was barking up the wrong mom.

Nowadays, Brent and Audrey and I are proud of that woman who refused X-rays and tonsillectomies, who wouldn't let us run behind mosquito spray trucks with the rest of the kids, cavorting in clouds of DDT. A woman ahead of her time, who sketched drawings of electric cars, she also claimed baking soda would whiten our teeth, and garlic would help cure colds. The foresight we now consider signs of her brilliance, you took as further proof of insanity.

No operation for me; I remained sick.

Yet after a month in bed, I couldn't help but get better. Or else she finally relented and allowed me antibiotics.

While I was ill, something earth-shattering happened. Susie, my childhood soul mate, best friend of my life, entered my sick room to bid me farewell. It felt like a fever dream, some fearsome nightmare, only it was real—she and her family were moving to Indiana, and she came to say goodbye. Tangled up in sweat-soaked sheets, I was too weak to sit up and hug her, too ill to even register my sorrow. Susie had been such a basic part of my life, such a part of *me*, that half my identity left when she did.

And while I lay there in my bedroom, week after week after week, our family continued to disintegrate. Did you choose that exact block of time to complete your emotional extrication? When you did come home, you were a stranger. When I finally emerged from my sickroom, the air in our house had been drained of life. It just hung there, dead.

I returned to school for the last few weeks of eighth grade. On my thinner, still wobbly legs, I felt like a different kind of creature, as though I was the one who'd moved away, and had to start over in a new school. Recapturing my former junior high social standing held little appeal. It didn't trouble me much; after nearly nine weeks in my bedroom, I'd become my own best friend.

I wasn't fully aware of it, but all that solitary confinement created in me a perception of separateness, a new loner attitude, which, although unfamiliar, felt not uncomfortable. I see now how this new sense of apart-ness undermined my self-confidence right when I'd need it the most and set the stage for the different girl I'd become in high school, making choices I'd live to regret.

Of course, other destructive forces contributed to that decline. Like the fact that soon I would hate you, Dad. Just like you hated me.

Sinking Sand

By the time I turned fourteen, you hated us all. Not just Mom whom you snarled and cursed at night after night, but you hated me, too. And little Audrey? Is that even possible? She was only seven. Away at college, Brent was spared.

I try to pinpoint the moment the love left your eyes, and that unbearable look of disdain moved in. What did I do? What did I do to make you stop loving me?

Back in August of 1967, your poisonous glare was still reserved only for Mom. Those last few days of summer before my freshman year, I still felt loved by you. We took our final family vacation, with our soon-to-be-sold boat, in Holland, Michigan. You were in good spirits. Browsing in an antique shop, I found an old Dutch Bible from 1843. Someone had pressed a wildflower between two pages, under a bookmark embroidered with the words: *To One I Love*. I longed to own it, and you bought it for me. You still loved me then.

A few weeks later you took us all to a matinee at the Martinique's Drury Lane Dinner Theater to celebrate my fourteenth birthday, the perfect gift for your daughter who shared your passion for theater. You still loved me then, right?

But, come to think of it, I remember— for the first time ever— feeling antsy during that play, thinking our family party might take too long, and I might miss out on whatever fun my new gang of high school friends was having without me. I probably didn't keep my fretting to myself; I probably grumbled aloud, and that would have offended you, hurt your feelings, as well it should have. It would have been unprecedented for me, and a perturbing turning point for you.

No two ways about it, in the fall of 1967 I was becoming a teenager and not the kind you must have hoped for. But please understand—I didn't expect to be my type of teenager, either. I'd planned on wearing bobby sox and poodle skirts. To have coke dates at the malt shop. I never pictured myself riding around in cars in bell-bottom jeans and some sailor's pea coat from the Army/Navy Surplus, smoking Marlboros, and drinking Colt 45s.

Two weeks before ninth grade, this transformation was nowhere in the cards. I was still your good Lutheran daughter. Consuming alcohol was the farthest thing from my mind. In our eighth-grade health unit, Miss Johnson described the countless brain cells killed by cocktails. No real cause for alarm since I had no interest in drinking, but I still took note of the brain damage business.

While I had no plans to drink or smoke, neither you nor Mom had raised me to shun these vices. The Surgeon General had not yet "… *Determined that Cigarette Smoking is Dangerous to your Health*" and I considered cocktails before dinner a gracious aspect of adult living. When we ate at upscale restaurants, I watched you order a series of Martinis and Mom her one Manhattan, with a maraschino cherry. On the rare occasions we had company over, those gleaming bottles came out of the liquor cabinet and joined the soda pop on the counter. (I still hadn't drawn a concrete connection between your profane outbursts of hate-spewing, and the many martinis you drank.)

When it came to health and injury, you might recall that I was a cautious child. I didn't even roller skate for fear of falling. But I did smoke my first cigarette, and drank my first cup of coffee, earlier that summer when I spent two weeks with Susie and her parents in Indiana. I did both to be polite. Sue's parents smoked and thought nothing of offering their pack to a recent grammar school graduate. It was not my idea. In fact, the prospect of exposing my poor, newly healed tonsils to any more hazards horrified me. Yet wishing to be both game and courteous, I gave it a try, then promptly rushed upstairs, and gargled for five minutes. That was the end of that. For the time being.

A miraculous result of visiting Susie that summer was that my two-year headache vanished. All it took was two weeks away from the war at 206 Grant. My headache never did return and I'm sure it's because I soon found more ways to stay away from the combat zone. Riding around in cars would be one of them.

I ended up in those cars, because the week before high school started, when we returned from Michigan, I found myself in serious friendship limbo. Susie now lived in Indiana. My other friends had fallen to the wayside when I stayed sick and out of school for so long. That summer I mainly read and baby-sat and walked around slightly dazed from the realization that our family was deteriorating. So, when Sally Brand called me up out of the blue, she offered a welcome connection. Ten minutes later she picked me up on her tandem bicycle, and we pedaled into Hinsdale to hang out with her new friends.

These friends of Sally's—I didn't know them at all. They ranged in age from older to much older. Sally and I were the lone freshmen. The rest were sophomores and juniors, and a couple had even graduated. The group consisted mainly of boys—cute, clever, rebellious boys. That right there was the draw.

I craved a boyfriend. In junior high, rumors of sexual escapades abounded, because lots of girls had steady boyfriends. I wasn't one of them. But I'd had mad crushes on boys since kindergarten, and boys I "liked," generally liked me back. Of course, my first all-consuming, hormone-fueled crush was on Davy Jones in *Oliver!* Only how would I ever see him again? Well, remember *The Monkees*? That sitcom that came out in September of 1966, when I turned thirteen? Four cute guys formed a rock band, and unbelievably Davy Jones, was one of the four. Also unbelievable was a chart-topping hit of theirs on the radio, a song called "*Valerri*." I mean, what are the odds? There's Davy Jones, *my* Davy Jones, on everyone's radio, singing "*Va-a-a-a-lerri, I love her ...*" At first, I nearly fainted and walked on air for weeks, but over time, instead of flaming my infatuation, watching Davy Jones be a "Monkee" cooled it. He wasn't the Artful Dodger after all, and I guess that's who I'd loved all along.

Anyway, I wanted a boyfriend *so badly*. I had read so many adult books by that time that I was ravenous for romance. Not all-out sex. That was for marriage. At least that was the plan. But I yearned to go steady. I yearned to be desired. Cherished. *Kissed.*

The cutest boy in Sally's group was named Terry Velling and looked like my new celebrity heartthrob, Dean Martin's son Dino, who played in a band called "Dino, Desi, and Billy." Terry became my first boyfriend. I was fourteen, he was fifteen, and we kissed for the first time on a bright September Saturday, kissed and kissed, perched high on the fire escape of an office building. So exciting, so scary.

And that's what being Terry's girlfriend meant—meeting up on weekends or after school to kiss. Kissing and talking on the phone at night, that's what we did to go steady. I loved "making out," as we called it, and was content to do just that for hours. Terry was not. He wanted more action. So, after two months of getting nowhere, he broke up with me over the phone. To be rejected by my first actual boyfriend hurt for sure. But although I'd been ga-ga over Terry, I hadn't, thank goodness, loved him. That made it easier. Plus, I heard through the grapevine that another boy was interested in me. That helped, too.

My new friends drank. They drank and smoked and swore, and a couple of them, including Terry, would end up in drug programs before long. But laughing with them was so much better than listening to you bellow at Mom. Because this was the year all hell broke loose. As if you'd been holding back until Brent left for college, the gloves came off, no holds barred. I much preferred being—and drinking— with my new friends.

We could get our hands on alcohol because the oldest and oddest member of this group was a twenty-one-year-old beautician named Mindy McNulty. Did you ever meet Mindy? She had an orange beehive hairdo, drawn-in eyebrows, a devilish wit, and a serious nervous twitch. It was Mindy who not only purchased all the beer and wine and cigarettes we wanted but hauled us around all night in her Pontiac while we imbibed. Even if you never met Mindy, you certainly knew of her, and both you and Mom must have had qualms. I don't recall you saying much about her, but I read your faces. It was a questionable relationship, and I'll admit, I found it peculiar, too. I worried about how it appeared to other students my age — to us, 21 was as good as 50—still Mindy was our friend, and we defended our right to be hers. And get rides and liquor.

In Mindy's car we mostly drank beer, but my first drink was wine. One smoky September night we sat around a bonfire in someone's backyard and passed around a bottle of Mogen David. Once again, I joined in to be game and courteous.

Euphoria.

I had managed a vital emotional distance while your fights with Mom worsened, but over time, it required more effort, which I maintain caused my two-year tension headache. The harder you fought, the harder it became to stay unaffected, and the tighter my internal knots twisted. By age 14, my nerves had stretched to the snapping point. Now half a cup of wine released them. Another half a cup, and a rush of comfort warmed my veins, bringing a sense of security I hadn't felt since sixth grade. Mogen David— childhood in a bottle.

I never drank during the week. I went to school and did my homework and talked on the phone at night. But by October of my freshman year, the agony in our house was palpable. The contempt in your eyes, the misery in Mom's, the furious fighting when you happened to be home, had me longing for the weekends when I could soothe my own sorrow with wine's sweet sedation. You and I were both using alcohol to deal with your fury.

You and Mom were too wrapped up in your own mess to notice. If you did, you were probably doubly disappointed in me. If you wanted to do anything about it, I doubt you had the energy to try.

Granted, I gave you no warning. For 14 years I'd been a model daughter. Year after year, I brought home top-notch report cards induced by neither reward nor punishment. I never even had to be told to go to bed. You had no reason to believe I was anything but a good, responsible girl, capable of making my own, correct decisions, and until then, you'd been right.

Had Sally never called, I might have been a different teenager. We both think I'd have been a better one. But you never know. I might have been worse. And yes, I took you and Mom by storm when I went from one kind of girl to another. But I could say you did the same to me.

Downward Spiral

During my freshman year of high school, you and I lost all respect for each other. I believed that you wanted to leave me as much as you wanted to leave Mom. I figured that I had become as big a vexation to you as she had, such a colossal disappointment it pained you to look at me. I had spent 14 years making you proud of me. Could it be that all I had to do to make you ashamed was grow up?

Looking back, I see it wasn't one large, unforgivable act of mine that earned your condemnation, only a series of small missteps, a compilation of errors. But so many of my sins were committed inadvertently, as I—like most teenagers— did what my friends did.

My shopping trip to Old Town in September of that year, 1967, gives an early example. Mindy drove the whole bunch of us down to North Wells Street, the hippie mecca in Chicago in the sixties. Piper's Alley was lined with cool "head" shops selling all kinds of hip novelties, with an emphasis on drug paraphernalia. I bought the things my friends bought, bringing home a silver cigarette lighter, love beads, and a giant mahogany fist, with one finger—the middle one— extended to the sky. I didn't even know what that meant. I only knew it was supposed to be cool and displayed it proudly on my dresser. That might have displeased you. And perhaps that silver lighter.

Maybe I kept changing in so many distasteful teenage ways, that you finally woke up one day and discovered you just didn't like me anymore. Your eyes, which had perpetually beamed affection; now flared hostility. I see you standing in our front window, framed by the golden drapes, regarding me with disgust. What were you thinking? That I wasn't the same daughter you'd been so proud of— the reader, the singer, the swimmer, the scholar, the sunny, uninhibited girl surely destined for greatness? I still got good grades and sang in the high school choir, only now I wore miniskirts and frosted lipstick. I lined my eyes with black pencil and hung out with older kids. I had a boyfriend. I smoked cigarettes, lit with my own silver lighter. A big "Fuck You Fist" sat on my dresser. I see your hostile eyes again and catch a glimpse of hurt. Did you feel your good girl had betrayed you?

If so, I am truly sorry, but I felt betrayed, too. And disgusted. No more turning a deaf ear to the foul way you spoke to your wife, my mother; I was perpetually horrified. Those two years—my freshman and sophomore years of high school— were pure pandemonium. As if the black storm clouds building in the distance, settled smack dab overhead and poured their pent-up poison straight down our chimney, filling our house with toxicity.

Although you were almost always out of town now, the rare nights when you were home were horrendous. After our usual sullen dinner, Mom took refuge on her ironing board chair in the corner of the kitchen and lit a cigarette. You stood at the counter mixing a fresh martini, and for a couple of hours you two would lay into each other.

More often than not, after you raged and swore for what felt like hours, you stormed out of the house, slamming the door behind you, and tore off in the car. You found your way back sometime in the night to sleep on the couch. Audrey and I had long since retreated to our rooms.

When the havoc began, around 7:00 pm, I typically withdrew to the basement where we had our stereo and another yellow phone, mounted to the wall. Here's where I'd listen to my records, talk on the phone, and smoke the single cigarette I managed to pilfer from Mom's pack of Pall Mall straights, blindly believing no one smelled the smoke wafting up the stairs.

One night, while talking on that yellow phone, instead of escaping the havoc, I got sucked into it.

Janet and I are talking about school that day.

"Did you see Carol? Did she say anything about Danny? Didn't you love Nancy's dress?"

Diana Ross and The Supremes are singing "Where Did Our Love Go?" I've cranked up the stereo enough to muffle the uproar upstairs, but still hear Janet. Diana sings, "Baby, don't leave me, oh, please don't leave me, all by myself..." when the racket in the kitchen ceases abruptly. Then BAM, BAM, BAM above. The basement door slams open, and you come crashing down the stairs, charge across the room at me, and in one fell swoop, you rip the phone out of the wall. The concrete wall! While I am talking on it! I stand there speechless holding the severed receiver, while you, saying not a word, turn on your heel and stomp back up the stairs. I think: Mom must have been complaining about me spending so much time on the phone and that was Dad's solution to the problem.

I got the sense that Mom complained about me to you often. Like "what are you going to do about it?" type of complaining, like it was up to you to solve whatever bothered her about me, such as spending so much time on the phone.

I can imagine her saying, *"Valerie is on the phone too much. She is on it every night from seven to nine."* Then she'd wait for the response you wouldn't offer.

"That's way too long for a girl to be on the phone. Who is she talking to for hours?"

"Her friends, probably," you might say.

"I don't know these friends. We haven't met any of them. They never come to the door. She just ducks out and hops into a car. A car driven by a 21-year-old woman and filled with boys. It's unseemly. What must the neighbors think?"

You say nothing.

"*Well, her phone use is excessive. Shouldn't she be doing something more constructive with her time? I wish you would give her some firm rules. She'll listen to you. I wish you would do something about this.*"

Anyone reading this imagined exchange, would conjure a voice not at all like Mom's. They would assume a crabby, crotchety voice, quick and clipped and shrill. Absolutely not Mom. She would have said all of this in a controlled and dignified voice, calmly and sensibly. But lacking any self-doubt.

She wanted you to do something about my excessive phone use. So, you did.

I never heard such a conversation, of course. But why else would you do that, pull the phone out of the wall? I've never stopped to consider what you hoped to accomplish until now. I always thought you were just furiously angry like you were every night, and this time you were angry at me. But you were angry at her, weren't you? You wanted to shut her up. *There*, you thought, *that ought to do it.*

*

Although Terry Velling was my first boyfriend, my first true love was Ed Dawson, the boy waiting in the wings. Because of Ed Dawson, no one can ever tell me that young love is not real. We were Romeo and Juliet. And then just Juliet, because he broke up with me in the springtime of my freshman year and I still wonder why.

The obvious answer would be that I wouldn't have sex with him. We kissed and, as Mom called it, "petted" ourselves into frenzies, but I knew how young I was, and kept my resolve to save sex for my wedding night. How I regret it.

That year, when I was fourteen and the loss of your love, Dad, left me bereft, Ed's love came like the sweetest of gifts. It replenished some of my drained security, and it kept my withering spirit not only intact, but buoyant. I can still relive the splendor of that all-consuming first love. As well as the cannonball to my gut when it ended.

My love for Ed overwhelmed me. Fall and winter, early spring, my love intensified into a physical hunger and a rapturous refuge. Because of Ed, I could almost transcend the strife at home. All I had to do was see him, talk to him, or even imagine him, and I felt safe and strong.

I didn't think I could survive a day without looking into his powder blue eyes. But Ed and his family vacationed each April in Florida; he would soon be gone for over a week. It was spring vacation for me, too, yet all I wanted was for it to end fast, so Ed could come home.

One of those vacation nights, I slept in Ed's bed. His older sister, also my friend, had stayed home because she worked as a secretary and couldn't get the time off. She invited me to sleep over. When I slid between the sheets of his neatly made single bed and lay my head on his pillow, I about burst into flames of bliss.

But a few days before his homecoming, I had a dream that made me wake up with a stomachache I couldn't shake. I dreamed I saw Ed walking on a beach, then meeting a girl in a yellow two-piece bathing suit. He took her hand and slipped off to a sand dune to make love, he for the first time. I woke up with the sickening certainty that it had actually happened, that I'd had a premonition. And I was right.

Ed returned from Florida on a Sunday, the last day of vacation. When he pulled into my driveway late in the day, I stood there waiting for him in a new summer dress, weak with anticipation. Our yard had exploded with purple lilacs, my favorite springtime fragrance; but as I waited, their sweet scent made me queasy. Something was wrong. Ed got out of the car. We went to each other, smiling. He put his arms around me and kissed me, but something had changed.

The next day he broke up with me. Down in our basement after school. He came over just for that. Without ever saying the exact words, he told me *even if I loved you before, I don't anymore.* Then he left. It took less than five minutes.

Something about being "free" was all the reason he offered me. But I did find out later that he had indeed met a girl on the beach, a girl named Kit who evidently had not made such vows about virginity. Although Kit was a spring break fling, he'd tasted what he'd been missing and what was surely available to him at Hinsdale High School, just not with me. Yet.

My stomach stayed sick for nearly a year. At school, on those muggy May days, Ed passed by me in the halls, and I couldn't help it, I broke down crying. It didn't matter that other kids saw me. I walked along, clutching my books to my chest, tears streaming down my face. When Ed drove by with his new girlfriend pressed up against him, I wanted to lay down and die. I could not stop loving him. How could he stop loving me?

My best friend, Janet, had been going steady with Ed's best friend, Mike. Mike broke up with Janet that same week, probably for the same reason, a choice the boys made together, like a business decision. Janet and I clung together like two Apocalypse survivors. We ousted our poor friend, Sally, the third member of our trio, without ever meaning to. We stuck together and licked our wounds and held fast to one another for years to come.

I say I regret that I did not make love to Ed back then, and I mean it. For how could it not have been about as perfect as first sex can be, at least emotionally? And the fact is, only a year later, I would lose my virginity anyway.

Bad to Worse

My sick stomachache wouldn't go away. A few sips of orange juice were all I could choke down before school, but it felt like I'd swallowed a bowl full of tears. I woke up sad, went to school sad, went to bed sad. I know it could strike a sensible adult as silly, but anyone who remembers their first heartbreak will understand. It is akin to grieving.

Only Ed was very much alive and dating other girls. I could not fathom what he saw in a single one of them. How could he possibly prefer any one of them to me? I forced myself to date other guys. I let myself kiss them, but it felt plain awful. It was Ed I wanted. When a guy asked me out, I usually said "yes" hoping Ed would see me with someone new and find out he missed me, maybe even want me back. He never did.

I don't suppose sadness is a good excuse for dangerous drinking, but it always has been and always will be, so I guess I will use it. Up to that point, our high school drinking was under control, so to speak. We got tipsy, bordering on drunk, but so far no one had fallen down a flight of stairs or blacked out or driven into a ditch. But on this June night, less than two months after Ed broke up with me, I made a big mistake.

Janet's parents were going out, so naturally we had to have a party. We hadn't been able to get our hands on beer or wine, so, while you and Mom were waging war in the kitchen eight feet away from me, I grabbed an empty Coke bottle and began to fill it with an assortment of alcohol from our liquor cabinet. This cabinet was located directly above our refrigerator in the very kitchen where you stood fighting. I stood there, too, pouring a little bit of this, a little bit of that, a little gin, a little bourbon, a little vodka, vermouth, whiskey, crème de menthe, until I had a bottle full of poison.

I sealed it up and headed over to Janet's where I sat down on her piano bench and played "My Faith Looks Up to Thee" while I knocked back this vile concoction or as much of it as I could, before halfway through "Alley Cat" I went blind and fell over backwards.

The rest of the night is a nauseating blur. I actually lost my vision. People talked to me—I could hear them, but I couldn't see them. They tried to take care of me. They held me up, laid me down, poured coffee and water into my slack mouth, tried to mobilize my legs. No one thought of the emergency room. And no one dared to bring me home, to spare me, I guess, from the wrath of my parents. We were so ignorant.

I was lucky that night. Not only did I survive, but I made it into our house and into bed, undetected. To do so, I had to walk past you asleep in a lounge chair on our terrace, and Mom, wherever she might have been. I would say asleep, but she always waited up for me, so I must have slunk in so quietly she never even heard me. Naturally I didn't announce my arrival. I slipped into my room and fell into my bed where I lay motionless for the next 12 hours. I woke up feeble and carved out, like a hand grenade blew up in my stomach, leaving my outline intact, but my insides hollow.

Other than that frightening drinking episode, my vices were relatively tame and my life during freshman and sophomore year much less dramatic. By sophomore year, the group of kids we palled around with my freshmen year had somehow disbanded. Janet's parents had forbidden her to hang around with Mindy McNulty, so I didn't either. Most weekend nights found Janet and me driving around in her mother's Mustang looking for parties, looking for boys—Ed and Mike namely, just to know where they were— seldom finding either. We would end the evening at Topp's Big Boy in La Grange, with a cup of coffee and a plate of onion rings. I often slept overnight at Janet's house. She had two twin beds and her own bathroom. We'd drift off to The Doors on her record player. That was about the extent of our fun.

Those were bleak months. Everything at home felt cold and grim. Everything at school felt pointless and stupid. Pep rally? Preposterous. I left the mindless joy behind, lit a cigarette, and walked home. I can find no photos of me that year. I guess no one wanted keepsakes. But I remember my face in the mirror—pale and expressionless.

*

If you still retained even a glimmer of respect for me, Dad, I guess it died for good when I got suspended for smoking. It was a Tuesday morning in mid-September of 1968, my sophomore year, a year of many firsts—none of them praiseworthy. But I never got to tell you what happened, did I?

School hadn't even started. The bus dropped me off each morning at 7:50. Classes didn't start till 8:10. I didn't know what to do with myself. So, as was my habit, I stood in a stall in the girls' room outside the gymnasium, smoking a butt. Me, the jolly girl crowned Snow Queen in sixth grade, with boatloads of friends in seventh, had become a loner, someone who grew panicky when facing the sea of students laughing together in the cafeteria. The stall and the cigarette calmed me.

I don't know why I didn't flush it down the toilet. Instead, I walked out to the sink with my lit cigarette, said something to a girl named Cindy, turned my back, turned on the faucet, ready to douse my smoke, when I heard Miss Larkin, my favorite gym teacher say, "*Give me your cigarette, Cindy.*"

To this day there is no explanation for what I did next. I remember thinking, "*She must have seen mine, too.*" I'd been taught to "fess up, always fess up" if I got caught in the wrong, and I thought I would make matters worse if I pretended not to be smoking. So, I turned around and turned myself in.

"*Do you want mine, too?*"

Miss Larkin's expression shifted from total surprise to utter disbelief, to complete dismay. It said, loud and clear, "*You stupid, stupid kid.*"

Miss Larkin ushered us to the principal's office. He called our mothers as we sat two feet away and we each began to cry when we heard our own mother pick up.

We received a three-day suspension as punishment—Wednesday through Friday.

You, Dad, had quit smoking and deplored the habit in anyone. Definitely in your wife. Certainly in your daughter. You happened to be home, that night, and your usual hateful countenance turned murderous. You didn't say one word to me, as if there would be no end to your wrath if you so much as opened your mouth. I don't think anyone had ever looked at me with such disdain. And no one's disdain could hurt me worse than yours.

Mom reacted with exceptional tolerance. She knew I was ashamed and sorry and after an adult discussion, she announced that this hiatus presented us with the perfect opportunity to redecorate my bedroom. We drove to various stores on Chicago's South Side, buying curtains, lamps, a chair, and pillows, all in shades of green and blue. I did my homework in my inviting new room and returned to school prepared and chagrined.

My teachers all had to sign the slip that acknowledged I'd been suspended and why. I quickly surmised the story had made the rounds. Teachers either rolled their eyes or shook their heads when I timidly handed them the suspension excuse. One actually repeated my own dumb words to me, "Do you want mine, too??" I was deeply embarrassed.

The year before, I'd been sent to the principal's office, too. One Monday morning, a couple of kids came to my Chorus room, asking for Valerie Kuhn. "She's wanted in the office," they told Mrs. Osborne. I nearly passed out. That weekend, I'd taken my first apprehensive hits off a joint at a party. I knew nothing about marijuana, but as always, game and polite, I took a couple of tentative drags. I felt nothing. I suspect no one else did either, still we all pretended, trying on a new far-out, wow-man type of voice. When those kids came to collect me at the Chorus door two days later, I was sure I was "busted."

Nothing of the sort. The school had selected one boy and one girl from each of the four grades, ninth through twelfth, to represent Hinsdale High School on Lee Phillip, a Chicago-based talk show. Eight students out of roughly 3,200. I was one of the eight. What a difference a year makes.

For our family, that year was 1968. That was the year that you and Mom plunged into the most vicious period of your ruptured marriage, and we all went to hell in a handbasket.

I picture Mom sitting there on her ironing board chair as you shouted and swore and called her names. "You son of a bitch! Drop dead! You louse! DROP DEAD YOU LOUSE!" It blows my mind that she did not grab a frying pan and deck you with it. Or at least get up and walk away. Why would she ever stay in the same room with you, let alone stay married to you? If *that* was your proof of her insanity, well, I'd be inclined to agree.

I do recall grilling her about this, some years later. As became her habit, and as if I needed to hear it, she was rehashing your cruel treatment of her. Ready to tear my hair out, I finally shouted, "WHY DID YOU STAY WITH HIM??" To which she said, very quietly, "I had nowhere to go." This blew my mind. "You have a brother!" I said. "A *rich* brother, in Arizona! You could have gone to live with him!" Poor Mom. What a dope I was, how arrogant of me, to think it was all that easy. There are monster spouses of both sexes, but society has always made it much easier for men to leave. Single, divorced, or widowed women couldn't even have their own credit cards until 1974. Even today, fifty years later, a woman without means, without a good job, especially one with children, has to think long and hard about freeing herself from an unhappy marriage. I know that now.

Anyway, you obviously didn't care how vile you sounded when you bellowed at Mom. I know your heavy drinking had much to do with this. I know you might not even have remembered the vulgar words you used, the demeaning names you called her, but I'm sorry, Dad, your drunken tirades had finally turned you into a monster in my eyes. You kept shouting, "*You're crazy!*" at her. "*Your mother is crazy!*" to me.

But at this point, I'd have sworn you were the crazy one.

War Torn

By December of 1968, you must have been hanging on by a thread. Mom, too. She had been married to you for a quarter of a century. You used to love her, now you despised her. It must have bewildered her endlessly, particularly since she could not recognize her own role in the demise. She even wondered aloud to me if you had another family somewhere. *Ridiculous,* I thought. *Impossible!*

Still, one evening I decided to ask you. We stood right there in that same front window, framed by the golden drapes. I don't know where I got the nerve. It just came out of my mouth.

"Dad, do you have another family somewhere?"

The malevolence on your face hit me like a bash to the teeth. You spat out one word: *"No!"*

Well, okay. But where were you all the time? I knew business couldn't keep you away so much, so long. And why, when you were home, did you act like a caged beast? Like we were your jailers, and the only way to bear us was to get blind drunk.

I have a hazy memory of coming home loaded myself one night. Not drunk, not stumbling or slurring my speech, just buzzed enough to wrap me in that warm protective shell that kept me cozy. You, of course, were loaded, too. You sat glowering in one of the aqua chairs in the living room, doing what? Plotting your escape? Wishing Mom dead? I drifted in and plopped down in a chair opposite you. We talked briefly about nothing I can remember, but what I do remember is thinking to myself *Huh. This is okay. This is what it takes now, for us to connect: get buzzed together.*

*

In 1968, our home might have felt war torn, but our country actually was. As a teenager, I was conscious of the upheaval, yet only recently did I consider how the turbulence must have affected both you and Mom.

Mom voted straight Republican, and you voted straight Democrat. There can be no way this philosophical division during that highly charged political era, did not exacerbate your already fractured relationship. In America today, people are willingly and righteously severing ties with friends and even family members, due to this divide. Morality matters that much.

More than that, though, I think of you, a World War II veteran, first absorbing President Kennedy's assassination in 1963, then in 1968 the assassinations of not only his brother, Bobby, but Martin Luther King, Jr. as well. You opposed the war in Vietnam, offered to drive Brent to Canada, if need be, and were passionate about civil rights. I think of you, reeling from all this violence, and then, less than three months later, I think specifically about the Democratic National Convention in Chicago, August 28, 1968. About those bloody riots.

Watching a documentary recently about the atrocious brutality used by the Chicago police force, even against innocent bystanders, I realized that this happened not just in your country, state, and city, but only three blocks from your office. Perhaps you even witnessed it from your window. Your company, Pro/Mark, located at 332 South Michigan Avenue, overlooked Grant Park, from where protestors and pedestrians moved to the Conrad Hilton Hotel, at 720 S. Michigan, just minutes away.

If you had observed any of this bedlam, I would think at the age of fifty and with your political convictions, it would have impacted your image of life and how you wanted to live the rest of it. Even if you did not watch it in person, you watched it on television — "the whole world (was) watching"— and the impact may have been nearly as life-changing. And if Mom's political views had clashed with yours at all (and how could they not?) it would have been even more intolerable. It has taken me fifty years to put this together, but I'd bet my bank account that I'm right—those shocking events and the political chasm between you and Mom were a catalyst for change; creating a tipping point, spurring you to action. If it wasn't that exact August night, I'll bet it was shortly thereafter that you finalized your exit strategy. You pulled it off five months later.

Gone

1968 was the last full year you lived with us. Those are woeful words to write, but by that time, you'd basically lost all resemblance to the father I had loved so well, so long. The imposter who'd taken your place was tearing us all apart and I heard myself praying to God to *please, make it end. Make him leave.*

But that was my second prayer. My first and most fervent prayer was that this angry man would turn back into my original father—my real, true dad.

That was also Mom's first prayer. Because once upon a time, she had loved you with her whole heart, too.

"*You're everything in the world to me,*" she wrote after you were married. "*You are part of me and yet you can't be—because you are so much better than me. You are a strange mixture of strength and sweetness. Guess what I am trying to say is that you are just plain wonderful, and I love you with all my heart.*

Yet twenty-five years later, Mom asked me to sit down and pray with her, reminding me how Jesus said, "*When two or more of you are gathered in my name, there I am in the midst of you.*" We had never done this before. At Aunt Kathie's house, devotions preceded every bedtime, always closing with the nerve-wracking need to individually pray aloud, even if you were only six. But Mom and I settled into the chairs in the front window, the one with the golden draperies. We bowed our heads and she spoke to God. I know she said more, but this is what I remember:

"*Dear God, we gather in Jesus' name. Please hear our prayer. Please return Ed to the way he used to be, to the man, the husband, and father, he was. Please. In Jesus Name. Amen."*

Well, it was too late. I do not doubt that Jesus was there in the midst of us, and I wouldn't even say that God ignored us. In truth, Verna's husband eventually did become much more like the man she had married, it was just … somewhere else.

Because a few weeks later, on a snowy Sunday night in January, God answered my second prayer.

I am coming home from the Oak Brook Movie Theater with my friend, Gary. I climb out of his car, wave goodbye, then crunch up the driveway, heading for the warmth of our house. I open the door, thinking what should I wear to school tomorrow? I decide on my striped sweater dress, step inside, shake the snow from my boots and in that instant the kitchen door flies open. Mom marches out, her ashen face a death mask.

"Tell Val what you just told me!" She is addressing you but looking at me.

It's a dare. She is hoping you won't have the guts to say the words aloud.

But no. You storm right in behind her and roar, "I am leaving tonight and I'm not coming back!"

I stand there in my parka and stocking cap, in the same little hallway where we used to hug you when you walked through the door after work. Now you grab your hat, coat, and briefcase out of the closet and leave through that door. Gone.

I remember not one more moment of that night. I hung up my jacket, and then? Mom walked back into the kitchen? Dear God, and did what? Did I go to my room and get ready for bed? Eight-year-old Audrey should have already been asleep, in the midst, I hope, of some sweet dream. Only how could she sleep through the ferocious climax that surely preceded that finale? All I know is that's how it happened, and you didn't mean maybe; you never came back.

Well, a few days later you slipped in for your clothes when no one was home, but that cold night is the last time I ever saw you in our house, the house you and Mom built the year I was born, the house in which you'd raised me.

I was relieved that the monster who had terrorized our nights was gone. But I wept for you, the father who had been there all our lives — reading to us, singing to us, calming us, adoring us. I wept for my old dad, my real dad.

We were fortunate; you didn't die. Nor did you disappear from our lives. Even so, after you left, it didn't matter if we lit every light in the house—no room ever felt completely bright again.

*

Dad. There is a certain memory of you I hold almost sacred. It was the last time I remember us being alone together before you left.

It is a dark winter's night. You have offered to drive me to LaGrange to pick up a pair of gloves I left at MacDonald's. Bundled in coats and scarves we ride in silence. You don't look at me; your eyes are locked on the icy road, and your hands in your brown, fur-lined gloves grip the wheel, but out of the cold silence I hear a voice I recognize from my childhood, from the life we've left behind.

In the tender voice of my original, loving father you say, "Val, in the play Hamlet, an old man named Polonius said some wise words to his son, Laertes. I say them to you now and ask that you please remember them."

You take your eyes off the road briefly to look fully into my face, as you say, firmly, finally, "This above all: to thine own self be true."

Fallout

So, that's it. You left. The end.

Hardly. The nightly battles were blessedly over, but like the ending of any war, we had rubble to climb out of, we had fallout. A period of recovery lay ahead. Things were far from finished.

Although you hadn't died, I mourned you. I don't suppose it was obvious to anyone. I went to school, I sang in the musicals, I soon had a job and a new boyfriend. But at home, I was a mess. I cried easily, endlessly, often. I lost my temper and screamed over any exasperation. I wanted to peel my skin off to let the anguish out. You would never have known, since I, like you, could put on a happy face. I would never let you know how much I hurt. Never.

With you gone, the fighting in the house fell to Mom and me. Some of it sprang from normal teenage girl stuff, like curfew and my tendency to break it, but also due to my defiant behavior, which I'm afraid I did direct at Mom, because, well ... she was there. Poor Mom. I hate it that I would never in a million years talk to you the way I talked to her. I even slammed out of the house the way you used to, then feel sick with guilt. On occasion, I remember asking whomever I was with to pull the car over at the payphone at Snacktime. I said I left the iron on and needed to call home and alert my mom. In truth, I needed to apologize.

I think Mom and I both took our hurt and anger out on one another. Me more than her. Maybe somewhere deep inside me, I blamed her for driving you away, as Brent still insists she did. She and I were both in mourning.

You made a point of seeing Audrey and me once a week. Late Sunday afternoons, you drove out to Clarendon Hills to take us to dinner in Westmont for Italian beef sandwiches. Gosh, it must have been tough for you. A dour 15-year-old and a bewildered eight-year-old, sitting across from you in a booth at Trieste. What did we talk about? Do you remember? I don't. I guess you asked questions and we gave answers. What more was there to say?

You did not immediately revert to my former merry father solely because you'd finally been set free. You still glowered and acted displeased with me. (Like when I lit a cigarette at the table at the Illinois Athletic Club.) Still, at least you wanted to see me.

You might wonder if I had prayed you would leave, why would I grieve over you?

It was for my real dad I grieved. My original father. I could never forget who you had been. I would never stop missing you.

You got an apartment in the city. I never saw it, but I sure wondered what it looked like. What kind of furniture did you have? I pictured it rather empty and you sitting there, all alone, maybe— just possibly— missing us.

Paul

After Ed broke up with me, I lost my appetite and a good ten pounds. After you left, Dad, I ate and ate. I gained back the weight I'd lost and then some. My battle with food had begun.

The summer after you left, the summer of 1969, one of the reasons that I cared so much about the shape of my soon-to-be-16-year-old body was that I was undressing it regularly for Paul Bellino.

Before I met Paul, if Ed had wanted me back, I'd have run to him. But he didn't. And after a year of wishing, I faced the fact that he never would, and forced my hopeless heart to move on.

Where Ed had been a beautiful boy, Paul was a sexy man. Tall and lean, Ed had the soft blond hair and softer blue eyes of a Scandinavian farm boy. Paul, with his flashing dark eyes, raven hair, and powerful build, came on like a seductive Italian prize-fighter, and I was readier than I realized to be seduced.

True, I had expected to remain a virgin until I was married. And not caving in to Ed took excruciating effort. When I forged my original plan of celibacy, I had no idea how my hormones would invade my being like some syrupy drug. That touching the skin of the boy I loved, his lips, his hands, his fingers on my body, could melt my every pore and render me powerless to the most delicious, primal urge. How I did not surrender to Ed, I'll never know. But then came Paul and it was all over. He was no high school boy playing the field; he was the real thing, a born lover.

I did my best to hold off, but one sultry summer night, slinging back Boilermakers and dancing to Creedence Clearwater, I found myself less determined. After that, we made love every chance we got.

Enjoying a full-scale sexual relationship as a high school girl, took me by surprise—shocked me, even. This was not my plan for myself. But Paul became so much more than the boy to whom I lost my virginity. We had fallen in love.

Our passion was not without drawbacks. I never expected to be 16 and scared I had syphilis, or afraid I was pregnant. And as much as I relished our physical relationship, I felt a secret shame over it, too. And a little regret. Like this instant womanhood had robbed me of what was left of my adolescence. I remember once taking the bus home from school as a junior, for the first time since the start of my freshman year. ("Cool" kids didn't ride the bus.) There was something so comforting about it. Walking home from the bus stop along my childhood sidewalks in my plaid skirt and navy-blue knee socks, a part of me just wanted to roll back time and be a girl again. *Please, just let me be a girl.*

I guess I thought I was an anomaly, that other girls didn't have sex until they were much older. When I was a teenager, sex was pretty private, not part of casual conversation, so I didn't know that I wasn't the only one having sex at my age. It wasn't until, as a 40-year-old woman, I attended a 16th birthday party a friend threw for her daughter, that I gained a new perspective. Twenty women of all ages gathered in a circle, and, one by one, we took turns saying something memorable about our 16th year. Almost to a woman, the story included losing her virginity. What a revelation! And every bit as fascinating, no one acted remotely embarrassed about it. But shame came easily to me. After all, wasn't ours the only house sick with strife? Mine the only mother who had shock treatments? Mine the only father who shouted vicious drunken obscenities at his wife, then left his family? I certainly thought so.

It stood to reason I'd think I was a sexual oddity, too. And, at sixteen, all of it left me with one injurious subliminal message: *I am no longer a good girl from a good family.*

There's no doubt in my mind that the truly advantaged teenagers are those who stay innocent as long as possible. Brent, for instance, insists he sailed through high school unscathed because he was oblivious to all social machinations. He didn't give a hoot about being popular or having a girlfriend. His idea of fun was coming home from school and playing Risk or Stratego with his buddies.

I obviously did not belong to his fortunate set, yet in my more seasoned circle I was unbelievably lucky. Not only did Paul remain my longtime steady boyfriend, he also turned out to be the best boyfriend a girl could have. And although one set of parents—mine —knew nothing of our carnal knowledge (Or did you? Mom sure didn't), both sets fully expected us to get married someday, and I guess we expected the same.

Paul was also five years older. We kept this age difference quiet in the beginning. In essence it didn't matter at all; we were a perfect match. Our love affair began that summer of '69 and lasted three years, and in all that time a cross word never passed between us. This largely because Paul had one of the sweetest, cheeriest, most loving dispositions I've ever encountered. I picture our faces and see endless smiling.

In fact, Mom told me how glad it made her when Paul came over because he filled our dreary house with laughter. I think for this, and a few other good reasons, she did not try to stop this "older man" relationship. She watched Paul take me to movies and restaurants and concerts, buy me nice clothes for Christmas—a satin blouse, a flouncy red skirt, an elegant white sweater dress—she heard him speak to me gently and respectfully. She saw the love in our eyes, the sheer adoration. It made her happy to see me so happy. Why would she stand in my way? As we knew, the future could be grim.

Paul and I spent all summer in love—feeling it, making it, professing it. Something else we did was dance. We could dance all night, every night. Creedence, The Rascals, Aretha, Frank Sinatra—you name it, we danced to it. Even though you had been gone a mere eight months, Dad, I started my junior year of high school in a much better emotional place. The kitchen was now peaceful at night, and loving Paul made my heart sing all day long. I wish I cared more about my grades, but I sat in school counting the minutes until I could walk out of the building and into his arms.

Paul and I had settled into this dreamy relationship right when the Vietnam War escalated, and you know all about that: if a boy wasn't in school, he got called to serve. Paul had finished one year of college, but now worked at his father's steel company. His number came up and he got drafted.

On a gray, pre-dawn morning in November, Paul and the other local draftees gathered at a bus stop across from the Tivoli Theater in Downers Grove, surrounded by somber families and friends. We kissed our boys and hugged them tight, then waved goodbye as the bus pulled away.

When they arrived at O'Hare Airport, an officer surprised the new recruits by pointing at some and saying, "You, you, you. Congratulations. You're in the Marines." Paul was one of them. He flew that day to San Diego and spent the next six weeks in Boot Camp at Camp Pendleton. Miraculously, when he received his orders, he did not report to a swamp in the Mekong Delta, but to a desk in Honolulu.

Off he went. There I stayed. We promised we'd write. I did. He didn't. Every day for the first two weeks, I sent him a letter. And every day I checked our mailbox the minute I came home from school. Nothing.

I remember the wintry day and how it felt on my skin. My long hair, wet from swimming in PE last period, hung ice-crystal stiff. The sharp smell of chlorine clung to my cold-pinched nostrils. My freezing knees tingled in my thin black pantyhose. I pulled my hand from my glove to check our mailbox one more time, bracing for the disappointment, yet compelled to look. There, crammed into the mailbox, were fifteen letters from Paul addressed to me. *Fifteen letters!* His own fingers had printed VAL KUHN, 206 GRANT AVE., in his neat block letters on 15 envelopes—one for each day he'd been gone. I held those letters in my hands, pressed them to my lips. *He loves me,* I thought. *Paul still loves me.*

We wrote to each other every single day for two years. I poured out the intimate aspects of my life to him. I pledged him my love and, applying fresh lipstick, sealed each envelope with a kiss. He described boot camp and then Hawaii and how much he loved and missed me. I longed for him and lived to be with him again.

When he came home on leave for the first time, he gave me no warning. There I sat in my pink quilted bathrobe, my brown hair up in a bun, face caked with Clearasil, about to go to bed, when the phone rang. It was Paul's deep voice, which I had not heard in four months. When he told me, he was not 3,000 miles away but ten minutes, my body commenced to shaking uncontrollably. I can still see the alarm on Mom's face as she absorbed this fact. I had only enough time to use my trembling fingers to pull down my hair and rake a brush through it when there he stood on our terrace. I still see him coming through our front door. His dancing brown eyes, his thick dark hair now a GI stubble. He wrapped me in rock-solid arms and stopped all my shaking.

We had three more of these ecstatic reunions during his two years in the service. Each one was like a two-week honeymoon. Yet Mom still did not suspect me of sleeping with him.

At Christmas time, I landed my first real job at the hosiery counter at Bonwit Teller in Oakbrook. Women still wore nylon stockings that came wrapped in tissue paper inside pearly white boxes. I worked three nights a week and all-day Saturday, saving all my income from my $1.75 an hour job to fly to Hawaii to visit Paul when I graduated high school. It's what kept me going. I saved and saved, and by the summer of 1971, I had a few thousand dollars, more than I needed for the trip. Only I never went because Mom forbade it. She considered it, what else? Unseemly.

I suppose she feared I'd lose my virginity.

Harmful Thinking and
A Gold Coin from God

That baleful belief—that I was no longer a good girl from a good family—did a number on me. A lifetime of feeling proud of myself had formed the foundation of my confidence and competence. I grew up proud of myself largely because you were so proud of me, Dad. When you weren't, I wasn't either.

I've always wondered what came first. Was I incorrigible and you and Mom had every right to be fed up with me? Or was I a normal teenager experimenting with normal teenage things, against a stormy backdrop?

My freshman year in high school, you and Mom both seemed so appalled by my appearance and my behavior, I quickly got the idea you considered me "bad." But I really wasn't. I know that now. Okay, I smoked and I drank and I swore. I was also on the brink of sex, but only I knew that. Where it *counted*, I was as good as I always had been, and would eventually be even better. My group of friends? We all grew up to be decent people. You gave up on me too soon.

Do you remember how seriously I took confirmation? I thought I would detest spending every Saturday morning of seventh and eighth grade in the basement of Christ Lutheran Church. I ended up loving it. It solidified my faith, which came originally from you and Mom, then deepened with Uncle Ned's and Aunt Kathie's Baptist ways. I loved all their praying and singing, and accepted Jesus as my Savior when I was eight and introduced to "altar calls" when I spent two weeks at Camp Letourneau in Upstate New York, where Uncle Ed was chaplain.

In confirmation classes, I listened so carefully and believed so strongly as Pastor Engel taught us from Luther's Small Catechism that when the time came to take our big exam at the end of two years, I got 100%. You may not know this, but when I knelt with the other 30 confirmands to take my First Communion, I physically trembled, so overcome I was by the sacred importance of this sacrament.

When it came to the Golden Rule and the Ten Commandments, I took them seriously. I never stole. In junior high, when it was the rich-girl rage to shoplift at Marshall Fields, I never even considered it. If anything, I considered it beneath me. I did not use the Lord's name in vain. I had no qualms about using, "hell," "shit," "damn," even "fuck," when the situation warranted it, but wild horses couldn't drag a "Jesus Christ" or even a careless "God" out of me.

I had learned the deeper explanations to each of the Ten Commandments and understood that even if you don't go around murdering people, to hate or wish someone harm is, in a spiritual sense, akin to killing, so whenever I found myself pounding with that feeling I'd ordinarily label "hate," I quickly switched to the many alternatives I deemed acceptable: "despise, loathe, deplore, detest ..."

Like Mom, I did not gossip or bear false witness and accepted that we should not "belie, betray, slander, nor defame our neighbor, but defend him, speak well of him, and put the best construction on everything." I made it my mission to give people the benefit of the doubt. If they proved they were undeserving, well, then I'd call a spade a spade.

So, yes, I was what you might call "wild" for a spell, but I also strove to do God's will. I knew my heart was fundamentally good and figured that God did, too. Despite my new vices, my morality, (according to me) was solid. Still, my vices did trouble me as they troubled you, and this sense that I was now bad—that you and Mom, but mainly you, viewed me as bad (and maybe everyone who ever knew me did, too)—stripped me of too much essential self-confidence. I once thought I might like to marry a minister. Or even be a minister. But now I knew I couldn't; I wasn't ... good enough.

I'd been a praying child all my life and kept praying right through those confusing times. The answer I got back was that God loved me despite my departures from the straight and narrow. I remembered our pact. I never doubted that God heard my prayers and would, in some way, answer them. Once in a while, I saw my prayers answered dramatically, which went a long way in confirming my convictions.

One such occasion was during my junior year of high school, when I found a lump in my right breast. My breasts were not big, so I could easily see it beneath the smooth skin. Nauseous with fright, I told Mom. This time, she did not bar me from the doctor; she made an appointment right away, bypassing Dr. Dreyfuss and heading straight to a specialist. The doctor examined me and arranged for a biopsy. I would check into the hospital one day, have the surgery the next morning and then—if all went well—I would go home the day after that. This was February of 1970. I was sixteen.

Mom, in her style, decided I needed presentable pajamas for my hospital stay. She took me to Marshall Fields where I chose two ensembles, both yellow. One was cotton and sleeveless, with a puffed sleeve cover-up etched in white lace. The other you might call a "peignoir," my first negligee-type nighty. The silk-lined chiffon skirt skimmed my knees, and two delicate spaghetti straps held up a frilly bodice. A sheer, long-sleeved robe completed it. Not all mothers would consider such attire necessary for surgery. Those two nightgowns, which I still own, speak to me of Mom's silent love.

Anyway, I checked into my room at the Hinsdale San where I'd been born and Mom confined, and as I settled in, the doctor dropped by to alert me to a problem: my mother would not sign the consent forms. He explained that it was standard procedure in a biopsy to run the tissue to the lab while the patient was still under anesthesia. If they found the lump to be malignant, they would perform a mastectomy then and there. Hah! Over Verna Kuhn's dead body.

The doctor sat by my bed and explained, "It's not a matter of keeping something you want. It's a matter of living or dying." His exact words and deeply sobering.

Naturally, this frightened me. The thought of having a breast removed at sixteen was terrifying. But dying was worse. I had no reason to doubt his words and I knew next to nothing about breast cancer procedures. The Internet wouldn't appear for another twenty years.

I didn't know what to do. It didn't surprise me that Mom wouldn't sign. She had raised me to never, *ever*, sign *anything* without reading every single word on the page. Besides, if she hadn't let them take my tonsils, she wasn't about to let them take my breast. I knew what the doctors were up against. But what should I do? Pack up my pretty pajamas and go home and wait and see what the lump decided to do?

The doctor walked out of the room and all I knew to do was pray. I paced around my hospital room and prayed aloud, "Please, God, don't let them do it. Don't let them do it. Please, don't let them do it."

Like magic, the doctor walked back in and the first words out of his mouth were, "*Well, we're not going to do it.*"

He continued, "We've decided because of your age, we will only do the biopsy, and take it from there."

Naturally, all I could hear and marvel at were the exact words that perfectly echoed my desperate prayer: *We're not going to do it.* I took this as God speaking directly to me. It deepened my already firm faith that the God I believed in was present, and sometimes came dramatically to the rescue. I call that "a gold coin." Along the way, you need to find one now and then to stay on the path.

As you know, the lump was benign.

Surprise!

When you moved out, Dad, I figured you were sick to death of being married. You used to love us, now you didn't, and you were through with wives and children.

I know it's naive, but I never even considered "another woman." Mom had either known or suspected the truth, (it was she, after all, who raised the original idea of another family) but I had not. It was the surprise of a lifetime.

A year has passed since you left home. I am a junior in high school and Audrey is nine. Mom is forty-eight. Brent is in college. The phone rings, I answer. It's you.

Your voice is kind and careful when you say, "Val, I have something to tell you. I got married last week to a terrific woman named Barbara. She's a wonderful, whacky redhead and you are sure to love her."

If you had told me you'd been swept up in a cyclone and were phoning from the land of Oz, I would not have been more astounded.

"NO!" I shout instinctively and so loudly that Mom and Audrey come running.

You give more information and then I hang up the phone. They stare at me, "What happened? What's wrong?"

"Dad got married," I say. "He married someone named Barbara from Connecticut. She has six children between the ages of six and twelve and they all live together right now in Winnetka." Was there more? Oh, yes. "They had their honeymoon in Nantucket."

We stand perfectly still, absorbing this impossible fact. Mom drops her head and stares at the floor. Little Audrey, tears rolling down her cheeks, splits the silence and nails the truth. "Now I don't have a dad, but all those kids have my dad."

Your weekly business trips had taken you to New York, but also to Connecticut where you indeed had another family, yours or not. That family consisted of six little children and their young, single mother. I remember standing by the golden draperies, and asking, "Do you have another family?" Mom hadn't been so far off after all.

You traded wives, Dad. I hated it, but I accepted it.

But the trading of children pulverized me. Didn't you remember who you were to us? Didn't you know that our light, our comfort, our courage, and confidence all came from you?

You packed it up in your suitcase and took it to them.

*

When I finally met Barbara, I couldn't help but like her. I didn't want to—meet her or like her—she was the enemy. I shudder to think how I dreaded that initial encounter. Still, I accepted your invitation to this all-important luncheon at Medinah Country Club.

But first—the ultimate horror—you actually drove into our driveway to pick me up with Barbara right there beside you in the front seat. There was Mom—*right there in the kitchen.* And there was Barbara—*right there in our driveway!* For the rest of her life, I fought to shield Mom from Barbara. While still in high school, I understood that I could never have a wedding— not a big traditional one, not even a small family gathering. Mom would turn into a pillar of salt if forced to behold her husband's new wife.

Still, no one could not like Barb. She was the life-of-the-party sort of gal. Vivacious, enthusiastic, and totally present, she dazzled and won over this teenage girl. As we sat there at Medinah, where Mom—just like that—would never be welcomed again, Barbara asked me engaging questions about myself and listened attentively to my answers. She was no bimbo. She was flat out magnetic. Especially her laugh— that jingle of a golden bell that slid a solid octave, starting high in her head and ending low in her throat. She was a blend of warmth and zest. Just like you, Dad. The original you.

We finished our Crab Louis and Elmer Sundaes then strolled out into Medinah's Great Hall, over to the grand piano where Barbara settled onto the bench and skimmed her fingers over the keys. Without warning, slow and swingy, she played Gershwin's "Can't Help Lovin' Dat Man" from Porgy and Bess. She sang along with a dreamy smile, her voice light and feathery but soulful. Exactly the sort of thing to captivate you, Dad. Me, too, for that matter. I sat down next to her and joined in — "Fish gotta swim, birds gotta fly, I gotta love one man till I die ..." You never stood a chance, did you?

Barbara was thirty-six years old. Mom was almost fifty. According to my calculations, that meant your new wife was a mere thirty-two when you met her, barely out of her twenties. But I liked that she did not try to be twenty, flaunting mini-skirts and long hair. Instead, she sported short red curls and dressed tastefully enough, almost matronly. I couldn't help comparing her physically to Mom. Barbara was a good four inches shorter and sturdier. Even though Mom had put on weight, she was still curvaceous. Barb was too, only more like a gymnast. No one could call her thin, but she was fit, compact. Both she and Mom had ample bosoms and sculpted calves. Light eyes, too, now blue, now gray. Unlike Mom, Barbara was covered in freckles, which on her looked good, in a cute, Peter Pan sort of way.

I didn't imagine, and still don't want to, that you cashed in my gray-haired mother for a younger model, yet it's hardly uncommon. Your eighteen-year age difference made Barbara forever young. You certainly appreciated her youth and good looks, but I truly think that her personality hooked you. "She's a gutsy broad," you'd say proudly and no doubt she was. She juggled a job and six little children. My mother, I am sure, appeared coddled and privileged by comparison. If Mom acted put-upon with a third child, Barbara's plucky ability to breeze along without complaint, *after six babies*, would have awed you. And won you.

As I grew older, you and Barbara became less guarded about sharing stories from your courtship days. One in particular featured the two of you on a couch, when the children were tucked in for the night. She would rest her silk-stockinged feet on your lap while slathering peanut butter and jelly on twelve slices of bread, a school lunch assembly line.

I'll bet you admired that about her. Mom fed us lavishly on soup, sandwich, fruit, and dessert every lunch time. Mom's extravagance in general had been under fire for years. She consistently chose quality over economy, another one of your battlegrounds. For a few months during my sixth-grade year, I remember you initiating Friday night grocery shopping dates with Mom. You were trying to teach her how to comparison shop. Mom didn't look at prices. She grabbed the brands she liked and the items she wanted. Had you already picked up some tips from thrifty Barb?

One story about Barbara's economizing appalled me. When the children got oatmeal for breakfast, if any of them didn't eat it, he or she would get the same unfinished bowl for lunch. If they didn't eat it then, they'd find it waiting for them at dinner. Or so I was told.

Mom may have been extravagant, feeding us from all five food groups at every meal, but the aging oatmeal is going overboard in my book. Mom did consider our likes and dislikes. Still on many occasions, if I turned up my nose at the food on my plate, she said, "If you're hungry, you'll eat." Thus, the ever-present bread and butter; in case someone didn't care for the liver and onions or Egg Foo Young.

Barbara was a powerhouse. She could get more done in an hour than Mom could in a day. Mom cared too much. Mom had ideals and got hung up on details. Barb had no such obsessive encumbrances. I'm sure you loved that about her. She cut corners and settled for "good enough" while Mom kept working on "perfect." Mom was the type to knock herself out on pineapple boats for her nine-year-old's birthday party while Barbara proudly served pies from the frozen food section on Thanksgiving. It rankles me that all Mom's painstaking attention to detail amounted to naught. Barb couldn't care less and still won the prize.

But like Mom, I would not have disparaged anyone for no good reason, and I had to give Barbara her due credit. I might have resented her very existence, yet I had to admit, if she wasn't your wife, I would have been her biggest fan. And you and she were plainly kindred spirits. You could not have been happier with her, and even in my own brokenness, I could be happy for you.

When you dropped me off at home that afternoon after lunch, I stood in our driveway and waved goodbye, then turned and walked up to our house thinking, *at least there is one parent I will never have to worry about."*

Poor Mom was a different story.

Me, too, I'm afraid.

Aftershock and a
Personal Renaissance

I could not accept that you had a new family. I knew it was true. I knew I had to get used to it, but it felt surreal. Unimaginable. Then one night in the summer of 1970, Janet picked me up from my job at Bonwit's in her mother's Mustang, with the plan to spy on you. I wanted to see where you and your new wife and all those children lived. I had your address and Janet had a road map.

We've been driving for forty minutes. It's past 10:00 pm and we are closing in on the swanky suburb of Winnetka. We're approaching the business district when we find your street. Slowing way down, we read the house numbers and bingo—there's yours. We crawl along now taking it in—a white Victorian on the corner of a tree-lined street overlooking the town green and village center.

"Want me to park?" Janet asks.

"Yes, park. Only not here. Back up a bit so they won't see us if someone looks out the window."

That's what she does, and we sit there in silence, staring.

How utterly bizarre this is, looking at the house where my very own father, who lived with me since the day I was born, now lives with six other children and their mother. I'm having trouble absorbing it. We both light cigarettes to calm down.

"Wow," Janet marvels. "So weird. Your dad is in that house, with a whole new family."

"Yeah," I say. "Yeah, I know."

Your house is pitch black inside. I don't see so much as a nightlight on. Everyone must be asleep. You, of course, and Barbara, whom I have met, and three little boys and three little girls I have yet to lay eyes on. What do they look like? What do you think of them? Did you tuck them into bed tonight and sing "Alexander's Ragtime Band?" Do you love them? Will you come to love them more than us? I know you fell in love with Barbara, but did you maybe fall for those little kids, too? I mean, none of them would be wearing eyeliner or smoking yet.

"His house is so big," Janet observes.

"Sure is," I say. "So much bigger than ours. They must be so happy."

I stare at your big, dark house and think: What's bad for us, is good for them.

"Yep," I say. "Life sure is strange."

*

It wasn't long after that covert mission that Audrey and I drove up to your new home in Winnetka announced and invited. It was time to plaster big brave smiles on our faces and meet your six new children. Smiling was not too hard for me because children have always delighted me. And these were cute children. The youngest, Kelly, was six; the oldest, Katie, was 12. I was 16 and Audrey was nine, the same age as the boy called, Chris. Today, my adult heart squeezes in sympathy for us all. Those little kids had moved a long distance—leaving friends and family—to a brand-new state and brand-new schools. They were excited to meet their new "sisters." They were ready to love us and be loved by us. Meg was the only one with dark hair. The other five all had hair of varying shades of red. I can't remember what else we did after we met. Ate a meal. Played a game. But I do know that six-year-old Kelly took Audrey's hand and brightly asked, "Have you met my father yet?"

That summer I alternated between weeping spells and tirades. It scared me when I cried because my body didn't relax with my tears but stiffened and shook in fury. I lay in bed at night, worried that I might be depressed, because I felt like a stranger to my own self. We want to believe children just roll with divorce; it makes it so much easier. Sure, kids will adjust, but not without paying a price.

Day after day, I felt either sad or angry, like Mom had so long appeared to me. Once during some miserable frustration, I burned with the need to hit something. I went to the basement and picked up a hammer and bashed the daylights out of the basement floor. I remember thinking the concrete could stand it better than my head.

*

That same summer of 1970, a week before my senior year, I lay in bed one hot August night, worrying about my brain. I had turned into such a flub-up in high school. Once upon a time I'd been a smart girl. What happened? Was I still smart and hadn't been trying, or was my mind gone for good? I thought I'd better find out and vowed to make an effort my senior year.

At that point, my favorite place to be was at Bonwit Teller. I loved the silky stockings, the customers, the cash register. I loved working. It took me away from the cheesy world of high school and allowed me to live in the real one, where I much preferred to be. I also loved the other girls who worked there. Most of them were in their twenties, and since I felt twenty-one, not seventeen, we got along great. I entered my senior year of high school feeling like a bona fide adult. I had a sweetheart—a lover— in the Marines, I worked and made money, I drove. I had nothing to prove to anyone, only myself. So, that's what I set out to do; prove to myself that my brain still worked.

School became my top priority. Ignited with motivation, I applied myself in every class. I focused, I studied, and it worked; my mind bounced back with a vengeance. As though my slump had never happened, I began to excel again. My self-esteem soared.

That last year of high school—1970 -1971— I lived a structured, disciplined life, and totally grooved on it. Because I never took a study hall, I had extra credits my senior year. This entitled me to "early release," which meant I left school at 12:50 and drove directly home (Mom generously gave me her car each morning), where I used the next four hours to do my homework. At 5:10, I wolfed down dinner, which Mom thoughtfully cooked before I left for work, yet never quite early enough. She routinely served it five minutes before we had to dart out the door and drive to Oak Brook. (Mom dropped me off and picked me up, feeling unsafe at night without a car.) By 10:00 pm, I was back home, in my pajamas, face washed, writing my nightly love letter to Paul. By 10:30 I was asleep.

In this new, organized, achievement-oriented world, I gained enough confidence to audition for a leading role in the high school spring musical, "Annie Get Your Gun." Despite my loner ways, I had stayed in the school choir and sang in the chorus of these lavish productions, known as "Operettas." I privately envied the upperclassmen in their starring roles, but never had the nerve to compete for big parts. Until "Annie Get Your Gun."

It's interesting to me that I didn't go for broke, didn't audition for the major lead, Annie Oakley. Because that's how it worked, you only auditioned for the part you wanted. The director did not ask us to read for any number of roles, only for the one role we specified. I know now I should have tried for Annie. But self-doubt still had me playing it safe, not asking for more than I deserved, so I auditioned for the second female lead, Dolly Tate, and got it.

I can see you thanking God when you heard the news. You must have thought *finally, a glimpse of my old Val*, and like old times, you bought me the Broadway cast recording so I could practice my music. I had no more than one brief solo, and also sang, "*There's No Business, Like Show Business*" with Buffalo Bill Cody and Sitting Bull. Still, your familiar, loving gesture meant the world to me.

Do you remember how at Hinsdale Central the Operettas were prodigious affairs? The usherettes wore full-length formals and long white gloves. I'd wager a good four thousand people attended the three performances staged over one single weekend. These shows were historically double, sometimes even triple, cast. The chorus was the same, but the leads typically got one night to shine. Saturday would be my night. If Mom managed to attend, she would, for the first time, risk running into you and your new wife. In an audience of a thousand people, it wasn't inevitable, but it wasn't impossible. What courage it must have taken for her to put herself in such peril.

I was made for the role of Dolly Tate. I practiced my lines backwards and forwards, yet I knew instinctively how to use my hands and body, how to deliver each line in precisely the right slinky, sarcastic manner for this conniving coquette. I remember standing under the stage lights after a full cast run-through, as Mrs. Osmond, our illustrious and formidable director, delivered detailed rehearsal notes. She got to my big scene and paused. She found my face in the crowd and smiled. "Val," she said, "That scene ... It's a masterpiece." In all four years of high school, that was my proudest moment. How gratifying to feel like a winner again; it had been so long.

In the grand scheme of things, that small role was not such a big deal. As an adult, I have directed scores of high school productions and watched kids perform leading roles to perfection, play after play. That it felt like such a crowning achievement to me, is a strong testament to my lost footing early in high school. The girl I used to be would have acted in all the plays, not only the operettas. The girl I'd become bowed out of things, as heavy-hearted people do.

My original group of friends had no use for drama. For some reason, they called it "queer," and I'd let that sway my own opinion. But there had been more to it, namely that perilous perception I had succumbed to early on: *I am not good.* True or not, it crippled my confidence and kept me from joining things. By senior year I had largely overcome it and turned things around. Even so, rehearsals found me sitting alone. While I must have appeared snooty or unfriendly, I was neither. I felt like an outsider, not belonging to any cheerful clump of kids. A freshman boy named Dave eventually took a chance on me. He sat down in the empty chair next to mine and struck up a conversation. He was smart and sweet and off-the-charts funny, and thus began a steadfast friendship that lasted for the next few years, until our paths finally veered too far.

Senior year was my renaissance, all right. My thirst for learning extended beyond school, and I resumed my organ lessons that year, which much have pleased you greatly. I had stopped abruptly in junior high, but now I located a new teacher for myself. Mr. Ackerman let me select my own music, songs I wanted to learn; I practiced incessantly. Yes, I was feeling like my old self again. I even taught Sunday School.

Mom and her Bible,
Mom and her Shame

I taught Sunday School because I loved children and aimed to be a teacher like Miss Lundgren someday, but also because I felt great at church. Mom, on the other hand, never went to church again after you left home.

She used to go regularly. Her attendance tapered off during my junior high years, those warring years when I, conversely, never missed a Sunday. Although I would have gone anyway, attendance was compulsory for us confirmation kids. Pastor Engel expected us to write a summary of his sermon each week and I, for one, enjoyed it.

That was during the school year. In the summer months, between seventh and eighth grades, there were no Saturday classes, but I still went to church—I went to church with you, remember? We sat side-by-side on those summer mornings, the Midwest humidity already steamrolling through the sanctuary by 9:00 am. Once it was so stuffy and airless that I fainted. You caught me before I hit the ground and had me sit with my head between my knees. On other occasions I recall you dozing during the sermon, gently snoring, sitting straight up. I loved being there with you, the two of us in church together. I've been back to Christ Lutheran a couple times over the decades, and I still look over and see us there, in the sixth pew on the right, me in a summer shift and sandals, you in your navy trousers and short sleeved dress shirt.

After you left, Brent came to church with me on special occasions like Easter and Christmas, and little Audrey, too, sometimes. Mostly, I went alone.

Since Mom was one of the finest examples of a true Christian I ever saw, it perplexed me that she ended her relationship with our church so finally. Even though she stopped going to church, she read her Bible every day. In fact, that's all she read. After years of all the popular magazines in America piling up on our coffee tables, and plenty of good literature on the bookshelves, she read her Bible and that was it. She did more than read it, she studied it. I'm sure you need no reminder that Mom believed the Bible held many clues supporting the existence of extraterrestrial life and that Jesus was quite possibly a visitor from a more advanced planet.

You probably know now, but didn't then, that she was not

alone in this view. In 1968, Erick Von Däniken wrote a book called *Chariots of the Gods*, in which he pointed to ancient artwork all over the world depicting astronauts, and air and space travel. He also maintained that extraterrestrial visitors created the Pyramids and other wonders, or at least taught humans how to build them. This made perfect sense to Mom. She scoured her Bible for evidence, drawing and writing notes in the margins, certain that she was unlocking those exact mysteries in the Good Book. She wanted us to thrill to these theories, too, and showed us her findings with electrifying enthusiasm. All this escalated during your last years with us. Probably each new bit of evidence she found in her Bible, was more proof to you she was off her rocker.

At the time, her convictions unnerved me a little, still I could also see how she could be right. Even as a kid, I did not expect our finite minds to comprehend the infinite, and I believed most anything was possible. I also didn't think it contradicted Christianity. Like Mom, I figured God could do whatever He wanted, and Jesus could come from wherever He pleased.

How I admire that free-thinking woman. I admire her ability to blend metaphysics and Christianity into a single, compatible philosophy. I admire how she poured over her Bible like a scholar and didn't shy away from ideas the status quo considered kooky. Along with her Bible studies, she created artwork depicting the unity and harmony she fervently believed all living creatures—not solely on earth, but in the whole infinite Universe—were meant to share. I will forever love that about her. And I am forever proud to tell people that my mother's favorite song was *"Let There be Peace on Earth."*

I guess one of the reasons she stopped going to church stemmed from shame. In your generation, divorce was not common. That fact carried tremendous impact. For Mom, certainly, but for me, too. Sure, when I got into junior high and high school, I met some kids who had divorced parents and even one girl who lived in one of those extraordinary households with step siblings. But divorce was whispered about like cancer in our community. Maybe it happened, but God forbid it happened to you.

That was then. Ten years later, divorce was as common as it had recently been atypical. This is not me with information bias. *These are statistics.* The divorce rate skyrocketed in the late sixties and seventies. The rate of 25% in 1966 had doubled to 50% in 1976 and was still rising. In a few short years broken homes abounded.

But poor Mom. Herself the first person she ever knew to get a divorce, she wore that stigma like a scarlet letter. And I guess, to a certain extent, I did, too. I grew up watching *Father Knows Best*, not *The Brady Bunch*. It's a good thing they started airing shows with blended families, because that soon became the way of the world. But it hadn't been mine. Or Mom's.

I knew Mom felt like an anomaly and an outcast in our community, and became reclusive afterwards, yet it never occurred to me until I was much older that it wasn't all about image. God's commandments and sacraments were ingrained in her and she did her utmost to honor them. Divorce wasn't only a personal and public failure, it was a spiritual failure, as well.

I never knew how truly ashamed Mom was about her divorced status, until the night before her mastectomy, the eve of her 61st birthday, her last birthday on earth. The hospital chaplain paid Mom a visit, and naturally asked her religion, to which Mom promptly answered, "Lutheran."

"So, your own pastor will be visiting you?"

Mom gawked at him like he'd asked her to an orgy.

"Oh, no!" she said. "No, of course not. *I'm divorced.*"

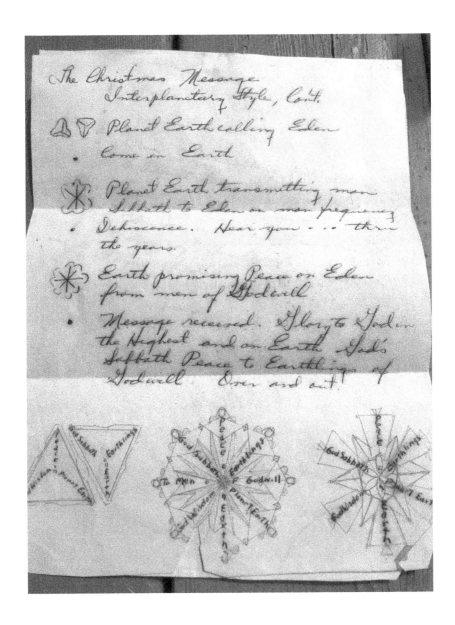

Poor Mom

I felt so sorry for Mom. I mean howling-like-a-dog kind of sorry. She seemed to me like a gentle dove with a broken wing. Her life, the way it turned out, made me heartsick.

Two years after Mom died, Uncle Roy's wife wrote to me: "I pause quite often to reflect what a sweet and gentle person your mom was. She added a lot of beautiful, special touches to our family during your early years, especially during the holidays." Yes. That was Mom. Sweet and gentle. Adding beauty. But things, for her, just … went wrong.

Today, reading the love letters she sent you before your wedding, I feel even sorrier. "… *our life together*," she wrote, "*will become more and more beautiful with every passing day, won't it? The success of our marriage depends on us two alone. With you, the kind of a person you are, it can't fail, and I will try so very hard to be everything you would have me be.*" Oh, Dad, she loved you so much. She had complete faith in your future. The end of your love … dear God, how it must have hurt.

Eventually, though, after you'd gone, the wince of acute injury so long frozen into her features, started melting. Something inside her relaxed and a certain peace seeped back into our jangled home. And here is the amazing result—she loved me again.

Mom seldom told me she loved me. She seldom put her arms around me. I was more apt to do both. She showed her love through her actions. Like the time she stayed up all night with me, typing. All night, all the next morning, and on into the afternoon. My first high school research paper was due in May of my senior year. It had to be typed. I'd taken a typing class that semester to prepare for college, but I still typed slowly and laboriously. The paper was for Sociology, and it turned into a book. Not only did I have reams of research, but I also included selections from plays and poetry and photos from magazines. I had no idea that typing this tome would take about a week not a few hours the night before it was due. I sat down to type around 5:00 and by 10:00 I still had ¾ of it left to go. Dear God.

Mom came to my rescue. She typed only slightly faster than me, yet she did her best and all night long we spelled each other. Neither of us slept. We got up only to use the bathroom, pour another cup of coffee, or smoke a cigarette. We finished that massive paper around 2:30 the next afternoon. I had to skip school to keep typing and brought it to my teacher right after school let out at 3:00. I got an A+. But think of Mom. What a selfless thing to do. And so exactly like her. Seriously—we're talking high school here.

I would never have dreamed it was possible, but I went from loving you and feeling estranged from Mom to precisely the opposite. The clouds had lifted and just as she could see me, I could see her. I saw her strength; her creativity; her goodness; her unwavering, unpopular, nonconformist beliefs; her unswerving adherence to the teachings of Christ, despite her internal stumbling blocks. I saw the way she found beauty everywhere. I admired her more than ever, and we two, at long last, became close friends.

It didn't happen overnight—I acted up and lashed out at her for another year or so after you left to raise your new family—but the rebellious teenager in me finally packed up and left, too, making room for the enlightened person I'd always wanted to be.

The loss of love is a killing thing. When I had love, I couldn't imagine losing it, but I did. Mom's love, yours, even Ed's. With it went a vital sense of security. But now, for me, love and security made its way back. Paul loved me. Mom did, too. Even you seemed to like me better.

Today, as I conjure your faces again—you, Mom, Paul, Ed—I see that it's all in the eyes. The presence or absence of love. The power to nourish or wither. When love is there, crystal clear, nothing in this world feels so fine. But when it's gone—when it leaves those loving eyes—well, I just don't know how we humans survive it.

*

One trade-off for this newly revived attachment with Mom was hearing things I'd rather not hear. Like all war stories, Mom's needed to be told; she had to get what had happened to her off her chest. To a point, that was fine. We'd sit with our cup of coffee in one hand, cigarette in the other, and talk like two girlfriends. Unfortunately, all conversations had a way of circling back to you and how poorly you had treated her. She had pain to purge. I understood, I honestly did, but I hated to listen. It hurt me to have to think worse of you than I already did. My shoulders would squeeze up around my neck, so I had to breathe deeply and keep pushing them down to stay in my chair.

Mom spoke her truth, from her own experience, but she would then go on to ascribe all valid criticism to the whole world of men.

"Men end up with everything. We give them our best years, all our youth and beauty, and then they cast us aside for younger women. We have no recourse. It's too easy for men to get a divorce. Men get all the money and spend it on their new wives and families. All the credit is in their names. Women lose out to men every time. Men stray. Men don't have to stick by you, even after 25 years of marriage. Men can do anything they want. Men have the upper hand."

"Mom!" I would plead. "Please don't say 'men.' Say 'some men' or even 'many men,' just please don't say *all* men!"

How could my fair-minded mother slander an entire gender? I knew her sweeping generalization stemmed from her own tribulations, still it irked me. I liked men and wanted it to stay that way. I loved Paul and had received only goodness at his hands. My brother had always been my best friend, and I'd gotten along famously with boys since nursery school. But my mother was not making things up. She was pointing things out. She was warning her daughter of what many women were up against.

I fought her observations. When you and Mom split up, Dad, I assumed you two were the weirdos. That the institution of marriage—of love and monogamy— was as solid as ever, just not in our house. But this divorce epidemic I mentioned earlier soon opened my eyes to the truth.

I remember a customer at Bonwit Teller, a tall, striking woman resembling Miss Kitty on *Gunsmoke*, who decided to sidle up to the hosiery counter like we were a saloon and tell us about a book she was writing. It was all about men cheating.

"*Girls*," she said, "*Make no mistake. There is not one man alive— not one—who hasn't cheated on his wife.*"

The other salesgirls and I looked leery.

"*Oh, don't kid yourself!*" she persisted. "*No matter who they are, how good they are, sooner or later they all cheat.*"

I wanted to throttle her. I did not need any more bad news. Still, what she said gnawed at me.

You happened to call later that evening. (With no caller ID, we took our chances and answered the phone no matter what. That meant Mom had to speak to you on occasion. God in heaven.) My outrage at that Bonwit's customer and her loudmouth claim simmered close to the surface. At the sound of your voice, I broke down. Hot tears of pent-up fury poured forth: "Is it *true*, Dad? Do *all* men cheat on their wives? Some dumb woman swears it's true. *Doesn't anyone actually love anyone anymore?*"

You answered me gently, though I don't remember what you said. I hadn't been able to keep this revolting revelation to myself and blindsided you with it, when you had merely called to ask Audrey and me to dinner. I marvel at my ability to be so candid with you in this instance.

The era I grew up in fueled my dismay. So much was changing, starting with the skyrocketing divorce rate. I found a high school English paper I wrote not long after you left home in 1969. It's title? "Despair." Boy, does it say a lot about my fifteen-year-old self. Here's a paragraph from it:

> The ideal future that many young girls look forward to is, by their standards, a perfect marriage, and the endless joy that such a life would bring. Next thing she knows her own parents' marriage is shattered, leaving them desiring only to never see one another again. This is only the beginning for despair to move in, but more now than ever, she becomes aware, by hearing constantly of just such instances and other behavior completely opposite to her dreams of marriage, that her hopes were too idealistic. Now she sees marriage as a gamble, and all the standard advice of "being sure" is no consolation. Hadn't they all thought they were sure? It's almost as if she is looking forward to a game of Russian Roulette.

I wasn't purely reacting to my own mother's plight; I observed things on a societal level. Both men and women had long been locked into stereotypical roles and at this moment in American history, a backlash had begun. Mom was a casualty being referred to as "Displaced Homemakers." Wives who found themselves— facing fifty and menopause—booted aside after a career of making meals and raising children. The injustice infuriated me. As did the apparent capriciousness. Like for instance this fact: When you left home, you had just launched your new business, Pro/Mark. As an advertising executive you had made a good living, but Pro/Mark made you rich, right in time for Barbara to reap the benefits. So, you see, although I hated hearing Mom's harangues, she wasn't off base. Which of your wives got a mink coat when she turned fifty? Not Verna.

From that point on, my spirit grew steadily heavier as I realized that what you had done was not such an anomaly. Even Paul's parents hit a rough patch and when he told me, I sobbed inconsolably. I was an idealist, forced to face facts. In my high school paper, I define "Despair" as "... *part confusion, part frustration, part loneliness, part helplessness, part hopelessness...*"

I guess I wrote about despair because I'd been fighting so hard to stave it off. In a couple more years, I'd lose that battle. Despair would pull me down like a lead cape.

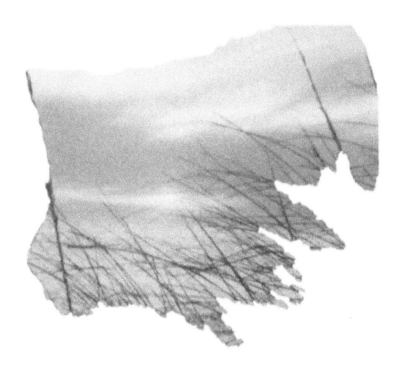

Part III

Look What They've Done to My Song

Harbinger of Hunger

"*What do you plan to do after you graduate?*"

This was not you, but Mom talking, as one jolted out of a trance. It was spring of 1971, only months before high school graduation. I'd always assumed I'd go to college, only I'd done nothing about applying. In a graduating class of 800, I guess the guidance counselors had their hands full, for when I finally talked with mine, it felt like an afterthought for both of us.

I do remember that when Mom broached the subject, she made it clear that no option existed outside the University of Illinois in Champaign/Urbana. I couldn't argue with instate tuition, especially when the school was a good one. Plus, it's where she went, and her brother, and my brother, too. I felt somewhat sorry that no other choices were available. You had convinced me once upon a time I'd be going to Stanford, back when everything was possible. Then again, I, too, had been jolted out of a trance. Doing anything about college at this stage, felt like catching a train as it left the station.

I hadn't known, but I came to find out, that my college admission rode on my performance junior year. Junior year—my worst year of all. It didn't matter that I'd snapped back to get all A's my senior year. My unimpressive grade point and class rank from junior year hindered me, but combined with respectable SAT and ACT scores, I did manage to get accepted into the University of Illinois. Unfortunately, the university was divided into colleges, each with its own separate admissions requirements. That's where I blew it. I missed my top choices—Education or Liberal Arts by one ACT point. Therefore, I began freshman year in the College of Agriculture.

Since the enchanted days of my beloved teacher, Miss Lundgren, I'd dreamed of teaching second grade. Remember the classroom I set up in our basement, complete with a seating chart of imaginary students? I played school and taught my phantom classes right through seventh grade. Standing there, drilling my pretend pupils on whatever I had learned in school that day, my body danced with endorphins. Starting college, I still wanted to be an elementary school teacher. My rekindled love of theatre, plus some encouraging words from various adults, also had me toying with the idea of an acting career.

But I landed in the College of Agriculture. And that small twist of fate affected me profoundly, largely since the only major I could reasonably declare in Agriculture was Home Economics, with its fascinating focus on food. Food—soon to become my full-blown obsession.

*

We did a whole lot of eating in our house after you left, Dad. Courtesy of Mom, bags of potato chips and tubs of onion dip appeared in my lap while I watched *Laugh-In*. I'd go to the kitchen before bed for a glass of water, and hot fudge sundaes with whipped cream and nuts lay in wait on the counter. Mom would run out for the newspaper and return with a dozen donuts. I gained twelve pounds in one month.

Not being much of a drinker, Mom took refuge in food, all aspects: the buying, preparing, eating, and feeding of it. The feeding part infuriated me, and I yelled at her. It was her fault, wasn't it, that my pants were too tight, and some obnoxious girl referred to me as "the fattest one in the group" after I downed three hot dogs in a row at a cookout. The truth is I'd been trim, so technically "fat" was inaccurate, but high school girls are notoriously cruel, so let's just say I was "fatter" than I had been. High school girls are also vain, so even though I weighed in at the high end of my ideal weight, my extra flesh had to be addressed.

I turned to The Atkins Diet, the big weight-loss craze in 1970. I consumed nothing but poached eggs, cottage cheese, and skinless chicken, and washed it all down with the mandatory 64 ounces of water, and all the black coffee I could stomach. I shed a miraculous ten pounds in four days. Then Mom decided to enter the Pillsbury Bake-Off and I came home from school to stacks and trays of newly invented cookies, cakes, and pies. They had to be eaten.

I yo-yoed like this for a time, losing weight, gaining weight, losing, gaining. Finally, in March of my senior year, I consulted Dr. Dreyfuss, who introduced me to the concept of counting calories. How effective! How exhilarating! How quickly it became my own personal gateway drug, setting the stage for the eating disorder awaiting me.

The self-discipline of my senior year revival extended to my diet now. I dropped the twelve pounds I had been gaining and losing and kept them off. I loved how I looked, how I felt, and I certainly loved my willpower. I had found the secret to dieting—counting calories!

The original goal was 1200 calories a day to safely lose ten pounds in one month. I did it in half the time. Magic! I could even organize my eating to feed myself *all 1200 calories at once* if I wanted, a truly heady experience. Instead of the recommended 250 for breakfast, 250 for lunch, and 700 for dinner, I could, for instance, skim through the day on coffee and a banana and then at night, devour a box of Girl Scout Cookies. Of course, this meant foregoing the mouthwatering beef stroganoff or tacos Mom (no longer vegetarian) was serving for dinner, but that, too, became an exciting aspect of my new identity. Who was in charge? Val was in charge. And looking noticeably slimmer.

This was long before the calorie content of every food was posted everywhere you looked. But I relished this challenge, too. I had to scout, I had to dig—calories were most mysterious. Dr. Dreyfuss had supplied me with a list of 30 common foods and their caloric values, things like an egg, a plain donut, a glass of milk, a hamburger. A hamburger and French fries contained a whopping 800 calories. Who knew? And yet two plain donuts and a glass of milk was half that. What a fun game! And, how marvelous it felt to exercise such control.

I soon had that list of 30 food items memorized and at my fingertips for instant calculating, which in itself was fun. And about a year later, of all the remarkable discoveries, I found my new Bible in a bookstore—a pocket-sized calorie booklet listing hundreds of items! I held the key to weight loss in my hands.

I knew that I still had to be ever vigilant because I really, really loved to eat. If I went to a party and drank beer and surrendered to a can of cashews or came home ravenous at midnight to make and eat an entire box of Betty Crocker Noodles Romanoff, the scale would shame me the next morning. I'd have to limit myself to 600 calories, until I shed those madcap pounds. And I did.

But I longed to someday be thin enough not to have to even think about all this, to be able to eat whatever I wanted, not afraid of gaining weight. To sip a cup of cocoa before bed and wake up weighing the same as the day before, not three pounds more. Exactly how thin would I have to be, though?

I'd soon find out.

Such High Hopes

1971

The summer of 1971—that glorious space between high school and college—shimmered with freedom and promise. Brent came home often, and he and I reestablished our closeness. Sometimes his quiet friend, Glen, would drop by in the evenings bearing a joint or two, so the three of us hung out in the basement, smoked a little pot to the Stones or The Beatles, and then, played Bridge for the rest of the night with Mom. For her part, Mom never bought booze again after you left home. All that sat in the liquor cabinet were the same old dusty bottles you'd left behind. I never touched them, either.

One reason I'd been able to plow ahead freely during my last year of high school was the lack of outside influence, including drinking buddies. With Janet and Paul gone, I seldom had the occasion. Not that they made me drink, of course. It's just one of things we might do together at night. Janet attended a community college for two years before transferring and took me along to the scads of parties her college friends threw, where everyone drank or smoked pot, or did both. When Paul wined and dined me, we ordered cocktails with our appetizers, and split a bottle of Lancer's with our entrees. At home, we drank beer with his buddies, or VO with his parents. But neither Paul nor Janet was around; and since they had been virtually my only companions, things changed.

A new best friend came into my life at that time. A sweet, smart, golden-haired girl named Debbie moved to Hinsdale from

California, but she'd been raised in North Carolina, so she spoke with a soft Southern accent. Debbie and I liked to spend evenings at Howard Johnson's, solving the world's problems over a pot of coffee. I still went to parties occasionally, but when I did, my new self-discipline carried over to my drinking. I was conscious of every calorie in a Michelob or a whisky sour. Gone were the days of guzzling with abandon.

Rationing my cigarettes was another way I practiced self-control that year. When I got the part of Dolly Tate, I worried that smoking would impair my singing voice. I'd heard a story about some overwrought woman being told by her doctor that smoking would calm her, but not to exceed ten cigarettes a day. So that's what I did—limited myself to ten. Then, during rehearsals, I brought it down to five. At college I would allow myself three, one after each meal. When I succumbed to bronchitis at semester break, I didn't smoke for ten days, so I figured why start up? I never smoked again.

The structured and productive life I had maintained my senior year had put me in the ideal frame of mind for college. That summer, I took my first college course at the local community college. I had quit my job at Bonwit's to be in "Annie Get Your Gun," but I still had all that money I'd been forbidden to use on a trip to Hawaii, so instead of working, I spent a portion of each day at the school Janet had attended—the College of DuPage, or as we called it: COD. I might have been stuck in Agriculture that first year, but I would transfer out as soon as possible, and that meant getting outstanding grades. Home Economics carried stiff science requirements for freshmen. Fairly certain my mind didn't work that way (the only high school class I ever got a D in was Biology), I decided to get the scariest requirement—Chemistry—out of the way before that year even started. I worried that if I took it at U of I, that one course alone could destroy my grade point. So, that summer I gave it all my brain power. Each morning, I attended the three-hour class, then holed up each blistering afternoon down in our cool basement doing homework, my papers spread out across Brent's pool table.

To my amazement, I clicked with chemistry. It didn't come easily, but I took to both the subject matter and the challenge, concentrated intently, and got an A. It felt grand to use my mind to master something so foreign and then receive the reward of that simple little letter grade on an actual college course. Of course, it was the only course I was taking. Still, I was proud of my ultra-effort, and that "A" fueled my verve for all the studying I would face in the fall.

I took a few trips down to Champaign/Urbana that summer and got totally stoked for college life. Brent's last semester coincided with my first. He was taking summer courses, and had an apartment in Urbana, so I drove down some weekends to acclimate myself to my soon-to-be new home. I loved the University atmosphere. It was everything I expected. I could not wait to join these hip adults—bearded men and liberated women—carrying important books and papers in and out of stately brick buildings, hanging at The Red Lion at night, drinking beer, listening to local bands like REO Speedwagon. I belonged here. I would be my best self in this place.

ONE STOP WEST OF HINSDALE

So now, to help you understand the girl who went to college fit and flourishing and came back a depleted skeleton, I will start at the beginning of that school year and describe what transpired.

First, I'll set the scene by describing an interesting aspect to my relationship with Paul. Even though we loved each other—wrote to each other every day, and fully expected to pick up where we left off when he came home—while apart, I sometimes hung out with other guys. I wouldn't call it dating; "palled around with" is more accurate. Because it was for fun, for something to do, not for sex, just companionship. I can't speak for Paul, but this probably applied to him, too. Often it was simply to have someone to go to a party with. It only made sense; we were too young not to. I told any boy who wanted to date me, that I had a steady boyfriend in the Marines—see his class ring on my finger?—and I had only friend-ship to offer. This may sound risky to someone else, but I knew I could keep things from getting out of hand. I had complete faith in my faithfulness.

Then on my 18th birthday, three days after I moved into the dorm, Brent took me to dinner at a Japanese restaurant. From there we walked a half a block to where Brent's friend, Mike, was having a party in the apartment he shared with a couple of guys. One of these guys was Philip. He wore his sandy-colored hair long but neat, like one of The Dave Clark Five. Tiny flecks of gold lit up his iridescent eyes and his smile was as honest as they come. We hit it off instantly. After the party, he walked me back to my dorm and that night Philip became my new best friend at school. Until November, that is, when Paul came back to civilian life and me.

I told Philip about Paul right away. I thought I was being upfront, but maybe he took it as a challenge. He had quite a bit of spending money and spent a lot of it on me. Well, on us, to be accurate. I mean, he didn't order me pizza then sit there, drinking tap water. Still, he did cheerfully pay my way as we gallivanted all over campus. I kept trying to split the bill with him, but he kept declining my money, so over time I stopped.

We had a routine. Since we both took studying seriously, we did it together. After my 5:15 cafeteria dinner at Evans Hall, Philip came calling for me. Laden with textbooks, we strolled to the Student Union where we sipped putrid vending machine coffee and studied for two or three hours. After so much silent concentration, we rewarded ourselves by splitting a pitcher of beer at Chances R, our favorite campus bar, where Rod Stewart was always singing "Maggie May." I deemed eight hours of sleep a necessity, so I was always back in my dorm room, in bed and asleep by midnight.

Sometimes Philip and I would go to Uncle John's restaurant which offered about a hundred different kinds of pancakes and toppings to choose from. This would be particularly satisfying after we had shared the occasional joint. On Friday nights, to celebrate our productive week, we'd wolf down deep-dish pizza at Garcia's then top it off with ice cream.

The only way I could do all this unrestrained eating with Philip at night, was to stop eating altogether during the day. My first couple of weeks at school, I'd taken advantage of my pre-paid meal plan by eating breakfast, lunch, and dinner at the dorm. But it soon became evident: calorie-wise, I couldn't afford to.

I'm sorry to admit this to you, and I did feel guilty about the wasted money, but maintaining my weight won over responsible spending. Soon, all I allowed myself from the breakfast and lunch line was coffee and a piece of fruit. Eventually, I didn't even go downstairs. Instead, I made instant coffee in my room and, if I happened to be back in my room at midday, I heated up a 200 calorie can of Campbell's Chunky Chicken Noodle Soup in my electric hot pot. Otherwise, I skipped lunch. I still went to the dining hall for dinner—Lord knows I was hungry by then—but I limited myself to two thin slices of meat and mounds of vegetables. I also walked a good eight miles a day.

Anyway, Phillip was a terrific person and a first-rate friend. And maybe I was naïve, but I did not consider a close plutonic relationship with a cute boy an anomaly. Maybe I was the anomaly. I should have understood that Philip had likely figured that by the time Paul returned, it would be Paul getting the boot, not Philip. By then, he would have made himself too lovable, too indispensable, for me to still choose Paul over him. This was not unreasonable. But it's not what happened.

It was an evening in November 1971 when Paul's mother called me in my dorm.

"*Val! Paulie is getting discharged this week and we're going to meet him in Las Vegas to celebrate and we want to take you with us! We want to make it a real homecoming. Can you come?*"

Of course, I said yes.

I hung up and sat there taking it in. *Paul is coming home! I will see him in Las Vegas in five days! I'll need to take two days of classes off. I'll need a new dress. I'll need to ... tell Philip.*

Oh, no. Philip. I had to call him and tell him that the dreaded day had come—Paul was coming home, and our time together was over. I picked up the phone and dialed his number.

His voice is still in my ears. All I had to say was, "Philip?" and he knew.

"*Oh, God,*" he said.

I tried to console myself by remembering that I had been up front from the start. I told myself that he didn't have to get close to a spoken-for girl. He could have walked away, not wasted his time. Others might say I should have been the one to walk away. Neither of us were old enough to be so wise.

I think back on it now and see that other girls might have done the opposite. Had there been no Paul, I'd have been lucky to be Phillip's girl. Only there was a Paul, and he was it for me. Philip was my treasured companion, but Paul was my man. I didn't want to hurt Philip, but there was no way around it.

I guess I hurt him more than I imagined.

A month later, before we all went home for the holidays, I wanted to do something nice for Philip, let him know I considered us friends still and thought of him fondly. So, I baked him a batch of Christmas cookies in the dorm kitchen and bought him a few little gifts—hand knit gloves, a leather bookmark, ceramic pipe.

But when I came to his door, festive and beaming, he recoiled as though I'd brought him a box of dead rats. I set the gifts on his table and left.

I did not see Philip again until the following May, when—if my eyes did not deceive me—I passed him on the Quad. He had lost so much weight I barely recognized him. He resembled a scarecrow, or a prisoner of war.

My heart stopped as I registered who it was. *Oh, NO. Did I do that to him?*

Life is so strange. After all that, after all of everything, Paul and I didn't even stay together. Before that summer ended, we had parted for good.

And when I passed Philip that morning in May, I was every bit the shrunken scarecrow he was.

Changing

Paul and I, as expected, resumed our love story. But in retrospect, I see how unrealistic it was for Paul or me or anyone to think neither of us would change while he was away.

When the war in our house finally ended, and they drafted Paul into the real one, I found myself immersed in the pleasant, solitary, unfettered act of reshaping my identity. It began my last year of high school and was in full swing at the University of Illinois. Finally, free to be me, I wasn't exactly the girl Paul left behind.

The 1960's was a decade of extreme change. When it began, women wore pillbox hats and strings of pearls, white gloves, and suits. When it ended, we were braless in bell-bottoms, our dresses so short they looked like tunics. We traded our Breck Girl pageboys and flips for long, straight hair parted down the middle, or bold, curly afros. For boys, the ubiquitous crew cut could now only be spotted on soldiers. The rest of the male population grew their hair down their backs if they felt like it. You didn't have to be an all-out, far-out, San Francisco hippie to embrace the ideals of the counterculture. A lot of us who didn't drop acid, or live in communes, or even march in protests, still embraced peace, love, and equality. But the counterculture opposed a whole lot, too, often whatever their parents had valued. Capitalism was under fire. Materialism was gauche. Ostentatious wealth? Not hip, man.

You might remember that Paul's parents were well off. His father had worked hard and done well. These were down-to-earth people, not pretentious, still they did live in Hinsdale, on the top floor of a posh new apartment high-rise, from which the Chicago skyline could be seen through sliding glass balcony doors. They walked on white shag carpeting and drove Cadillacs. When Paul came back from the Marines, he went back to work at his father's steel company and bought a new Corvette. They lived large and I, for one, loved the luxury. But that first year of college, exposed to new views and alive with fresh knowledge, my social consciousness began to morph.

After you left, Dad, Mom struggled financially. Your alimony and child support settlement may have been fair. But for 25 years she had operated on a certain amount of income and when it decreased, she had some big adjusting to do. And remember, your payments were calculated on your salary *before* your business boomed.

In 1971, Mom turned fifty but appeared to be pushing seventy. Ageism is still a problem today, but it was worse then. Despite her college education, she'd been out of the workforce for nearly three decades. She had more than a few disadvantages when it came to jumping into some kind of career. So, she didn't. Instead, she found fulfillment in familiarity—caring for her sixth grader, her house, her garden, cooking, sewing—while adjusting to her own new socio-economic status.

She had some big ideas. *"Let's get into the storage unit business!"*

I wish we had. They were in their infancy, and she had the foresight to see they would one day be a cash cow.

"Let's go to Alaska and homestead! We can get land for free and start fresh!"

Neither Brent nor I wanted to own storage units or move to Alaska, and we were all she had for cohorts. She thought about using her art and her sewing skills to make upscale doll clothes. But she didn't. She needed a partner, she needed encouragement. (When Audrey graduated high school, Mom did go to work. First, as a cashier at a big toy store. I'm not sure what happened there. I have this idea she talked to customers about the toys they were buying, and it slowed her down, and they let her go. She next took a job making donuts in the middle of the night at the nearest Illinois Toll Road Oasis.)

At one point, when I lived in the dorm in Urbana, she had our household phone disconnected to cut costs, using the phone booth at the drugstore for emergencies. Maybe it did save her a bundle but maybe it also kept her from hearing your voice when you tried to reach Audrey. Maybe it kept you from *reaching* Audrey. It also sent you a pointed message: *Look how poor you made us.*

Anyway, about that trip to Las Vegas. It thrilled me no end to be with Paul again, and that was all that mattered, but I found that watching people play with money turned my stomach. Although when Paul and his father won, and a man appeared with a suitcase of jewelry I was happy to accept the star sapphire ring Paul bought me. Still, for the most part, I abhorred the smoke-filled, windowless casinos, where we never knew if it was day or night. The only time we left our casino was on Sunday morning, when we piled into a cab to attend a brunch and floorshow at Caesars Palace, squinting and blinking like a family of 'possums, assaulted by the sunlight.

That first night in our hotel bedroom, I felt unexpectedly timid. Eleven months had passed since we'd last made love. Paul felt just a tad foreign to me. And so much restructuring had been going on inside me, I felt a little foreign to myself. Since September, I'd been going to classes, sleeping alone in a dorm room. Suddenly I'm in Las Vegas sleeping with a man in a hotel room. Thank goodness the strangeness didn't last long.

Through winter and spring, Paul and I kept on loving each other. Every Friday afternoon after work, he hopped in his Corvette and drove down to Urbana. Once or twice, he stayed the weekend at the University but more often he took me home with him, where we laughed and made love and he'd treat me like a queen, then turn around and drive me back on Sunday afternoon. It was a three-hour trip one way. Of course, he'd rip down old Rt.

47 and make it in just over two; still, it was a long way to go. But that was Paul, the best boyfriend a girl could have.

For some months, it worked well. Now, though, I see how this arrangement wore away at me. That first college semester had been idyllic and yes, part of that was Philip's companionship. Plus, Brent still lived on campus. I'd found a balance, a groove. My days had been orderly, productive, *and* fun. I loved learning, I had always loved learning, but now I felt about school the way I had as a child: passionate. Absorbing knowledge, building the foundation for my future career became all-consuming. Paul was set; he worked at his father's steel company during the day and wanted to have fun at night. I still liked fun, but it had to take a backseat to my studies. I wanted to be a productive woman, not a party girl.

I still loved Paul as much as ever but bridging two different settings produced a sense of vertigo in me. I had made such a smooth adjustment to campus life. And now, instead of spending the weekend in my college home, I raced back to my old life, my old ways. I wanted to be with Paul, but eventually the back and forth created an agitating limbo, like being incessantly yanked between two worlds, belonging to neither.

Maybe even worse, I began to miss Mom and Audrey terribly. It felt like acute homesickness, but for them more than me. I regarded Mom from a distance now and remorse pummeled me. My poor, poor mother. Her husband left her and now, when she and I had become so close, I left, too. And poor little Audrey—no dad in the house, no brother or sister. The weight upon my heart grew oppressive.

So, when I went home with Paul for a weekend of love and sex and fun, an insufferable guilt consumed me. Mom and Audrey *were only three and a half miles away*, all by themselves, believing Val to be back in her dorm room. Instead, I was right there, in my *hometown*, not even stopping in to say "*Hello.*" It mangled my conscience.

Something else happened during this period of intense sensitivity—I began to lament the way I had grown up so fast, the way I had drop-kicked myself into adulthood. I was beginning to regard my high school years as temporary insanity. I felt mortally sorry for so many things I had once done to cause Mom even a moment's worry. I regretted those times I had lied to her, told her I was sleeping at Janet's, when I was at the Ramada Inn with Paul, praying no one would recognize me in the elevator. The lying had bothered me, but I told myself that I knew what I was doing, that Mom couldn't understand and would only be upset, so to my way of thinking, my deception protected her.

Now, though, the larger picture of what had happened in our house, to my mother, my little sister—the loss they endured—grew into chronic heartache. I wanted to go back and change it all. Knowing I couldn't, made me want to stand on a cliff and howl for eternity. Maybe then I could purge my pity.

I'm not saying any of this was healthy or correct. Up to a point, my sympathy and remorse made sense. Beyond that, it approached deluded and dangerous proportions. Still, it's how I felt, and this guilt-ridden grief provided a fertile field for a developing depression.

So, there I was, going home with Paul, who hadn't a clue that these deep disturbances were gutting the girl he loved. But he might have noticed she was getting thinner.

And thinner.

And thinner.

Tracing an Addiction

Everyone noticed my weight loss, including you and Mom. How could you not? Mom addressed it, you didn't. Up until early 1972, my dieting could be considered risky behavior, not yet the full-blown eating disorder it would lead to. I guess it all began with my acceptance of the foolish but widespread notion that thin equals beautiful.

You left Mom for any number of reasons, but as a teenager, I couldn't help wondering if her weight gain was one of them. When Audrey was born, Mom had for the first time, a "pot belly" she never lost. She wasn't obese and didn't even lose her basic contours. Still, this protruding potbelly was conspicuous. Picturing her now, I would call her zaftig. She had shapely curves, but her body had widened, loosened up, turned jiggly, after she gave birth for the third time and turned forty. I am ashamed to say that it did occur to me that maybe you didn't love her so much anymore because she wasn't so attractive to you anymore.

I know several women who say they stay thin, fearing that they—like their mothers—will gain weight and their husbands—like their fathers—will lose interest. On the other hand, I know scads of women who are not at all thin and are cherished by their husbands. In fact, Barbara was not thin. She was young, but she was not thin.

Anyway, for me, this thinner thing started to take on a life of its own. I had arrived in Urbana, after my disciplined senior year, weighing 138 at 5'9". Who could ask for more? No one ought to.

But some wire got tripped in me at a certain point, and dieting became a habit— "an acquired mode of behavior that has become *nearly or completely involuntary.*" Programmed into you. Damn hard to stop.

The first true sign of doom came in February of 1972, when Mom sent me a box of cookies for Valentine's Day. Eighteen big, thick, Swedish butter cookies, shaped like hearts and topped with creamy pink icing. I ate one. I ate another. Then I ate them all.

When I was starving, I could do that. (I once ate an entire pecan pie in one sitting. It hurt, but it happened.) When I'd swallowed that last cookie, horror consumed me. What could I possibly do about this? Run, that's what!

I never ran. I walked. I walked for miles all over campus. But run? I didn't even own sneakers. I put on my regular leather shoes and hit the pavement. I ran and ran, up and down the dark streets of Urbana, I ran like the wind, a girl inside a gazelle, knowing that nothing else could forestall the barrage of calories assaulting me. I ran for two hours. And it was no hardship. I remember it as slightly euphoric. Problem solved.

The next month, Paul's parents invited us to their new vacation home in Florida, during my spring break. In those days, Easter still figured into spring breaks and if I took the trip with Paul, I'd be there for Good Friday and Easter Sunday. A heavy decision for me as I secretly longed to be home, with Mom and Audrey and Brent, go to services at my childhood church. Still, I knew the normal and expected answer was *Yes, let's go!* So that's what I said.

Mom sewed me an Easter dress. I picked out the swirly, pastel fabric and pattern and she sewed it to fit me to perfection. Mom, I hope you know, constructed clothing like a Vogue designer. Yet her immense talent got no further than the back bedroom of 206 Grant Avenue.

At that time, I weighed 130 pounds. Yes, eight pounds down from the perfect 138. Must have been all that walking. But also, I had noticed that whenever I went home and ate like a regular human being, I gained five pounds, so I reasoned that 130 was the safe weight which would allow for that. Worried that one decadent vacation week would pack on the pounds, I decided that only by losing *another* five pounds could I permit myself to eat to my heart's content on vacation. So, I made sure to drop an extra five before we left. I had that power.

All I had to do was limit my calories to 600 a day and the scale rewarded me each morning with another full pound gone. By the end of the week, I'd lost the five leeway pounds and weighed 125. That, I believe to this day, was my moment of no return, because nothing could match that exultant sense of accomplishment. I hiked into downtown Champaign and bought a silky purple bikini.

Vacation came and Paul picked me up in his Corvette and we whipped down to Florida in a night and a day. We flung our bodies down on the beach when we arrived and immediately fell asleep. Even though it was four in the afternoon, the tropical sun was so powerful that my pale body got burnt to a crisp and I spent my first two days in Tierra Verde in fiery pain, soaking in vinegar baths, and avoiding the sun.

Paul cared so much for my feelings. I wanted to go to a Good Friday service, so he took me to the nearest Lutheran church about twenty minutes away. I wanted us to have an Easter Basket, so we went to a local mall and created the most elaborate basket known to man. We colored Easter eggs and on Easter morning we sat on the dock eating them and drinking champagne with Paul's mother, as the rising sun lit up the Gulf of Mexico.

While in Florida, I noticed something unusual happening to my body. A certain brittleness began seeping into my bones. I felt breakable, snappable. Physical touch felt oddly uncomfortable, even a little dangerous. Starvation in its early stages changed the way I felt inside my skin. Too much of me was missing.

On the drive back to Illinois, I ate nothing but candy from our Easter basket. I could eat food, or I could eat candy—one or the other—and I chose candy. We checked into a hotel overnight and because I'd eaten so much candy, I spent half an hour before bed doing jumping jacks and toe-touchers in my underwear. I saw nothing peculiar in any of this. Poor Paul.

All in all, it was a grand vacation. After my sunburn abated and I could wear clothes and move without whimpering, Paul and I enjoyed solid sunshine and the usual love and laughter, not only together but with his family, who treated me like a treasured daughter.

I gave strict attention to what I ate during the day so I could live it up at night. Till then, fish sticks and canned tuna had been the extent of my seafood experience. I pluckily sampled lobster, crab, shrimp, and grouper, even escargot, and became a fan for life.

When we returned and I stepped on my scale, not only had I kept those five pounds off, I'd *lost five more!* Of course, I had; I had a dieting habit I couldn't kick, not even on vacation. So, there I was at 120, ten pounds below what my relatively still rational mind considered the lowest side of ideal. Nice!

Since dieting was now a way of life and unmonitored eating a physical impossibility, I soon dropped another five pounds just by living. One night a sweet girl named Billie came to my dorm room. I wouldn't call her a friend, exactly. By now, I had no friends. I had no time for them. To spend my weekends with Paul I needed to study nonstop during the week. But she was a warm-hearted girl whose conscience led her to knock on my door to voice her concern. Her timid, soft-spoken delivery belied the courage it took for her to speak her mind to someone she barely knew.

"*I hope you don't mind,*" she said, "*but I need to talk to you. I remember what you looked like when we all moved into Evan's Hall back in September. I thought you were thin then, but now, well I think you've gotten way too thin. Scary thin.*"

No one knew yet about eating disorders. Maybe a few doctors, certainly not the average person. Still, Billie knew something was wrong with me. She had noticed my body disappearing.

I can still see her wide, worried eyes. What a brave, caring girl.

I'm not sure what I told her in response. It shocked me to hear someone call my svelte figure scary. I registered it and probably said, "*Oh, I know, I'm down about five pounds. I won't lose any more.*"

I wonder if Billie grew up to be a doctor or maybe a minister. I'm sure she grew up to be a force for good in the world.

Obsessed

My overzealous studying had paid off; I'd gotten straight A's my first semester. Mission accomplished. Now it was more crucial than ever to finish the year with a perfect 4.0 grade point average. Not only did I need those grades to transfer out of Agriculture, but a new mission had materialized—support Mom for the rest of her life. The picture of poverty she painted had me wringing my emotional hands. On top of everything, she would live out her life indigent? Not if I could help it!

This time my classes presented a more rigorous load. Last semester, I'd taken courses like Sociology and Psychology—people-centered subjects I took to naturally. Now I had Economics and Physiology to contend with, subjects I believed my brain had not been built to grasp. Could I keep up the pace? Lately my mind had been feeling ... clogged.

That spring of 1972, the heat was on in the race for A's. Now I hadn't a soul at school—not one single friend—to distract me. That helped. But my study schedule lost two full days and nights by spending the weekends with Paul, ostensibly having the fun I so sorely needed. To make up the time, I had to cram all my studying into the weekdays. I still went down to the dining hall at dinnertime and ate my sliver of meat and piles of vegetables, but I ate and left in under ten minutes. Tarrying or talking I deemed a frivolous waste of time. I mean—I could be studying.

From that point on, whenever Paul and I were together, he had to know that my mind was not on us, but on what we might eat. I had moved into the embarrassing stage of eating disorders, where you lay your obsessions out in full view for everyone but yourself. The stage where you can legitimately be called "sick." After our Easter trip, my mind and body had crossed that line. Food ruled my thoughts. If my brain wasn't memorizing anatomical definitions or analyzing the gross national product, it counted and recounted calories all day long, planning what I might allow myself to eat at the end of the day. Hadn't I watched one full pound of flesh drop off the scale every morning when I limited myself to 600 calories a day? How do you walk away from a kick like that?

Confining my daily food consumption to 600 calories, especially when I wanted to fit ice cream in there, became an art. Cough drops helped. Gum, too. Until I discovered sugarless Trident—a smart option, at only twenty calories a pack—I chewed Bazooka Bubble Gum while I studied. I could chew seven yummy pieces a night for 105 calories, but the next time I went to the dentist he found thirteen cavities.

Sometimes I took the Illinois Central home on a Friday afternoon and never looked up from a textbook the whole ride. Paul would pick me up in Chicago, ready to begin our typical carefree weekend. One time, I salivated the whole train ride imagining an enormous bowl of peppermint ice cream covered in hot fudge. Knowing I'd be expected to eat with Paul that night, I ate nothing during the day, so I quivered with anticipation for that heavenly sundae, and could barely think straight. When I got in Paul's car, that was our first stop— the Jewel/Osco, to load up on ice cream and sauce. Like a junky, I trembled with desire and gnawing hunger until our bowls were piled high and at last, I sank my spoon in for the first orgasmic bite. Paul was such a good sport. He never made me feel remotely foolish for these cravings. He never questioned my odd eating habits or my obvious weight loss. But if he wasn't worrying, he had to be wondering.

I exhibited classic symptoms of starving people. I lost all interest in sex. It felt neither normal nor right. But I couldn't tell him that, or that during sex I often wanted to scream. My body felt stiff and breakable, like I was made from balsa wood, not living tissue. Experts say that a subconscious need to not be sexual, to return to a former child-like innocence, often drives such drastic weight loss. I would not argue that. In a female, it removes any signs of womanly sexuality; my breasts and bottom shrunk, my period stopped. It's like reverse puberty.

How hard this must have been for Paul. His vivacious, curvaceous girlfriend, who used to love making love (as we actually called it), now shied away from physical contact and babbled incessantly about what to eat next. I realize now that my shrunken naked body not only felt different to me, it also felt different to him. And looked different, too. Yet he never said a word. Not one word.

That weekend of the ice cream, Paul drove me back to school late Sunday afternoon. My heart sank with the sun. The guilt and pressure I kept heaping on myself became too much to bear. Once more, I'd been minutes away from my unsuspecting mother and sister and hadn't gone to see them. I had to return to mountains of homework and no friends. I was happy nowhere, and miserable everywhere.

The next weekend, Paul had some commitment and would not be coming for me. It didn't occur to me then that the poor guy probably needed some time with his buddies. He was only 23 years old, fresh out of the Service. He couldn't put a name to what was happening to me, but I'm sure he needed a break from it.

Maybe the best part of our entire blissful relationship had been our ability to be our genuine selves with one another. I have never felt so cherished for exactly who I am—*so approved of*—as I did with Paul. (Except with you, Dad, when I was young.) Now, though, that very self *itself* was changing. The strangeness of me, inside and out, must have bewildered Paul. We never talked about it, his affection never wavered, but it was clear—I was not the same. I was unraveling, physically and emotionally. And although we never discussed it, there was no denying—our love story was unraveling, too. Such a mournful realization. Everything solid was slipping away.

Somewhere around then I slid within the parameters of clinical depression. My mind and body felt so feeble and altered, my heart so hopeless and heavy, that in a flash of understanding, I knew I had lost myself; despair had finally won. I felt sick. Sick in my spirit, sick in my soul. The disillusionment, the loneliness, the guilt, the grief, the studying, the starvation, flattened me under its weight. I was helpless to contend with any of it.

Then something remarkable happened.

You called me, Dad. You called me from your office on Michigan Avenue one afternoon to say "hello." It so happened I sat in my dorm room, studying.

"How are you, Val?" you asked.

I hadn't the strength to pretend.

I said, "I'm horrible, Dad. I'm scared and sad and sick. I think I'm really sick, Dad. I think I'm sick in the head."

And you did the most amazing thing. You believed me.

You did not try to cheer me up or talk me down. You believed me.

"*I will be there to get you,*" you told me. "*I'll bring you home.*"

You got into your car and drove the three hours down to Urbana. You took me out to a nice restaurant for a hot meal, making me feel safe and cared for. Then you drove me the three hours home. Not home to your house, with your new wife and children, which would have made me sicker, but to my own home, where my own lonely mother and sister waited for me.

I will never forget this. Never as long as I live. What hope and reassurance you restored to me simply by taking me seriously and coming, unbidden, to my rescue. Who would do that? You. My original, loving father.

*

You brought me home, but of course I couldn't stay there. I might have been hanging on by a thread, but I still had to go back to school.

I rested, soaked up Mom and Audrey's love, slightly soothed my guilty conscience for all the times I'd been nearby and hadn't visited. Still, I had to finish out the year. I was not so far gone that I would allow myself to tank this close to finishing freshman year with a solid A average. My super-human willpower was nearly, but not entirely, spent. Your loving act kept me holding on, then something happened to grease my grip.

Mom still did not know (or perhaps, did not accept) that I had been having sex with Paul for almost three years. It seems implausible, but she was of a different era and ilk.

Another weekend passed in the usual manner: Paul picked me up from school on Friday and drove me back to campus on Sunday night.

It is Monday evening and my roommate, Linda, and I are studying at our desks. We've opened our one large window and sit in a sauna of May humidity. The phone jangles us out of our drowsy concentration. I pick up the receiver and hear Mom's flustered voice.

"Val! Where have you been? I called and called all weekend and you never answered! I've been so worried! Where on earth have you been?"

I cannot keep it up anymore. I tell her the truth.

"At home, Mom," I hear myself say as I watch Linda's eyes fly open, her hands and head shaking, "No!"

It's too late. I stare back at Linda's wide eyes and say, "I was at home with Paul, Mom. I stayed with Paul for the weekend."

Linda's head drops into her hands. I wait for Mom to react, while a motorcycle revs and backfires, then buzzes off into the distance.

"Oh, Valerie," she says at last. "I don't approve."

You might think that's a mild reaction. You might think, "Well, that's good, right?"

Well, no, this was Mom. This was me. I'd been craving her approval all my life. During my teenage rebellion I couldn't let myself care so much, but now this girl, this girl who stood on stork legs, who dragged around a heart full of *mea culpa*, was felled by these simple words.

I tried to stay light and breezy and adult about it.

"It's fine, Mom. We love each other. I'm almost nineteen, you know. I'm on the pill. It's all okay. I'm sorry for worrying you."

But the damage was done. I'd lost her love again.

Sunk

When it came to sexual morality, my generation was caught between two worlds. We were raised by parents who condemned premarital sex, at least in theory. Lack of effective birth control had something to do with it, but so did the prevailing conventional attitude. We daughters were given the impression that the swiftest way to bring shame on ourselves and our parents was to get caught having sex before marriage. Get pregnant and life is over. Maybe Mom was overly fearful about this, but books and movies and TV programs all reinforced these traditional beliefs. On the other hand, we belonged to a generation who came of age during the "sexual revolution," so we naturally gravitated toward the new ideas of our own liberated culture. There we were—there I was—confused and conflicted. Damned if you do, damned if you don't.

I had no doubt that Mom dreaded the possibility that I might be one of those girls who engaged in premarital sex. I don't fault her. I know she was driven by a strong need to protect me from the dire consequences. Yet it also established an ironclad standard, that, should I fail to achieve, would cast me into a pool of supposedly hapless, inferior young women. I did not believe this, but I knew *she* did, and while she dreaded it for me, *I dreaded it only for her.*

So, now that she knew I had lost my virginity, I could not find a moment's peace. I had failed her in her greatest expectation. At least that is what *I believed* she believed.

The following weekend was Mother's Day. I had wanted to honor the day with as much fanfare as possible. I'd invited Mom and Audrey down for the weekend, booked them into a nice hotel, and made dinner reservations at an Italian restaurant. I also got us tickets to see the University's production of *Fiddler on the Roof* at Krannert Center for the Performing Arts. (Where did I get the money? It's possible it came from that stash of cash I'd saved from not going to Hawaii. It's also possible you paid for it. Maybe both.)

Mom would be coming soon, and we were sure to talk about sex.

I want to say it was all my imagination, that I expected to see disappointment written all over her face, so I conjured it up where it didn't exist. Actually, it was the other way around. I told myself she couldn't possibly let this recent revelation affect her opinion of me, me—the daughter who loved her so much and missed her so much. Who studied so diligently so someday I could make her proud and restore her dignity. I told myself I would see the same love for me that I saw three weeks ago when I surprised her with a visit. But I didn't. Her face had hardened again into the stony grimace of *disapproval* she'd worn for so many years. The love that I had re-earned over the past few years had been rescinded all at once by my bold admission to pre-marital sex. I thought it might finish me.

Mom arrived with a picnic basket full of food. At this point, my bony body alarmed her, and she induced me to eat. There were thick ham salad sandwiches on fresh bakery bread and homemade chocolate cake. The temperature climbed above ninety and the food felt straight from an oven, yet I remember losing all control and cramming this feast into my mouth like the starving person I was. Horrified that I had succumbed to temptation and consumed all that rich food, I yearned to go running for a couple of hours, but of course I couldn't. It had made Mom glad to watch me eat her food with such gusto, and we were off to a good start, though her stiffness was apparent.

Over dinner, I tried desperately to keep a *bon vivant* attitude. I talked up our plans for the weekend and pretended not to notice any tension. I so wanted us to be happy together, in our booth under the twinkly fairy lights, eating our lasagna.

She chose to talk about it, though, which in a way reassured me. She felt an urgency to impart all the information she hadn't expected to share until the night before my wedding. With eleven-year-old Audrey sitting next to me, we talked practicalities—birth control, hygiene, and her own peculiar worry—that I be wide awake, not asleep, for the action.

On one level, it bolstered me to talk like this, woman to woman. Like maybe we now shared an intimate connection, which could bring us closer. I hoped she might feel the same. Years earlier, when I read the term "sexual intercourse" and asked Mom what it meant, she gave me a glowing explanation. "When a man and woman love each other, they want to get even closer, and it is the closest you can get to another person." She called it "one of the most beautiful experiences a human being can have." Yet, sitting in that Italian restaurant, I noted an air of distaste in her manner. Instead of some new bond between us, I felt this distaste now extended to me. My heart sank. Emotionally, I could not afford that.

The play on Sunday didn't measure up to the impressive treat I'd planned. *Fiddler on the Roof* is a three-hour musical. Mom saw only the first 20 minutes before the cloying perfume of the woman seated on her right drove her from the theatre. At intermission I insisted we leave, but she said, *no, you paid for the tickets; you and Audrey should at least enjoy it. I'll stay out here in the lobby.*

Snapping

At 115 pounds I began to feel the effects of malnutrition. My period had stopped, my shiny dark hair had turned dull and coarse and fell out here and there. A new and persistent pain pressed deeply into the center of my forehead so I could often be seen walking around cradling my skull. Thank God, I had only a few weeks left of school; I couldn't have lasted any longer. It was getting harder to retain the endless information I daily forced into my brain. It, too, was starving.

The sense of being half-there troubled me. I remember sitting on the grassy lawn of the Quad one day, eating a tomato for lunch, because a tomato has only 20 calories, and repeating over and over the first line from a poem my high school English teacher admired: "*What I wanted was to be myself again.*"

In physiology, we were assigned a research paper on a topic of our choosing. I chose "*The Effects of Malnutrition on the Brain*" Of course I did. Maybe I couldn't see that I was so thin as to be repulsive, still I did know that my brain and body didn't feel right, and probably because I'd stopped feeding them properly. Many of the symptoms now plaguing me were, sure enough, classic effects of malnutrition. I had the research to prove it. But I could make no changes.

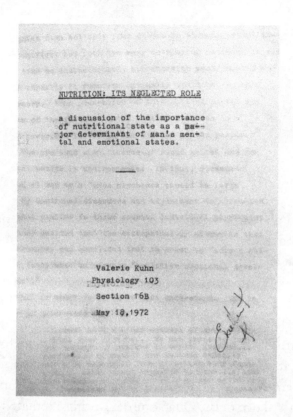

NUTRITION: ITS NEGLECTED ROLE

a discussion of the importance
of nutritional state as a major determinant of man's mental and emotional states.

Valerie Kuhn
Physiology 103
Section 16B
May 18, 1972

June arrived. Final exams approached. I crammed and crammed but nothing stuck, as if the pain in my skull came from a hole in my head, through which all the facts I jammed in there leaked back out.

One night I snapped. In my room I tried with all my might to retain key points for my economics exam. Something let loose in me, and I heard myself half-gasping, half-wailing, over and over like a stuck tape recorder: *"Help me! Help me! Help me!"* I could not stop. It was as though someone else took possession of my voice. It was also eerily like a nightmare I'd had about a year earlier, where I came home to find our house filled with blood and body parts; my entire family murdered and dismembered, even the dog. When the police arrived, I lay at daybreak face down on our driveway, seeing only black shoes and cement, powerless to lift my head or stop screaming that same exact sentence, *"Help me! Help me! Help me!"*

A knock on my door. Billie, again. I don't say "come in;" I can't stop saying help me long enough. She opens the door, assesses the situation, walks in, and stands by me.

"What's wrong? What's happening to you? Are you okay or do you need help?"

I shake my head and try to catch my breath. "I don't know, Billie. I don't know. Maybe I'm having a breakdown. I think I'm coming apart."

"What can I do? Should I get help?"

"I don't know, I don't know what happened. I couldn't stop saying that. But I think I can breathe again, like whatever had hold of me, dropped me when you came in."

Now I'm crying. "I am so exhausted. I'm just so exhausted. I don't know how to keep doing this."

She stayed and talked until she saw I was calm. Then I closed my books and crawled into bed.

The next day I took my economics exam. I knew nothing. I did the best I could but afterwards, I could not remember even one question, let alone how I answered it. I went and spoke to my instructor, hoping to do a retake, explaining I'd been sick. He told me there was no need—I'd gotten the highest score in the class. My poor brain felt disconnected from my body, as if my head floated far above my shoulders, a balloon on a string. Yet my mind still operated on autopilot, it appeared. I didn't know any other explanation for even passing that test.

Blessedly, exams were over. I had made it to my last weekend at the University. I'm not sure what Paul and his friends were doing there, because that following Monday Mom and Audrey moved me and my belongings back to Clarendon Hills. But he'd driven down with his buddy, Dennis, and Dennis's girlfriend. Like they'd come down to celebrate the end of the year with me.

On a bright Saturday morning, the four of us piled into a sunny booth at Uncle John's. Like normal people, they all ordered something delicious, the way I would have earlier that fall with Philip. Strawberry crepes with whipped cream or German Pancakes with cinnamon apples. I couldn't make up my mind. I could not decide. Dear Lord, the *calories* that food represented, didn't they know? So, while they dug into their pancakes and blintzes, I carefully sectioned off my half a grapefruit.

Who's crazy now?

Part IV

Needles and Pins

Ending Things

Freshman year of college was finished. Praise God.

Back home in Clarendon Hills that summer of 1972, I knew for certain I could not go back to school in September. I could not pick up one more book, memorize one more fact, or so much as touch a typewriter. I made the all-important 4.0 and almost perished in the process. Someday, after I recovered, I would go back. I'd try a different school, somewhere far away, a more prestigious college, perhaps. After all, I had this perfect grade point from the University of Illinois. That ought to count for something. But, at the time, I could not even write a letter.

I dreaded telling you, Dad. My academic achievements made you proud of me. *You were proud of me again!* Still, I eventually screwed up my courage and admitted defeat.

"I can't go back to school in the fall, Dad. I'm kind of burnt out. I think I have to take this year off and work."

In the manner of my old, easy-going father, you said, *"Val, all a parent really wants for his child is happiness. If staying out of school will help you be happy, then it's a fine decision."*

Just like that, you absolved me of my "failure." You further bolstered me by informing me that four years of college is an arbitrary number derived from some medieval belief that it took that long to groom a gentleman. You chuckled and assured me, *"You have all the time in the world."*

Going on nineteen, I was now back home, again sharing a bedroom with my little sister, because as soon as I left for college,

Mom had turned our three-bedroom home back into its original two-bedrooms, by knocking down the wall you'd built in 1958. Audrey was twelve at this point.

Paul lived a couple of miles down the road, but we saw each other less and less. Mom's displeasure over our intimacy did a deadly number on our already unravelling romance, not to mention my own beaten-down self. When he asked me to go camping with him and a few other couples, I baffled us both by saying, "I can't. My mother won't let me."

What a strange situation. Paul and I were finally back together in the same town, not separated by miles. I was a legal adult, not a high school girl. He rightly assumed we were now free to do as we pleased as a couple. But I lived under Mom's roof, with the objectionable truth of my sex life hanging in the air between us. I felt like some kind of guilty runaway—caught, sins exposed, returned to maximum security. I had so little left of my old fire and spunk that I simply surrendered. It was too painful to buck her.

Janet and I got waitress jobs at a new Italian restaurant in Westmont for the one-hour lunch crowd. The pace was break-neck and I had never waitressed before. I wanted to like it, but I couldn't stand it. For one thing, I was perpetually cold, and the place was like a meat locker, and since I had no flesh to keep me warm, I wore a bulky white cardigan over my black nylon waitress dress and still my teeth chattered. I gave serving my best effort, but the chef swore at me in both English and Italian. The pain in my head drilled deeper. I dropped soup on someone and couldn't live it down. We made no money at all. It was the first month of a new business, so it lacked clientele, plus lunches were cheap, so tips were meager.

On top of all this dreadfulness, I had to wear my long hair either up in a bun, or in a ponytail, which provoked me to tantrums every morning in front of the mirror. I COULD NOT GET THE BUMPS OUT. I guess they were the outward manifestation of the thousands of things I could not control, because I lost my ever-loving mind over them.

Damn it all to hell! Everyone in the world has smooth hair that lays flat, but MINE has BUMPS. I can't even put it in a ponytail without these hideous bumps appearing!! I try again and again and again, and still, I GET BUMPS. I can't stand it I can't stand it I can't stand it! I scream and scream and pound my arms with the evil, wretched hairbrush. "Fucking bumps! FUCKING, FUCKING BUMPS!"

Mom comes running and stands there looking at me, beyond horrified. I can't help it, I scream and swear and hit myself as she watches, frozen, wringing her hands. Audrey runs to see what is happening and watches me for a second then rushes to me. Her little girl arms enfold me, and she lays her head against my bony chest. I stop screaming and start crying.

She turns to Mom. "Mom! Hug her! She needs you to hug her."

Oh, Audrey, how right you were. I had felt unloved by our mother since I told her I had sex with Paul. It didn't make sense to me that she should not love me over this, but I accepted the fact that she didn't, and it tore me apart.

Mom stood there helpless, stricken, and then she obeyed her young daughter and moved towards me, too. Against her nature, she opened her arms and I walked into them. My rage and frustration melted into relief and remorse. I cried and cried for all the lost love. I wanted it all back so badly. I wanted everything back, for all of us.

*

A few weeks later, I found another lump in my breast. Since the skin on my breast now stretched as flat to the bone as the skin on my wrist, it appeared like a flesh-colored marble, under my existing scar. It needed to come out.

This time I knew the drill. I stayed in the hospital for the same length of time, but there was no argument over consent, maybe because I was eighteen. Once again, it was benign.

I was sitting on our patio, my gaunt chest and ribcage wrapped in a big sterile bandage under a white and brown striped halter-top

Mom had made for me, when Paul dropped by to say "Goodbye." He now wore a full beard and his buzz cut had grown down to his shoulders. He'd traded his Corvette for a Harley Davidson and was taking off for Pennsylvania, alone, to visit one of his Marine buddies. He didn't know when he'd be back. He thought he might stay there.

This is how we ended. No real break up. We simply parted. How could that be? "*Marry me and bear me many children as beautiful as you,*" he'd once written to me. I could not imagine loving anyone else. We kissed goodbye. He turned and left.

I sat in my chair and watched him go. I sat there for an hour. Then another. The light left the sky, and still I sat there. How had this happened to us? We had loved each other so fully, so *earnestly.* What had happened to me that I should be so numb, should feel so little? My senses felt swathed in cotton and it's probably an awfully good thing. Had I been healthy, I could not have endured his leaving.

Though we never quarreled or even addressed it, Paul had watched me fade away. When people asked what happened to us, as I'm sure they did, what could he say? "Something happened to her. She wasn't the same girl. I think she became mentally ill."

Funny, that's what you would have said, too, about Mom: "She changed. She was mentally ill."

The curious thing about my mental illness is that it did not actually impair my intelligence. It altered my judgment, my perception of reality, but it didn't alter my IQ any more than it did Mom's. Yes, depression and "burnout" affected my ability to concentrate. My mind felt like mush, encased in a thick layer of gelatin, but it kept right on ticking. Maybe the Jell-O swathing my brain and nerves was a defense mechanism, a shield, advantageous after all.

I sat on our terrace long after Paul drove away. The sun left, the stars came out, and still I sat, in the dark, fashioning a plan. What should I do next? Shivering there in my bandage and sun top, I figured it out; I'd go away, too.

Nantucket Via Greensboro

I couldn't quit my job fast enough. Since I wasn't returning to school, I could travel without deadlines. I called Susie in Indianapolis and asked if she could join me. She couldn't. Neither could Janet. Both were going back to school in September. I'd have to go alone. I apprehensively ran this plan past you, Dad. You were so in favor of the idea that you even offered to help finance it! (Yes, it saved you from paying for another year of college, which you were doing as the divorce decree stipulated. Still, it was also an overtly loving gesture, and I am forever grateful.)

So where would I go?

Where else?

Nantucket.

Finally, I'd make my way back. I'd check myself into a charming guest house, where I'd relive that last delightful vacation, when our family was as whole and happy as we'd never be again. Nantucket, where I had been myself before I, too, turned into someone else. I pictured my own cozy room—in what I saw as a cross between a quaint inn and a sanitarium—with a view of the ocean, streaming sunshine, and clean, white sheets. Still, I couldn't idly do nothing. My job would be to rest and restore my health, yes, but also to screw my head on straight and make plans for the future. I would legitimize my trip to Nantucket by visiting schools in Boston, where I'd surely be happier. Champaign/Urbana sat in the middle of cornfields. This time I wanted a city nearby, so academia wouldn't get another chance to swallow me whole.

What a sensational plan! The night I crafted it, (the night Paul left? The next?), I stayed up all night and watched the sun rise, too jazzed to sleep. For the first time in a long time, I felt hopeful and galvanized. The fact that you stood behind me, Dad, and would subsidize me, filled me with an off-the-charts elation. What I didn't realize was that you had plans of your own.

Cousin Donna was now a wife and mother living in Greensboro, North Carolina. You suggested to me that I begin my travels there. I suspect you and Donna agreed that I would be content there and that would be the end of my traveling. There was even a college nearby. Simple solution. Send the girl to Greensboro.

So, on August 1, 1972, you and Barbara saw me off at O'Hare Airport as I flew to North Carolina. Mom had opposed the plan. She'd campaigned against it since I described it to her. Her reservations, at least the ones she voiced, stemmed from the "young woman on her own, anything can happen" mentality, which is certainly grounded in reality. I went, regardless.

By now, because of my full-blown addiction to dieting, I floated in at around 105 pounds. I arrived at Donna's house still not comprehending how scrawny, how actually hideous, I looked. I simply felt finally thin. They had a pool at their condo complex, and I snuck in forty laps a day. I say snuck, because now people were watching me, watching what I ate, and I had to fool them.

Everyone in my life had a mission to make me eat. Some were subtle, some just short of force-feeding, but I now had to sit at Donna's dinner table each night and politely eat with her and her husband like a normal person. I got out of breakfast and lunch by sleeping till noon. I went to bed around nine and read for about an hour and then poured through recipes in magazines and cookbooks until after midnight. Porn for the starving. I must have been a disappointing, even burdensome, houseguest. You probably said I would repay my room and board by helping care for their adorable toddler. But I didn't.

I'd been with my cousin close to a month, when I started feeling nervous about the fact that I was in Greensboro, not Nantucket. It began to dawn on me: this was not a temporary stop on route to Nantucket; I'd been sent here to stay. Nantucket was the dangling carrot. *Oh, no you don't!* I thought.

Through some careful planning, pre-world wide web, and an iron will, I managed to make my next move towards my pilgrimage to Nantucket. I flew to Boston in time for Labor Day Weekend, 1972. I found lodging in the YWCA on Tremont Street and for one week I covered every inch of Boston, visiting every college within 20 miles. I told myself that this was my quest: to find my next school. (At this point, my food fixation ruled me, so all thoughts of teaching or acting were gone; I would be studying nutrition or restaurant management.)

Eating all my meals out presented a challenge. I economized well but keeping the calories under 1000 was tricky. My oddball eating requirements led to some awkward moments. One mortifying memory took place in a bustling deli near Copley Square. I sat down around 2:30 to eat my one and only meal of the day. The waitress presented me with a menu that made my head swim. More like a book, it offered page after page of mouth-watering items. I couldn't decide! Truly. *I could not decide.* I sat there for an hour agonizing over my options, like my very life depended on this decision. 3:00 came and went. 3:15. 3:30. I still couldn't choose. The concern on the face of my motherly server grew as the clock ticked. When I finally made up my mind, she rushed to the kitchen to place the order, then came back stone-faced to break the news:

"Listen, Honey, I hate to tell you this, but while you were making up your mind, we went from our lunch menu to our dinner menu and I'm very sorry, but that particular dish is only offered on the lunch menu, so I guess you'll have to pick something else."

My body slumps onto the table in defeat. I shake my head and silently beseech this kind woman with my tearful eyes: What do I do now?

Thank God, she tells me. "Get an omelet. It's the perfect meal. You've got protein, dairy, vegetables, and it comes with toast. It's a complete meal, dear. It's the perfect choice. Order an omelet. A Western omelet."

I took her advice and to this day, if in doubt, I go for the omelet.

Another less pathetic, more humorous, experience occurred at an all-you-can-eat fish fry at a Howard Johnson's. I sat at the counter and ate all I could eat, which for a tall young woman with an empty stomach is a staggering amount. I kept ordering one plate after another, after another, until the frazzled cook emerged from the kitchen in his stained apron, looking for the big galoot who was devouring all this fish. Visibly startled to see it was me, he nevertheless waved his spatula and hollered, *"That's it! You're done! No more!"*

Well, okay. But the sign did say "All You Can Eat."

A few days later, I woke up deathly ill, unable to swallow and nearly delirious with fever. Leaning up against buildings to steady myself, I made it to Mass General, where they informed me that I had mono. How could that be, I wondered; I'd already had it. Still, they insisted my blood test confirmed it.

I called Mom and told her. She immediately promised to put Audrey and our dogs, Ivy and Oscar, into the car and drive the thousand miles to Boston to fetch me.

These surges of courage from our retiring mother will eternally awe me. Luckily, she didn't need to make the trip. In a few days, I felt well enough, to take the Greyhound down to nearby Norwalk, Connecticut, where Uncle Ned and Aunt Kathie now lived.

I went there to rest—the doctor they brought me to claimed it wasn't mono, but "fatigue and exhaustion"—still, in true Aunt Kathie fashion, she pulled me out of bed each morning at 7:30 to jog with Uncle Ned at eight o'clock sharp. I turned 19 at their house, and instead of celebrating in Nantucket like I'd hoped, with a plate of bay scallops and a glass of champagne, Aunt Kathie invited three teenage girls from their church to join me in her living room for a maple-flavored birthday cake.

As soon as I could, I made my break for Nantucket. Uncle Ned and Aunt Kathie packed a picnic lunch and drove me to Cape Cod themselves. While still at their house though, I did the resourceful thing and drove up to Springfield, Massachusetts, where I visited UMass and Smith College, which would ultimately be my first choice.

I arrived in Nantucket — *our Nantucket, Dad* — on a splendiferous day in mid-September and stayed for a month and a half. By the end of that time, there was no doubt about it: I needed professional help.

The Reckoning

In many ways, I did recapture the glory of that heavenly childhood summer. The September days rolled by long and mellow. I rode my bike to every corner of my beloved island, my spirit revitalized, singing into the wind. I swam in the ocean and dozed in the dunes. I visited The Whaling Museum, the Library (called The Atheneum)—and read everything I could about the island's history. Its Quaker ancestry fascinated me. I visited churches, too. Since there was no Lutheran church on Nantucket, each Sunday I sampled a different denomination.

My first Quaker meeting stands out. Nine o'clock came and went. No one said anything. 9:05. 9:10. 9:15. Did I have the time wrong? I sat near a window and watched branches dance in the wind. Finally, someone spoke. Someone from a seat behind me, not from the front we all faced.

"Isn't it lovely the way the trees are swaying in the breeze today?"

Silence. Silence for another five or ten minutes, until someone else felt an inner urging to say something. It moved me, this alien form of simple worship. I kept studying and forming a love of Quaker ideas. The concept of God dwelling in the heart of each human being spoke to my own beliefs. No better place to feel the Quaker spirit than on Nantucket, founded by Quakers who fled religious persecution on the mainland.

Each morning, I carefully selected one of the many acclaimed restaurants that lined the cobblestoned streets for my one fantabulous dining experience of the day. Most people would look at me and think I consumed nothing, but you will remember, Dad—because most of our visits together were over a meal— restaurants were my happy place. They figured prominently into my strategy for staying emaciated. My eating was highly selective; I meticulously preplanned what scrumptious treat I would allow myself each day. Did I want a platter of fried shrimp at night, or a bowl of creamy chowder at noon? Or did I want breakfast at the Indian Room at the Overlook Hotel where I could gorge on a big plate of funnel-cake? I could do any of it because that would be my only eating event of the day. Before and after, I drank coffee and sucked on cough drops and pedaled my bike for hours and hours, to make sure that daily feast, that daily fifteen minutes of ecstasy, added not one ounce of flesh to my frame.

Although the island was particularly glorious in early fall and the weather exquisite, this time—being 19, on my own, and off-season—I saw a certain underbelly I never suspected existed on Nantucket. For example, one bright morning, riding my bike near town, a boy about my age who was sitting on the curb in front of a house, called out to me.

"Hey! What's your name? I'm Rusty."

"I'm Val." Well, he's friendly enough. I'll stop and talk.

"You live on the island?" he asks.

"Nope. I'm from Illinois. I'm visiting for a while. How about you?

"Yeah, I'm from Pittsburg, but I'm living here this winter. Living right there." He points to the house behind him—a small cape, with weathered gray shingles, like most buildings on Nantucket. "Where are you staying?"

"Over at Haddon Hall. I've got a great room with a fireplace."

"Yeah, I know where that is. Must be expensive."

"No. I don't think so. I love the location."

"Well, you could stay here, I'll bet. It would cost you way less. This older woman, Darla, it's her house and she lives here, too, but she rents out rooms to people our age. Kind of like a commune. We have an empty room right now. Want to see it?"

Well, no, not particularly, but he acts so friendly and proud of this house he's living in.

"Okay," I say. "Sure."

Darla's commune is nauseating. My stomach literally turns as I behold the squalor. The stench of garbage assails me the instant we open the door. The kitchen defies description. Food-crusted dishes fill the sink and cover the counter. An overflowing trash can spills rancid slop onto the scummy floor. Drunken black house flies swarm over everything. I cannot get out fast enough.

I still wonder at that boy who was pleased to live there and thought I might be pleased to join him. I never dreamed such a place could exist on this perfect island. I met other offbeat characters who gave me pause, and I concluded that when the summer people move out, another type of person moves in—those who are hiding from something. Was I one of them? In a way, yes. You could say I was hiding from real life. But more than hiding, I was hunting. Every day, everywhere I went, I searched for the girl I'd been back in the summer of 1965. The real me. Like Peter Pan's lost shadow, I wanted to sew her back on.

There is no question that this retreat did me a world of good, and I will endlessly thank you for giving me the chance to return, Dad. Yet I also came to exhibit some of my most bizarre behavior to date on the island. First, since I had no bathroom scale to monitor my weight, I asked the men at the local seafood market if I could stand on their fish scale each morning. They permitted it, but I can still see the looks that passed between them.

More outlandish was the skim milk incident. I kept a carton of skim milk in the refrigerator of Haddon Hall, where I rented a room. The single lady who ran it had befriended me and allowed me certain kitchen privileges. Well, sickly thin as I was, a few men on the island took an interest in this curious newcomer and one of them, a friendly carpenter, invited me to a nice restaurant on Straight Wharf for lunch. As I said, I compulsively designed my daily eating and obsessively required certain things with certain meals. I don't remember the meal I ordered but I remember that in my opinion it required milk. However, only skim milk could pass my lips and they didn't offer it. Without batting an eye, I informed my date I would just hop on my bike and ride back to the boarding house and retrieve my skim milk from the fridge. Yes, I actually did that. I have little recollection of what happened when I returned. I know he never called again. I am not even sure he was still there when I got back with my milk carton.

But the moment of truth for me arrived one evening when I rode my bike back and forth, on Centre Street, as I vacillated between two restaurants to eat at. I rode one way after deciding on fried clams at one place. Then, changing my mind, I rode in the other direction, as I settled on quahog chowder at another. Or did I want clams? Yes, clams. No, chowder. Wait, clams! Back and forth I rode, back and forth, over and over, trapped inside my illness. At that moment, I saw the insanity of my actions, the insanity of me, and I wished a car would mow me down and put me out of my misery.

The next day I called you collect from a phone booth.

"I need to come home, Dad. I need a psychiatrist."

In My Own Words

There was no getting around it: I was a wreck.

Recently, I stumbled upon a pile of papers from those days—me, trying to explain myself to myself. Me, trying to figure out what the hell had happened to me. Oh, what a pitiful girl came home from that first year of college.

"*I am a failure," I wrote. "I feel worthless...I am not a good person ...I feel so sad all the time at home—I never think of others—I'm inconsiderate ... I make others miserable. ... I have no patience. I hate this house. I get completely irrational and say what I don't really believe and hurt people. I hurt people! Me, who never hurt people because I knew how it felt. It was built into me without thinking ... When I am at home, I go BERSERK. On purpose?? I have no control. Over my body or my nerves ...*"

When I'd been in Greensboro for a couple of weeks that August, I wrote Mom a twenty-page letter, describing in my best handwriting, every little thing I had done and seen so far. I also, for a page or two, wore my poor, plaintive heart on my sleeve.

> *Oh, Mommy, I just hope and pray with all my heart I'm helping by being away—you know, please know, I'm sure you do, that that's all I wanted to do, but somehow I made it so I wasn't capable of what I wanted to do the way I wanted, so my only consolation is to think I'm doing what I can for you by being gone and not subjecting you and Audrey and Brent to whatever it is that happened to me, and while I'm gone I'll build myself up again so*

*I can sometime come back and do good by being pres-
ent rather than absent. Oh, I want to talk to you about
so much. Why did I have to come home like I did? Oh,
I have to not go into it now. When I come home again,
Mom, I'll be fine again, really. I'm trying so hard; you'll
be happy to have me around. That's my goal. I'll be a
person that's good to have around ... Mommy, just please
still love me, even though all this happened to me. I know
you must, but I love you so much, just so very much and I
know the person that somehow got to be me isn't the kind
you really (I mean the kind anyone) would particularly
adore. I think I used to be, before whatever did it, but I
know it would be easier just to wish, someone like me—
oh, I don't know. Just know I love you and I'm going to be
my same old self again and the same girl you all always
knew. I am still, right? Just underneath, huh?*

I think I sound drunk in this letter. I'm not; I'm just utterly
bereft. It stupefies me today, to read this girl's excruciating need for
her mother's love.

My "being away" merely put off the inevitable. I needed help.

When I called you from Nantucket to admit it, you asked no
questions and wasted no time. That same day you arranged for a
plane ticket out of JFK. I packed up my giant yellow suitcase and
carpet bag, took the ferry back to the mainland, a bus back to
Norwalk, the train to the city, and a cab to the airport. I returned
to Chicago on October 24th, 1972, with the intention of finding a
job and a good shrink. The funny thing is the adults in my life were
not so sure that I needed psychotherapy. Mom was most apprehensive, and our minister, after listening to my plight, suggested
that I was merely caught in the throes of growing up. Even you,
who did not stand in my way, expressed some doubts that I was
as unhinged as I knew myself to be. Reverend Engel did have a
recommendation for me, though. He said a nice fellow who called

himself a "family counselor" had dropped by and left his business card. Trying to build a practice, he visited local churches advertising his services. His name was Larry Jones.

I think Mr. Jones saved my life.

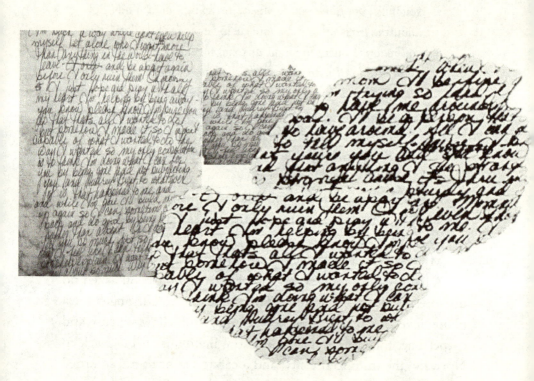

Two Jobs in Chicago

Fall, 1972

Once again, I lived in my sister's bedroom in my mother's house.

You and Barbara tried to prevent that, at first. You feared that my psychological progress would be impeded by living with such a lunatic as Mom. Mr. Jones, on the other hand, considered it the ideal place for me to tackle my problems—where they all began.

When I flew back to Chicago, you two picked me up at the airport and brought me to your house, because it was late at night, I thought. Actually, you expected me to stay. This made me uneasy as hell. I didn't wish to be ungrateful, but I couldn't do that to Mom. She'd made it clear than any loyalty to you was a betrayal of her.

Besides, Mom and Audrey needed me; you and Barb did not. I didn't want to offend you, Dad, and I genuinely liked Barbara, but when we sat on the couch and she insisted that living with the two of you (and all the children, of course), was my only choice, I had to firmly remind her that my actual family still lived at 206 Grant Avenue and that's where I'd be going.

I found work as a receptionist in an advertising agency—the perfect job at the perfect time. I fell into it serendipitously. After taking the train in and out of the city for a week, seeking employment with no results and becoming more and more anxious, I happened to overhear a girl on the train ride home one evening, saying she'd been promoted out of a receptionist job, and they were hunting for a replacement. I decided to butt in and tell her I might like to be that replacement. The next day they hired me.

Among other selling points, this job was convenient. Every morning I walked, jogged, or sprinted the two and a half blocks from our house to the Clarendon Hills train station. Then I rode for 30 minutes on the commuter train while reading the Chicago Tribune like everyone else, mostly men. I emerged at Union Station and merely crossed the street to arrive at my office building at 120 S. Riverside Plaza.

The city that belonged to you and Mom now belonged to me. The noise, the crowds, the bustling action—it all exhilarated me like Disneyland for adults. I spent most lunch breaks on foot, exploring as far as I could get and back in one hour, soaking up the atmosphere, getting to know my city. I knew where to find chocolate macaroons, Flaming Greek Cheese, the largest selection of raincoats, the cheapest selection of lipstick, I knew where they played jazz on Wednesdays, folk on Fridays.

The job itself rejuvenated me. I sat all dressed up behind a polished desk under flattering lights in a swanky reception area where cool, creative types came and went all day long. I had hectic hours, of course, phones ringing nonstop, memos flying off the desk, people stacking up in front of me demanding this and that, but I also got enough downtime to do plenty of reading. Top-notch magazines fanned out over the glass tables in my reception area. I kept one of those or a library book on my lap at all times. I even knocked off a political science course at the College of DuPage when I finally felt up to facing a textbook again. I can't imagine a better place to be at that exact moment in my life.

Since you worked on Michigan Avenue, we met for lunch on occasion, just the two of us. We frequented all kinds of first-class restaurants, but my favorite was Trader Vic's at the Palmer House. Once upon a lovely time, all five of us used to eat there as a family. Brent soon worked on Michigan Avenue, as well, and he and I liked to meet up after work some Fridays, for deep dish pizza and a movie. My skinny 19-year-old self could still only partake in these delicious meals because I so stringently limited the rest of my daily consumption, and because I seldom walked anymore if I could run. I had gained back enough weight to somewhat appease a few people, but not enough to rile me. Although at 114 pounds I still looked emaciated, it was almost ten pounds more than I'd weighed in June, so people construed it as progress. I'd hit a plateau I could live with. Maintaining that weight still required extreme tactics, but I had it down—the eating, the not eating, the exercising.

It was at this stage that I got it into my head I could be a model. Why not? I was 5'9" and rail-thin, so I might as well take advantage of it. You, Dad, had a photographer contact in Chicago, whom I called. He kindly recommended an agency downtown that signed girls my age and I made an appointment.

How demoralizing. The people who worked there were not friendly in the least. They were all business and brutally honest. The scowling middle-aged woman who took me into a small room to assess me, needed no more than thirty seconds, to say, "You're too thin." She took about five more seconds to study my legs and say, "Your legs are the only part of you I might consider, but they're actually too thin, too."

My *legs?* Unbelievable! My chubby thighs had been my lifelong cross to bear. Even as a little girl, it's where my fat settled. I'd once heard the word "hefty" used to describe them. Yet here sat this woman—a modeling agent, no less— telling me my legs were *too thin!* While I didn't take it as a compliment, I didn't exactly take it as an insult, either. I was, however, dashed to be told so bluntly I had no future in modeling. And in case any delusions remained, the snooty girl at the front desk looked me in the face as I left, wrinkled her nose, and said, "Why did you ever think you could be a model? You don't even pluck your eyebrows."

To lift my spirits, I stopped at the big downtown Bonwit Teller on North Michigan. I felt a slight thrill when it occurred to me that I could now probably shop in the preteen department. Why would that excite me so? Well, I do remember thinking that the clothes would be less expensive and that this was quite clever and resourceful of me. I also think it might have been one more way to connect me to childhood. As I talk to you, Dad, as I tell you this story, it becomes increasingly apparent that my subconscious wanted me back there.

The saleswoman eyed me like a store detective when I carried three pairs of preteen pants into the dressing room. My slight frame had not been noticeable under the bulk of my coat. No sooner had I slid into one of the pairs of pants than she drew open the curtain to check on me. She did an almost comic double-take, as she beheld my preteen body fitting perfectly into preteen pants. then mumbled something like, "Oh. I … didn't … I didn't think you were so … small." She closed the curtain.

When I joined the ad agency in November of 1972, I still had another job ahead of me—the bigger, much tougher job of psychotherapy. But the stimulation of my new work environment infused me with fresh energy for the challenge. Living at home was harder than I expected. I still fiercely protected my right to starve myself and entered into mortal combat with Mom who used weapons of homemade cooking on me. I had tactics of my own, though. On the rare occasions I succumbed to temptation, I ran straight out the door and jogged for a couple of hours, looking fairly foolish, since jogging was not yet the normal pastime it would become. I didn't care a whit; I had a Habit with a capital H, which I would cling to for another six months. Then my counseling kicked in and forced me into a period of awareness, conflict, and excruciating withdrawal.

Therapy

I couldn't stand Larry Jones. Not at first. I detested him for the first full month of therapy. More specifically, I detested what he said about me, what he arrogantly asserted—gross misperceptions, not remotely true. I felt demoralized and engaged in a desperate effort to accurately represent myself against his egregious misconceptions. He didn't know me. How dare he think he did?

"Did you know that you speak in a very affected way?" This was one of his first observations. I wasn't sure what that meant, "affected." At least not in that context. He explained, "It means pretentious, artificial. Meant to impress. I hear you put on a voice I don't think is yours. Out of nervousness, maybe, or self-consciousness."

Did you notice that, too, Dad? Did I do that around you, or did I only do that with strangers? I think just strangers, because a girl I met in Nantucket had asked me if I was from the South. Well, no I was not but I did, bizarrely, speak at times with a slight Southern accent. It came from that good friend, Debbie, I had senior year. Her Carolina accent charmed me and got caught in my ear. I adopted it when she and I were together, like an inside joke we shared. Now I noticed myself slipping into it when I was meeting people. Maybe to put myself at ease. Still, it was weird. I'm glad Mr. Jones pointed it out. It embarrassed me to be told I sounded "pretentious," and I worked to change that fast.

Even though I initially thought I'd made the wrong choice of therapists, my early visits went just well enough to keep me going back. Mr. Jones gave me two intriguing homework assignments. The first— describe in writing the two people who have had the most impact on my life so far. I wrote about Mom and Paul. Not Mom and you, but my mother and my boyfriend. I wrote several pages about each. Why did I not write about you, Dad? Perhaps because I did not yet know how to even begin to explain you. Or perhaps it was my subconscious attempt to downplay you, to assert that you hadn't been that important to me after all, so losing you had been no big deal. Today I shake my head in wonder at it, but I have to believe that my subtle attempt to minimize or negate you, was a neon sign to Mr. Jones, pointing to the root of my problem.

It fascinates me now that I chose Paul, since by then we were no longer lovers, no longer a couple. He had called me once at Donna's house in North Carolina in August. He'd been thinking about me, he said, and we spoke sweetly to one another. It left me shaken for a day or so, but my pressing goals—get to Nantucket, get to Boston, find a college— held center stage in my head and shoved aside any feelings of regret. Still, choosing Paul to write about proves the paramount role he'd played in my life to that point.

The second writing assignment was to describe my most humiliating moment. I chose the shame of wishing a car would hit me and kill me as I rode my bike back and forth, unable to decide where to eat in Nantucket.

That first hour of therapy with Mr. Jones, a total stranger, felt hopelessly futile. How could I ever get him to understand who I had been? That *this me was not me!*

"I used to be so capable," I may have said. "At school, I was at the peak of my brain power, but then it got smashed all to hell."

"Describe what you mean, please."

"At school, I worked so hard. I forced my brain every second to reach its potential. And then my brain just went on strike. Like it… broke. And I can't seem to do even the simplest task. At school, I left nothing undone, no matter how hard it was. Now I can't even pick up my clothes off a chair. Everything is … overwhelming. I am so tired. No matter how much sleep I get, I am so, so tired. And scared."

"What are you afraid of?" he probably asked.

"Of wasting my time, of wasting my life," I'd have answered. "I feel this constant panic that time is running out. I can't get rid of it."

As I spoke, I would have been touching my face. I couldn't keep my hands off my face and my mouth during that year. I clenched my mouth, too. And gritted my teeth.

"So, you often feel scared?"

"Yes, and sad. So awfully sad. I used to have bad lows, and when I did, I couldn't bear myself. It worried me. But I would always rebound. Now those lows have… taken over. Sometimes I just lay down and cry."

"Did you cry often at school?"

"No, I never cried. Never. It's only now that I am home. I'm not sure I feel happiness at all anymore. I feel no peace ever."

"Are you angry?"

"Yes, I have tirades. Absolute tirades. And I cry then, too, but I am not actually crying; I'm shaking and stiffening with rage. I've got fury inside me. I'm scared of that, too."

"What do you see when you envision your future?"

"I see black. Everything looks tragic and hopeless. My parents, my poor little sister … And I don't know if I'll ever be all right again. I think I killed myself at school. I think I ruined my brain. I used to think clearly and straight, now I can't, it's all scattered. My memory is shot; I can't remember something from one minute to the next. And I can't make decisions. It takes me fifteen minutes to decide what underwear to put on. I'll stand somewhere for ten minutes wondering if I should take a photo or not. I think I have ruined my brain for good."

At the end of my first hour of therapy with Mr. Jones, he told me he would accept me as his patient for three reasons.

"First of all," he said, "You definitely and genuinely want help. Secondly, you possess the intelligence necessary to do the work required. And finally—you are unquestionably sick."

What must Mr. Jones have thought of me, this preteen sized nineteen-year-old sitting across from him? He was new at this. He had a day job, a wife, two baby daughters, and practiced psychotherapy in his little attic office at night. It was one thing for a girl to come to him for help with emotional or mental issues, but when that girl has a skeletal body, a whole new and troubling dimension is added to the case. I may not have been his last emaciated patient, but I was certainly his first.

Mr. Jones requested I see him twice a week in the beginning, that my situation warranted it, and he was correct. At the right juncture we settled into weekly sessions for the next year.

We began by arduously deconstructing my tangled relationship with you and Mom. And Barbara. And her children. I tried to explain my crippling heartache for Mom. I canonized her; she was blameless. I demonized you, Dad. I told Mr. Jones how my good-natured, loving father had turned into a seething, swear-shrieking beast who bellowed at my mother and called her vile names, and how she sat there quietly taking it, periodically saying, "temper, temper."

"My father stopped loving me," I explained. "Then he left us. Now that he's remarried, he's more like his old self, and acts like he loves me again and wants me in his life. But whenever I do spend time with him, or say something even slightly positive about him, my mom reacts like I pushed her down a flight of stairs. When I cry or yell, she levels me by saying 'You're acting exactly like your father.' I am like my dad in a lot of ways, good ways, but I can't stand it when she compares my temper to his. I guess because it's true; my temper is bad. It's so bad I don't think I could ever get married."

"That will change," he said. "That will change when your

environment changes. When you've ironed out your problems, some of that temper will disappear."

I desperately wanted Mr. Jones to appreciate how deeply it hurt us—not just me, not just Mom, but my sweet little sister, your other biological daughter, Audrey—that our father was now the father to six other kids and would soon adopt them. (Brent was unaffected. He tells me to this day he never felt that he lost you, the way Audrey and I did. His relationship with you never suffered. But his with Mom sure did.)

Mr. Jones knew a thing or two. He knew how to listen, but he also knew when to pipe up and give me his two cents. Once we found level ground and I had succeeded in expressing my real self to him and he actually "got" me, he stood squarely on my side. He also worked to correct my skewed judgments where he spotted them. I think he struggled originally to accept that I believed in God to the extent I did. He pointed out one day, "Do you realize that every good thing that has ever happened to you, you attribute to God? And every bad thing that's happened you blame on yourself?"

No, I did not realize that; still, I saw what he was getting at it. How guilty did I have to be?

He asked you and Barbara to come for your own sessions with him. He even brought in an apprehensive Verna, about whom he said, "She is deeply in touch with her subconscious." I wasn't entirely sure what that meant, but it sounded like a compliment, and I was grateful for his observation into Mom's deeper nature, something few people saw, let alone appreciated.

Soon Mr. Jones felt like my champion. Like my guardian angel, common-sense-guru, bodyguard, all rolled into one. I gave myself over to his care as I began to fathom how knowledgeable and astute he was, and how sincerely he wanted to make me well again. I liked how he validated me, and my reluctance, for instance, to leave Mom's house on Thanksgiving or Christmas to mingle with your new family. Good grief, your gang of eight had each other.

When we left Mom, she sat there all alone. Instead of urging me to buck up and be equitable, he shook his head and agreed, "That's not right."

I will never forget something he said to me midway through my therapy. He had a look on his face— bemusement maybe, or wonder. As if this understanding afforded him a new level of insight into my strife.

He said, "*I have never met anyone with a greater capacity to love.*"

Well. It's a mixed blessing.

Naming It

In that year of 1972, I know it shocked you to see me with forty pounds of my body missing. Like Paul, and unlike Mom, you never spoke of it. The closest you came to addressing it in front of me was when you told a waitress who carded me, "Oh, she's lost so much weight, she doesn't look her age." That's it. None of us had a name for it.

Then, in the spring of 1973, during a lull at the agency, I sat at my desk flipping through a *TIME Magazine*. On the last page I found an article describing a little-known disorder in which young women were so hell bent on becoming thin, that they dieted until they lost up to one-third of their body weight and still believed themselves to be fat. They were walking skeletons, whose menstrual periods had ceased, whose frightened families begged them to eat, and still they chose to starve. They called this affliction "anorexia nervosa."

I had a session with Mr. Jones that evening and brought the magazine along.

"I think this is me," I told him.

He had not heard the term either and we both considered it rather miraculous that I'd stumbled across the article and hand-delivered a diagnosis.

Those words—anorexia nervosa—had not been heard or even read yet, by anyone we knew. In the coming years, articles, essays, and books would be written about it. Movies and TV shows would be made about it. Medical facilities would spring up to treat it. But not before 1972. To my knowledge, the first book on the subject in our lifetime, came out in 1973— *Eating Disorders: Obesity, Anorexia Nervosa, and The Person Within*, by Hilda Bruch. I only learned of this book in 2019. Although rare, the practice of starving oneself was not unheard of in history. But documented cases of anorexia and bulimia escalated during the 1970s and 1980s. To explain it, experts point to several cultural correlations—fashion, for one. I can't help but point to divorce rates. They escalated then, too.

I'm sure you and all who knew me wondered, *"How can you not know when you look like a skeleton?"* But I can tell you that what an anorectic sees in the mirror is not what others see. As if some sort of sorcery bewitched my brain, I saw what wasn't there. Some warped lens covered my eyeballs, or maybe, like Kai, a splinter from the troll's mirror got lodged there, turning every reflection into a funhouse distortion for me alone. Studies using lie detectors have confirmed that while the world sees skin and bones, an anorectic honestly sees fat.

Although the scale told the truth and Brent wouldn't eat with me if my bare arms showed, I still had the anorectic's skewed perception about my size. Yet, I must admit, I'd put a few things together during this illness. Like being told my legs were too slender for modeling. Also, my gorgeous friend Janet, who I secretly thought was too thin to be fully perfect, gave me a pair of green pants that were too small for her. *Too small for Janet?* And when I learned that Paul was now dating Sandy Harmon, my first thought was: *What? No! She is way too skinny!*

That is yet one more embarrassing thing to admit because of the poor light in which it casts my otherwise functioning brain. Yet that is exactly the point. This disorder altered my brain in a specific and dangerous way. Yet my intact basic intelligence and those fleeting moments of clarity kept my perceptions at least tenuously connected to reality. I could still manage to ask: *What does that say about me?*

Beginning with this article, Mr. Jones and I began to learn

about the disorder called anorexia. I could attest to much of what we gleaned in the article, from my own experience. For one thing—*dieting becomes an addiction.* This is the fundamental truth in the entire situation. It's crucial to accept. Who would dream it possible? Eating is pleasant, not punishing. But here's the reality—the anorectic can't stop dieting because it *feels so good.* It feels so good because of the euphoric sense of *achievement.*

Initially, the pleasure, the rewards, were exactly what I'd expected. My clothes were no longer snug. I could wear hip huggers and midriff tops, the bulge on my thighs disappeared and I looked a whole lot like those models in *Seventeen Magazine.* Ultimately, though, it was the morning scale, visibly rewarding yesterday's efforts—declaring *Touchdown!* with every pound dropped—that delivered my fix, shot me up with all the reinforcement I needed to starve myself another day. I want to shout it from the rooftop: IT'S A HABIT. IT'S AN ADDICTION! And every bit as gut-wrenchingly difficult to stop.

The medical world confirms that this intoxicating feeling of control is central to the motivation behind anorexia. Most anorectics will acknowledge, as I do, that at a time in our life when things moved beyond our control, dieting was within our reach. I was a classic candidate for this syndrome—an overachiever by nature who had watched her family crumble, helpless to do a blessed thing about it. I hadn't a shred of control over that debacle, but I could control the daylights out of what I put in my mouth.

The soothing rush I got from watching the pounds drop off, (and from the A+'s awarded to my papers and tests)—the direct result of my own indefatigable efforts— produced in me a high as powerful as any other substance which relieves human anxiety. And like any other substance, anorexia nervosa has the power to kill. After more than 50 years of research, anorexia nervosa has been identified as having the highest mortality rate of any psychiatric illness. The addict literally diets to death.

I'm telling you all this now, Dad, because I'm not sure that in your remaining 16 years on this planet, you ever learned any of it. We certainly never revisited this period of my life together. If you ever read up on it, educated yourself after the fact, you never talked to me about it. I've only now, decades later, sifted through the research myself. Once I found my way out, I stayed out. So, I'm telling you what I know. It's key information.

Your daughter had a confounding disorder. The solution must have looked so simple to you and Mom, to anyone who saw me—JUST EAT ALREADY! I know it defies logic and the strong human urge for self-preservation, and in a world where people do starve, it is exceptionally obscene. Who would choose to starve? No one in her right mind, confirming that anorexia is a mental illness. It's also hard to understand that no amount of raw intelligence protects anyone from this disorder.

I was one of the fortunate ones who sought help and got it. I will forever thank God that I found Mr. Jones, because I needed successful psychotherapy to recover. My anorexia was a symptom of underlying psychological issues, *a symptom that became an illness in and of itself*, like so many other addictions. To recover, these issues had to be resolved. Only first, they needed to be uncovered.

The Way Out

I call them insidious seeds, the fears and suspicions Mom planted in me. A few were innocuous. Like "Don't walk backwards." A girl she knew walked backward in a barn, tripped, broke her neck and died. That's understandable. It's a safety precaution, like "Never be alone in a public place at night." Especially the school. Or under the bridge. That's where bad guys lurk.

But other fears were less benign, and I discussed them with Mr. Jones. Like her strong aversion to the idea of me ever staying overnight at your house after you moved out of ours. When you lived with Barbara and all those children, Mom got it into her head that something sinister would happen to me at your house. I allowed her this peculiar worry, and only once did I challenge the notion, that October night in 1972, when you brought me from the airport to your house in Winnetka. I guess I internalized her fears because even though I did not share her unsavory suspicions, I couldn't double-cross her. It would have been a flagrant betrayal and I lived in terror of betraying Mom. I feared it would destroy her. And this, I would later learn, was the weapon she wielded over me. Until I figured that out, she had laid down her law: to be on her side, I could not, I dare not, defend my father. You were a villain and lest I forget it, she made sure to tell me stories depicting you as not only bad but maybe even evil. Like the rat poisoning business.

Mom found rat poisoning under the kitchen sink. Did it appear before you left or shortly after? At any rate, since she hadn't put it there, where did it come from? We didn't have rats. So why did we need it? She concluded you meant to poison her. I know it sounds ridiculous. Still, what was I to think? What was she to think? I had heard you swearing at her, bellowing DROP DEAD to her face. Could she possibly be right? This assertion caused a clamor of confusion in my brain.

But not as much as the lock on my bedroom door.

I don't know precisely when Mom installed it. I am thinking it was when I was eleven and started menstruating, which is an early age, and I think it shook Mom up. Most girls get it in junior high, but I was in sixth grade, still at Walker School. Only something tells me the lock arrived in fifth grade, when I was ten, and showing the first signs of adolescence and Mom came home from her shock treatments. Anyway, right around then, Mom put a new lock on my bedroom door. There already was a lock on the handle, the kind you push in. But now Mom installed a hook and eye lock. Why? Who was she protecting me from? An intruder? An intruder who might walk into our well-locked house? Walk into our locked house, and into my room, and rape me? Rape me and as soon as I menstruated, get me pregnant? I do not doubt Mom believed this could happen. But what I was forced to wonder when discussing it with Mr. Jones was if it was you that she feared.

Dear God, it is ghastly to say, but I'm afraid she genuinely believed that you were capable of molesting me when you were drunk. This all leaves me grasping for words to try to explain how bewildering that was. She never *said* it was you she feared. If she did, I have blocked that out, thank God. But the *implication* was there, and took root in my consciousness, and that was destructive enough. It was at this time she also forbade me to wear nightgowns.

You knew she put that lock on my door. What did *you* think about that? Did she ever point-blank say, "Ed, you get so drunk at night I don't know what you are capable of and I'm not taking any chances?" Or were you, too, left with the sordid accusation hanging over your head?

On the one hand, if she truly felt her daughter was in danger, it was a brave move on her part. Back then, I didn't know how that kind of abuse is all too rampant. But as far as I'm concerned, the chance of you harming me in that way was nonexistent, while the message sent by the lock did immediate and long-lasting damage. She gambled; she must have thought *better to suffer from the insinuation, than risk the reality.* But how was I supposed to ever forget that? Or that Mom walked around believing that of you? And maybe she didn't! But again—*what was I to think??*

Enough real stuff was happening to erode my opinion of you, without adding *alleged* crimes to the list. It's amazing to me how long and how well I fought against the defamation of your character, even when you yourself did the besmirching and I had my own observations as evidence. Aspersions like this, though, did genuine harm. To me, for sure. *But what about you?*

I can almost not bear to say this, Dad, but I felt forced to hate you. Hate, I now know, is too strong and simplistic a word, but for our purposes, I'll use it. Yes, you had in certain ways made yourself hateful, and before you left home, I despised who you'd become and how much you despised my mother and me. Still, a child's first response is to love and forgive a parent. I wanted to and I was ready to and yet I couldn't. If I did, I would break faith with Mom. She'd had too much of that already.

You now had a wonderful life; she didn't. I felt sorry for her and wanted to shield her from further hurt. But when I went to see you, it upset her. She complained that I was belligerent when I came back. Maybe so. I was pretty mixed up. And whenever I expressed my anger and frustration, and she accused me of acting like you, it angered and frustrated me even more.

Mr. Jones led me to some crucial understandings. Like about the way I vilified you, Dad, in order to support Mom, not knowing it was at my own peril. For how could I truly hate you and be entirely healthy? Part of me *was* you. Mr. Jones explained it was like hating myself.

The years of feeling compelled to denounce the father I once revered decimated me. As did the notion, subconscious as it may have been, that if my parents deplored one another, they must deplore the other within me. With Mr. Jones, I was getting closer to the essence of my distress. *I had to stop taking sides and find a way to love you both.*

Before I could do that, I had to extricate myself from my misguided belief that Mom was all good and you were all bad. That she was fully innocent; you were fully guilty. Mom and I shared this tacit agreement. And it had felt honorable to be so piously in her corner. Like a sacrifice. Yes! It *cost* me. *It cost me my right to love my father.*

With this new and infuriating awareness spinning inside me, I stood at the kitchen sink one night, doing dishes. Mom stood to my left, putting food away in cabinets. We were squabbling about my therapy. She never approved of it, badmouthed it even, almost as if she feared what I might learn. I could usually shrug it off; it was her issue. But on this night, something defiant festered close to the surface. Something began clawing its way out of me— the buried truth that she was not perfect, not without fault, like we kept pretending. It rushed from my gut into my throat and out of my mouth. "*I hate you,*" I told her.

We froze in stunned silence. I had said this to you once, but never to her.

Mom stared at me. She uttered a sort of half-hearted rebuke; she probably felt too shocked and too hurt to admonish me much. (Maybe that's what she feared I might learn in therapy and semi-expected this rebellion sooner or later.)

I hadn't planned on saying it. I had not once even *thought* those words regarding her. I loved her fiercely. But I guess I also hated her. I hated her for insisting I couldn't love you. I hated her the same way I hated you, Dad. Both of you taught me to mistrust the other. Both of you had sabotaged my love for one another.

So, it really wasn't hatred at all. *It was love, badly bruised.*

*

In the coming decades, I would read nothing about anorexia. I'd lived it, what more could I learn? But since I've been talking to you here, I chose to glance at some of the literature on the topic, and I learned something new, something that explains so much: there is a proven link between anorexia and the mother-daughter relationship! I read that "... it is usually the case that the foundation of eating disorders is an unhappy mother-child relationship, in which the mother shows lack of love or is over-protective."[1] I read that "...these children face the constant pressure of having to fulfill their mothers' expectations, but rarely succeed in making her happy. Fear of failure and feelings of powerlessness are thus common characteristics of anorectics and bulimics."[2]

According to Hilary Beattie in her 1988 research, food and nourishment symbolize our mothers, so a daughter refusing to eat can be viewed as an attempt to shirk a mother's control and separate from her. She decides to shut her mouth, "rejecting what her mother gives and hurting her in the most powerful way she knows how."[3]

It is a do-or-die struggle for autonomy.

All this fits me to a "T." It is extremely validating, of course, yet also painful. I only wanted to love Mom. Even more, I wanted her to love me. I wanted to make her happy again. Why did we keep clashing? Why did she make me want to tear my hair out? She was merely being herself, a caring mother. Why, oh why, would I *ever* tell her I hated her? She was the Good One. Blameless. She was the victim. Only a monster would yell at her.

But I wanted to love you, too, and she wouldn't let me. Believing that I couldn't—*that I shouldn't*—injured me terribly. My work with Mr. Jones eventually set me free from that ruinous thinking.

That summer, I made you a Father's Day card out of a big piece of cardboard, folded in half, like a play program. On the outside I'd written NOW PRODUCING: SMILES, PRODUCED AND DIRECTED BY MY DAD. On the inside I glued about 30 photos of my smiling face, from babyhood to the age I was then—19. Some pictures showed you and me together, but mostly they were of me, the happy girl I wanted you to remember and never forget. On the back, in the center, I wrote in big, bold letters: I LOVE YOU.

With Mr. Jones's help, I came to understand that no one is all good or bad. I had to accept that my saintly mother had played her own role in The Tragedy at 206 Grant Avenue. And even though it was natural for her to feel that sides must be taken, it wasn't fair to her children. When she implied that I could love her, or I could love you, but I couldn't love you both, I had to stand my ground and say, "You're wrong. I can. And I will."

And when I finally did, I finally ate.

[1,2] Petra M Bagley, Francesca Calamita and Kathryn Robson, *Introduction: Eating Disorders or Disordered Eating?* 8.
[3] Susie Orbach, *Fat is a Feminist Issue,* 160

The Snow Queen Melteth

My withdrawal from anorexia was like an exorcism. An overpowering force dwelled inside me. I had to drive it out and it hurt like hell. I had to force myself to do something anathema to my system—eat normally. I suffered months of internal conflict and sometimes pure horror as I loosened my iron grip on eating and gave up the awesome control I held over every morsel that went into my mouth. Until I came to terms with my late-night food frenzies—gorging, *positively gorging,* on peanut butter and vanilla ice cream, shoveling it into my mouth like a woman possessed—I suffered the shame, and resorted to running for miles the next day, and then found a new and desperate strategy—laxatives. I would never be bulimic—I abhorred throwing up—but along the same lines, I deduced that if I could expel what I'd consumed before it turned into fat, I could thwart these uncontrollable binges. But eventually my body came to obey a new master. It insisted on health. Despite my desperate objections, it had a mind of its own.

"*Enough!*" It commanded me, "*I will survive. And if you are too stupid to feed me then, by God, I will feed myself!*"

I ate and ate and ate.

Someone else, some invisible force, has control of my right hand. I wail and moan in protest as I watch it shovel spoonful after spoonful of peanut butter into my mouth. Oh, now peanut butter isn't enough! It goes for the enormous jar of plum jelly, piles great globs of it on top of the peanut butter. Now it is dragging me by my hair to the freezer and shoving my face into the gallon of vanilla ice cream Mom won't stop buying! I am miserable yet I am powerless to stop this force-feeding until my stomach is so rock-hard and distended, all I can do is creep down the hall and into my bed where I fight for sleep while my body does its utmost to absorb this onslaught of nourishment.

Poor Mom stands transfixed, watching these horrific wrestling matches—me trying with all my might not to eat, while I keep right on eating! She pleads with me to go to bed, "Please, oh, please, Val, just GO TO BED!"

It took months, but one day, the emotional healing and the urgent eating overlapped. Like two separate currents moving in the same direction, they finally converged, flowing at last into one healthy river of straight thinking. I believe my body had been racing to achieve a certain crucial weight, the weight at which basic physical fitness resumed. My period started up, my hair stayed in my head, the pain in my forehead vanished. The warped lenses fell out of my eyeballs, and I could see myself once more. At the same time, through my work with Mr. Jones, I saw you and mom more clearly, too. I had learned to separate my being from yours. I had learned how to love you both, and thus myself.

In late September, I remember a warm Sunday afternoon, when I let go and allowed myself *without guilt*— to eat and savor every bite of the midday meal Mom prepared: roast beef, mashed potatoes, green beans, gravy, rolls, butter. When, as Mom would say, the food hit bottom, a wave of astonishing well-being flooded my veins. In this state of near euphoria and deep contentment I did not get immediately up and do jumping jacks or fly out the door to run. Instead, I lolled about, talking and joking with 13-year-old Audrey. (She had always been a little girl to me, only now I saw her as an equal, a friend. My best, in fact.) And then, I experienced a most wondrous sensation—laughter. I felt myself genuinely laughing for the first time in over a year. Audrey and I laughed and laughed, uproariously, uncontrollably. It was epic.

Like Kai's frozen heart melting with Gerda's tears, my wooden being had melted back to life. It took food, love, and laughter, but mostly it took understanding. Necessities all.

Moving On

In late November of 1973, I dreamed a distinctly vivid dream about Larry Jones. At our next meeting, I described it to him.

"You wore a clerical collar, like a minister. I wore a white gown, like a choir robe. You pointed to a bright light in the distance that came closer as we stood watching it until it enveloped us. Then you sent me off to walk in a cold, clear stream that flowed uphill."

Mr. Jones listened attentively.

"That dream means we are finished here," he said. "We've completed our work together. I've had other people describe that same dream to me at the same point in therapy. There are variations, of course, but I'm usually in a priest's or minister's clothing, and there's light and water. Amazing."

And he was right. Our time was over. We had nothing more to accomplish. Our work together had made me strong. The Jell-o sensation in my head (the classic "brain-fog" of Anorexia) had dissipated. I was ready to go back to school.

My first choice, Smith College, had rejected me. One year of superior grades at the University of Illinois did not an Ivy League school make. Seems high school mattered. A pertinent question would be how on earth I expected to afford Smith in the first place. I guess I was banking on scholarships. At any rate, it didn't matter. Smith College didn't want me. Now what?

As I resumed my healthy self, I resumed some former activities, like teaching Sunday School. After church one morning, I decided to stay and be sociable. As I stood alone, clutching my Styrofoam cup of coffee, a tall, striking, blonde couple—husband and wife—engaged me in conversation. They brought up their alma mater, the University of Minnesota in Minneapolis, and heaped so much praise on this institution that the next day I called their admissions office and requested a catalogue. The catalogue alone sold me.

I found myself enthralled by the options for designing my own major. They offered a slew of alternatives for accumulating credit and in general, tailor-making my education to fit my goals. In addition to Miss Lundgren, I also wanted to be Mrs. Campbell, the remarkable woman who had offered "Creative Dramatics" to the children of Clarendon Hills in the early sixties and introduced me to improv and acting at the age of eight. It wasn't Children's Theatre I wanted to do, but theatre with children, and this catalogue pointed the way. I'd found my school.

To be certain, I had to go to Minneapolis and have a look around, see if I could picture myself being happy in this place I'd never been. So that summer, Mom and Audrey and I hopped in the old aqua Oldsmobile and drove the eight hours from Clarendon Hills, through northern Illinois, the rolling hills of Wisconsin, into the farmlands of Minnesota. We stayed in a motel outside Minneapolis and cut down on costs by making our morning coffee with hot water from the tap and instant coffee from a jar. We explored the campus, walked across the Mississippi River over the pedestrian bridge linking the East and West Banks, appreciating how the Minneapolis Skyline sat right on top of it all. Oh, yes, I could live here.

Back in Illinois, I applied, got accepted, and began making plans to move to Minneapolis right after Christmas of 1973.

*

Paul and I had seen each other only a few times since I'd come back from Nantucket in October of 1972. First was an ill-advised, ill-fated dinner at the Millionaire's Club on November 11th, Paul's birthday. He'd no idea I was back in town, and I chose to announce it with a homemade chocolate birthday cake. I didn't have his phone number, so I called his mom to say I wanted to bring it over. I honestly wasn't expecting more than that. But I suspect she urged him to ask me to the dinner party his friends were throwing for him, and I am pretty sure he had to break his date with whomever he planned to bring.

It was frightful. I'd had only one or two therapy sessions under my belt by then and was still a skull-cradling stick figure. It was made clear to me, not by Paul, but by some of the women, all older than me, that both my appearance and my presence disgusted them. I sat at the table clutching a whisky sour, probably using my Southern accent, wishing I'd never made that cake.

It was many months before I saw Paul again, in late spring of '73. This time we double-dated with my friend Janet and Paul's friend Dennis in Greektown. Nothing came of it. And then in early fall, I think he took me for a ride in his new boat, after which we had dinner alone at the Country House. Nothing came of that, either. But I do remember saying to him, "We sure did love each other back then, didn't we?"

"We sure did," he said.

*

Back in high school, when Ed broke up with me, I fantasized that he and I would get back together, if not as teenagers, maybe we'd meet again years later and get married. Back when I loved him so desperately, I tried to console myself with this slim possibility. You never can tell ....

Well, in early December when I was gearing up for Minnesota and finishing up with Mr. Jones, I had another dream about Ed. It, too, came true.

I woke up one morning still wrapped in the warm glow of this dream of meeting Ed again, smiling into his face, him smiling at me. I sat at the table with a cup of coffee and described the dream to Mom. Then off I went to work.

On my lunch hour, I ran eight blocks to State Street to a new store Mr. Jones told me about called Eddie Bauer, in search of a heavy coat for Minnesota. I found the store, opened the door, and walked smack dab into Ed Dawson. There we were, face to face, just like in my dream.

Ed worked there as a salesman. We said "hello" then chatted like two polite strangers for a matter of seconds, I think, I just don't know because all the blood in my body rushed to my head and blotted my brain. I looked for a coat, didn't find one, and left. All in about three minutes. That was that. That's all we were to each other now. How does that even happen?

I admit that I still feel cheated that the time granted me to love and be loved by such a boy as Ed was so brief. Still, that's my side of the story. Ed's choice to date other girls, may have been hard on me, but it was right for him.

*

In January of 1975, Ed died. I answered the phone on a Sunday evening, in my apartment in Minneapolis, to 14-year-old Audrey on the other end. During our chat, she remembered, "Oh, Val, Ed Dawson died."

I openly wailed, surprising us both. I got off the phone and cried so hard, so long. No one ever knew how much I had loved that boy.

I never learned what happened to him. The only story I ever heard was that he'd been out on a date and returned early because he felt unnaturally tired. He lived at home, and went up to his childhood bed, the one I had nestled in back when he loved me. His mother found him there in the morning. It may or may not be true. He was 22 years old.

I like to think that Ed had premonitions, too. That somewhere in his soul he knew his days on this earth were limited. I like to think he got to cram in as much love and glorious sex as a boy could handle in the seven years he had left. Those last seven years he got to live, after the sweet, short time I got to love him.

Minnesota

On December 30, 1973, I packed up my brown Buick Skylark and moved to Minneapolis.

Susie and a friend of hers drove up from Indianapolis to Chicago, and Brent and I led a two-car, eight-hour caravan across winter highways. It was 25 below zero the night we pulled into town. For Christmas, Dad, you and Barb and the kids gave me a huge care package, so I could set up housekeeping and, at least for a while, ensure I ate.

A couple of weeks before Christmas, I'd flown from Chicago to Minneapolis to attend the orientation and to secure an apartment. My very first. It came with some low-end furniture and a cupboard full of cockroaches. I loved it. I was twenty years old.

Being of sound mind and body, I no longer gravitated to a career in the food industry. I would study what I had been drawn to from childhood. I did not need to design my own major, because a double major in theatre arts and elementary education would cover it all and prepare me to be anything I'd ever want to be, including what I became, a theatre teacher and play director. You died before you could know this, Dad: In addition to second grade, I taught high school theatre for 20 years. I've directed over 80 plays. I've been hoping you've had a chance to see a few.

You might remember that my frantic eating did not magically lead me back to my ideal weight. Once I started eating, I had trouble stopping and put on about fifteen more pounds than I needed. It bothered me, but not too much. I knew that once I got to school and walked miles each day back and forth to classes, those extra pounds would drop off, and they did. Besides, I had better things to think about.

Aunt Kathie sent me a white alarm clock for my 20th birthday. Each new day I awoke to its music box playing "Oh, What a Beautiful Morning." The same happy song you sang to us all those years ago.

On January 7, 1974, I marched through knee-deep snow to my first class—Oral Interpretation. Though the temperature was 22 degrees below zero when I left the apartment at 8:45 am, my exultation warmed me body and soul.

I pictured myself as a brightly burning candle, lit up and aglow throughout childhood, then sputtering down to a mere flicker. Nearly out, but not extinguished. And now my flame blazed with a brilliance and a power—with a purpose—that would light my way for years to come.

I would thrive in Minneapolis. At twenty, I was light years older than the girl I had been in Urbana, only two years previously. I would live well, have friends and fun, and still manage to get, almost, straight A's. It would be three of the best years of my life.

It is my first day of classes. I leave my cozy apartment in my navy goat-hair coat and white mohair scarf. I am a Nordic queen claiming her sparkling new kingdom. I glide across the East Bank campus, the heated walkway above the Mississippi River to the West Bank Campus, and in this brilliant white landscape I see a most spectacular sight stretched out before me—the rest of my life, vast and dazzling.

Part V

Farther Along, We'll Know More Aout It

Farther Along,
We'll Understand Why

Mom died in 1982, two weeks before Christmas. You died seven years later. We three grown children have been making pilgrimages to Clarendon Hills since 1992. That's over thirty years.

Often Brent goes alone. Sometimes only two of us make it. Best is all three—Brent, Valerie, and Audrey. And when we are together, we talk about you and Mom like a cold case. Again and again, we study the two of you from new angles. *How come...? Why would...? What if...?*

We wander up and down our childhood streets like we're walking home from school, or from a friend's house, or from the Dime Store toting new school supplies. What do people think? It would be one thing if we strode briskly from one destination to the next. But we stroll, stopping in front of one house then another, putting our heads together to confer. We are remembering that Bonnie Gordon lived in that house, Kenny Edwards in the next one, and here's where Mr. Paidar parked his '61 Thunderbird convertible for all the boys to ogle. But when someone looks out her window, or pulls into his driveway, we must look to all the world like burglars. Or land developers. Plotting to steal the silver or make an offer.

The first time Brent went back in 1991—nine years after we sold our old house and moved Mom to Maine to live out her final months—he took the train from Union Station to the suburbs and stepped off around noon on a Tuesday. At that time, as in our day, it was a town of mothers and children. The fathers were at work in the city. But there walked Brent, a tall, thin man in a dark, wool suit, clutching a giant portfolio, looking and feeling like some kind of well-dressed pervert. Even so, he walked and walked.

That's when he called us and said, "You have to come back. You won't believe how wonderful it feels."

So, we keep coming back. We never grow tired of it. In fact, our nostalgia grows the more we visit. We can't get enough.

Nadine's Dress Shop is now a coffee shop. We sit there with Chai Tea lattes where Aud and I once bought sundresses and bathing suits. We eat dinner at the restaurant on the corner, which should be Grocerland, where Brent worked behind the butcher counter in high school. Or we go to the new place where the Towne Kitchen once stood, where I ate lunch with Mom the day Kennedy was killed, because she had locked us out of the house. We enter the News Agency, still called the News Agency, and I plant my grown-up feet in front of the invisible spinning metal comic book rack, where every Saturday I picked out two 12-cent comic books or one thick 25-cent edition. Then I head over to the imaginary candy counter where I'd spend the last quarter of my 50-cent allowance on no less than five candy bars, including, always, a Clark Bar and a giant Tootsie Roll. You are there, too, Dad. I see you by the counter, buying a newspaper, waiting for me. Once back home and stretched out on the living room rug, I luxuriously sucked the candy to make it last, savoring the divine combination of Archie, Veronica, and chocolate.

We always end up on The Big Hill at Walker School, overlooking the school itself and the baseball diamond where Brent played Little League. It shocked us when they knocked down our house at 206 Grant and built a "tract mansion" in its place, but maybe worse was the demolition of our beloved elementary school. We find it unthinkable that such a sacred building should be annihilated, as if our childhood souls still walked those halls. Sure, they

built a clean, new school in its place. They even tried to dupli-
cate the original in design and materials. We aren't fooled. And we
don't forgive them.

So, we sit on The Big Hill, considerably less big than it used to be, but still the same hill we sledded down many a snowy twilight. Now the age our grandparents were then, we sit cross-legged on the ground, remembering.

This is where our minds work best. We sit for hours, watching the sunlight fade over the rooftops of our childhood, reliving the same old memories, which, like any good war story, we can't stop telling. We wonder, we marvel, we guess. We hunt, we search. For what? What are we looking for? Us, I think. Us back then. Like we should have been forever.

We search on.

*

While I am writing to you, we take another trip back to Chicago, and because I have been swimming so long in the deepest end of my sea of memories, you and Mom treading water by my side, answers bombard me. I have brought you both to life again, as if I've conducted my own successful séance. I wake up in the hotel room, turn on the light above the sink and find Mom's eyes looking back at me in the mirror. They tell me something she wants me to know. She had not wanted a third child.

*

Why have we never considered this before? Maybe because, as her children, we wanted to believe she considered motherhood her greatest calling. But it was only one calling. And maybe, when she was ready to pursue other callings, she found herself ... prevented.

I have known women who were less than pleased with their third pregnancy, one even outright enraged. Thirty years earlier, could this not have been the case for Mom? Maybe her third pregnancy—when Brent and I were ten and six and she was nearing forty—was not exactly glad tidings. Maybe it felt like some sort of

242

jail sentence delivered out of nowhere. Maybe she consoled herself with the fact that her own mom was nearby to help out, but then her mother died. Maybe she couldn't bear to do it all over again.

In 1960 Mom had already been married to you for 17 years. She had survived wailing infants and terrible twos, sleepless nights, and dirty diapers she washed by hand. Now it was her time. Time to put her mind to use, develop one of her many talents, maybe begin a career. Well, no such luck. She was pregnant again and not by design. And with a baby at home in 1960, home is where you generally stayed for the next twelve years.

Here's how I see it: For 17 years, you and Mom lived and loved together. For the first seven years it was just the two of you and I'll bet it was blissful, since she wrote things like this to you:

"I love you ever so much more dearly than when we were just married ... Sweetheart, I realize more and more each day how much you mean to me... "PS. I love you. I love you. I love you."

These letters break my heart, knowing she hadn't an inkling of what lay ahead. But the point is, yours was a strong foundation.

In 1949 you became parents for the first time and then again in 1953. In my opinion, you met those demands and challenges with aplomb. Brent and I were happy, healthy, *oh so lucky* children. We had everything we needed and most of what we wanted, and best of all, we had your love.

For all those years, Mom did her job *so well*. She strove to be the best mother she could be, as well as the perfect homemaker. And she succeeded. She was, after all, a perfectionist. I see this in my memory but also in the snapshots from those early days. They show a storybook family: a spotless new home; a beaming young couple; their two lighthearted children; laughter, picnics, and parties. All of it, pre-1960.

You had risen through the advertising ranks, Dad, one promotion after another. Now the time had come for *Verna's* promotion. She may have been dreaming of fashion design. Or landscaping. English or art. Maybe she wanted to be a journalist, an architect. Open a restaurant. Anything was possible. And then it wasn't.

If Mom had wanted to be more than a housewife, she—like so many women of her generation—would have kept it to herself. Admitting to it flew in the face of propriety. Instead, these women did what was expected of them. They stayed home. And sometimes fell apart.

Maybe Mom was just one more woman in the eternal parade of females, who—until recently— watched the doors to dreams close and lock with pregnancy. If Mom truly did not want more children, finding herself pregnant at that stage of her life, against her wishes (the Pill did not yet exist), could have easily pushed her into a well of despair. And resentment.

This leads me to another conclusion, one I can only consider now that I have lived long enough to see old roles reversed, see moms out making money while dads raise the kids. Maybe you were the one who should have stayed home, Dad. You were the one who rolled with our punches, our imperfections, our tempers. Well, my temper since Brent didn't have one.

As a fascinating side note, I recently learned that neither Brent nor Audrey experienced Mom's disapproval the way I did, if at all. What a revelation! Why me? Well, a rambunctious little girl after an even-keeled boy would try any mother's patience, especially a mother who is juggling grief and depression and a newborn.

But back to kids and you. There's no doubt about it, any man who could jump right in and raise another man's six children after raising two, almost three of his own, any man who would willingly do the whole thing over again, loved kids. (You even took in foster kids!)

So, this is my answer to the mystifying question: What did Mom have against you?

Her third pregnancy.

It may sound exceedingly wimpy in view of all the women in all the world who bore eight, ten, thirteen children. But who says they were all thrilled about it? Or didn't crack up along the way?

And as unpleasant as it is to acknowledge, and although she never called it rape, you know that Mom maintained that Audrey's conception happened against her will. When she was asleep. I don't know the details, yet it does explain why she felt so oddly compelled to warn me, first with Paul and then with my husband, against the dangers of sleeping through sex. I scoffed—*how on earth is that even possible, Mom?* Well, I think that happened to her. And I know that is your business, but it changed her world.

And when it changed hers, it changed yours. Maybe it ruined your sex life. Ended it even. I can see Mom, fearing another pregnancy removing herself from the possibility. I can see you struggling with that plan. Maybe you patiently cooperated, but maybe Mom did not eventually become more willing, but *less* willing. And held a grudge, to boot. Made pregnant against her wishes—yes, she could easily hold that against you.

Maybe you faced a future without sex if you stayed with Mom. In a rock-solid relationship, it might not have mattered too much. In a floundering marriage like yours, though, it is no surprise you would follow the same advice you'd given me: *to thine own self be true.*

For the record, I believe the vast majority of humans born on this earth were not planned, and that the circumstances of one's conception do not, in the long run, amount to a hill of beans. And in case you didn't know it, Dad, expected or not, your daughter Audrey was her mother's darling. Mom could not have loved her more.

Mom Was Not Alone

If you live long enough and ask the right people the right questions, new information surfaces. Last summer en route to one of our Chicago pilgrimages, I called my childhood pal, Susie, from the airport. I told her I was digging around in the past and asked her what she remembered about my parents.

"Think back to Nantucket, Sue. You spent three weeks with us in close quarters. What do you recall?"

"Well, Val," she said almost apologetically, "I remember thinking that your dad wasn't very nice to your mom. He acted impatient, intolerant, like anything she said or did irritated him."

Sue's right. I'd forgotten— your scowl when she wanted to stop for coffee, your obvious annoyance. It's what we do when we are sick and tired of someone, right? Every little thing gets on our last nerve and the other person can't win. I guess I had adapted to it.

"Yeah," she said, "I remember being surprised that he would act that way in front of his kids' friends, because we had it drilled into us not to air our dirty laundry in public."

"Wait. Dirty laundry? You had dirty laundry?"

"Val," she said, "My parents fought all the time."

This left me speechless.

"They went all out once the boys were gone. Made me swear I wouldn't tell my brothers how much they fought."

Amazing. Just like when Brent left for college.

"My mother was difficult, Val; she had her own troubles. If my dad had been a different sort of man, she might have had shock treatments, too. Probably been divorced by any other husband, but when Joe Shuster said, 'I do,' he did. And really, they always loved each other."

I was thunderstruck. Fifty years later, I am hearing that my idols Ann and Joe Shuster, the epitome of marital bliss, lovebirds who kissed and cuddled openly and often, had their own battles. Who knew?

Even so, theirs was a love that triumphed. Joe did not leave. Right on into his seventies when his Parkinson's might have sent him to a nursing home, he stayed put. Instead, he and Ann swallowed barbiturates and lay down together to die. He succeeded; she did not. Poor, dear Ann.

"*As for my dearest, beloved Joe,*" she wrote, "*I'm happy he has no more pain. ... We wanted to be together in death, also, but it didn't happen that way and I still feel sorrow over that. However, it wasn't to be and when I see the pain the family felt it makes me realize there is a reason I am still here ... Remembering all the good times and deep love we had far outweighs the bad times any marriage has.*" I never knew they had any bad times.

Susie and I kept talking and together we concluded that in the sixties, every seventh house in Clarendon Hills had the same sort of thing going on. (Why seven? We liked the sound of it. And it's a safer bet than "every other" house, which was tempting.) In other words—our family was not the passel of freaks or pariahs I thought we were.

So, Mom wasn't exactly "normal." But even though we saw moms who were—hey, maybe their nervous breakdowns were just waiting to happen—there were others who weren't so normal, either. There are no fairy tale towns.

And think of this— our mom was not an addict or a drunk or a bully or a shrew. She didn't hit us or swear at us or call us names. She wasn't even catty or petty or shallow like some mothers I knew. Yes, she had mood swings. Yes, she would go without talking to me when I disappointed her, or when she slipped into a black period. She was depressed. Let's face it; that's who gets shock treatments, right? And although the phrase "postpartum depression" and "complicated grief" would later become household words, in 1960 they had yet to be introduced. Mom was likely a textbook case of each. But she was also good and kind and smart and honest. And always, *always*, there.

We, her children, feel that some outside job or a hobby might have kept her afloat emotionally. Yet in 1960's suburbia, like it or not, most mothers stayed home. In my seven years at Walker School, of all the 44 children in my grade, I knew only three mothers who worked outside the home. Two were nurses, and one—Sky's mom—was a widow. Besides, until seventh grade, we all came home for lunch every day. How far could those women get?

I will now go out on a limb and say that housework is boring and lonely. That, of course, is my opinion, but I'll bet more people share it than don't. It's one of those things that folks prefer to pay for if they can, and do pay for even when they can't, because it is that boring and lonely. Taking care of children at the same time—again, my opinion—adds purpose and pleasure to housekeeping. Yet it can also be exhausting. Endless. And thankless.

In the book *The Second Sex,* Simone de Beauvoir says it better: "Few tasks are more like the torture of Sisyphus than housework, with its endless repetition: the clean becomes soiled, the soiled is made clean, over and over, day after day. The housewife wears herself out marking time: she makes nothing, simply perpetuates the present ... the years no longer rise up towards heaven, they lie spread out ahead, gray and identical ...."

Seriously, Dad, your life was a whole lot more stimulating and fulfilling by comparison. That's certainly not your fault, just something to keep in mind when evaluating Mom. More than once she remarked about your air-conditioned office, the well-dressed secretaries, the fancy lunches. Eating another summer sausage sandwich with us at the same old table in the stifling summer heat, how could she not envy you? The highlight of her day was when you came home at night. But business took you away three, sometimes, four nights a week. How could she not resent it? Yes, Mom got out of the house, but only, as far as I know, to shop. She did not go out to lunch with girlfriends or meet them for drinks. Or bridge. Or a walk. Or a book club. No wonder she loved shopping; she equated it with freedom and fun. You might say her lack of friends was her own fault. I say, fault or not, it's a fact.

You know, Brent maintains that the worst thing Mom did was stay home with us. If he were king of the world, he would make all mothers work outside the home. Not because he thinks they need to earn money. It's because he thinks they can't be mentally healthy if they don't. He has a point. Still, today's children might say the reverse. That they wished their mothers didn't work so much, wished they were home more. We can't forget that we got the benefit of a stay-at-home mother who fully devoted herself to her children.

Verna Kuhn was an artist at heart. Also a scholar, a thinker, an achiever. And I believe being *solely* a wife and mother was not enough for her. I think she expected it to be, and even enjoyed it initially, then grew disillusioned over time. She was intelligent, educated, and creative. But as a housewife she had nowhere to turn her considerable talents except to pour them into pineapple boats and Easter ensembles and seasonal drapes and bedspreads; render her skills up to us as the perfect homemaker, as she tried to hold on to the promising person she remembered being.

I heard an interview in which the director Richard Linklater said, "Creativity thwarted is probably the most toxic thing in the world." Isn't that Mom in a nutshell?

Think back. I see photos of our house, spic and span, decorated for Christmas and fifteen—count 'em— fifteen kids crammed in for a party. Mom threw parties! Kids' parties! With gingerbread houses, and hand-made paper hats, and games and prizes!

For seventeen years she knocked herself out. (It only took me one year of zealous studying to burn out at college.) Eventually, the string of dirty coffee cups strewn across our counter, signaled surrender. "*What's the use?*" she used to say. I understand, don't you? Thwarted. By obedience to social expectations, her own sense of duty, and eventually, by her own handicaps.

*

I talked to Janet, too, that week. She reminded me of another housewife who lived two doors down from her, Mrs. Brand, our mild-mannered Girl Scout leader. One day she came down the stairs into their living room laughing and crying at the same time. She couldn't stop. Her daughter, Sally, later explained it matter-of-factly, "My mom had a nervous breakdown."

I knew about this. Then Janet told me something I didn't know. The woman who lived next door to Janet on the other side, had a nervous breakdown, too. Joan Sheridan was a housewife who had once been an artist and an intellectual. She put an end to her frustration by stepping in front of a train.

Now I Understand Depression
and I Trust You Do, Too

As an adult looking back, old enough today to be your own parent then, I am ready to believe that you tried everything you could to help Mom, but nothing worked so you gave up. Fair enough. You had that right. Only I sure wish you hadn't called her "crazy." That hurt too much. "*Your mother is crazy.*" That's how you explained Mom to Barbara, isn't it? And her children. That's what the youngest ones told me. Not to be mean, just stating a fact. Repeating what they'd heard. "*Your mom is crazy.*"

I have fought against that epitaph my whole life. "Ahead of her time" is more like it. "Too good for this world" is fair. Still, I know what you meant, Dad. We say, "mentally ill" now. Or "in distress." Or we use the proper term — depressed. I understand that in those days, even thoughtful, educated people still said "crazy" or "nuts" and you called her crazy because you truly thought she was. I wish you had been less crass about it, but I guess you couldn't look at her without seeing sickness. My perception of her was filtered through my love for her. I had the ability to see beyond her mental quirks into her mental beauty. You did not, or perhaps once had, but no longer could. You were a husband; I was a daughter. You thought she'd lost her mind. I get it.

I've learned that in the 1950's and 1960's depression was considered a rare condition, that depressed people were often feared and rejected. It was scary and embarrassing, wasn't it? Unacceptable, too. Mom was no longer one to impress your cronies at cocktail parties. Zesty Barb was a shoo-in for that role, a veritable asset. Mom became a liability with her talk of alien life forms and electric cars.

Mom might have been the first person I knew with depression, but she was by no means the last. I myself am on the list of friends and relatives who have suffered from it. Even bullet-proof Barbara, after your death, found herself depressed. She got counseling and took medication and plowed on. Like you said, she was a gutsy broad. But depression pummels even the gutsy.

I know you and Mom tried counseling. I got the impression you pushed for it and Mom, after a few sessions, rejected it. How disheartening for you. But how good was the therapist? The first one isn't necessarily the right one. I wish she knew that and kept looking. I wish she had been receptive to medication. Then again, if she did not think she was mentally ill, it must have felt wretched to be told she was. Maybe if she'd found a therapist she trusted, there'd have been no need for shock treatments.

Friggin' shock treatments. Yes, I know. They were hailed as the panacea for a time. But I've read a lot on the subject. Chilling, permanent side-effects belong to the controversy. Among the chief complaints is severe memory loss and disturbing personality changes. Yes, I remember. We saw it first-hand.

I've read that many people believe that ECT ruined or damaged their lives. They used words like "humiliated," "assaulted," and "degraded." I've also read about permanent intellectual damage.

Up until the 1970's, ECT could be administered without the patient's consent. Usually, a desperate spouse or parent gave permission. I believe this happened in our house. I'm sure you were led to believe it would help her, Dad. I think it hurt her and altered her. But who's to say?

I want to tell you about my friend, Julia. She reminds me so much of Mom, although Julia was way more depressed. She wasn't depressed until she lived through the sudden death of her 30-year-old daughter. A warm wave of sympathy and support kept her afloat the first year. Then came the one-year anniversary of Olivia's death and Julia went downhill fast. Grief incapacitated her. She stopped eating, sleeping, driving, leaving the house; indoors she couldn't cook, read, knit, or even watch TV. All she could manage to do was listen to podcasts about life beyond the grave. Mostly, she lay on her couch clutching a heating pad to her aching stomach, staring at the ceiling.

After many failed attempts at treatment, ECT was recommended. And I suddenly understood about those shock treatments. It's what you do when there's nothing left to do. I never thought I would hear myself approve of ECT, yet knowing Julia I can see why a family chooses it: they're out of options. And it worked. For a few months, Julia was much better. She could eat and read and converse the way she used to. Her dull eyes brightened, and we all felt new hope. Then, I guess it wore off, because the light left her eyes, the stomach pain returned, she stopped eating again. And then she died.

Of what? Pill overdose? Starvation? A broken heart? We'll never know. She said she couldn't go on living in her pain, and her body complied.

Knowing Julia, Dad, I have an entirely new slant on your position with Mom. I have a new empathy for your consenting to Mom's shock treatments. My heart aches for you both.

We know so much more about depression now. Maybe Mom was an anomaly in 1960, but she sure wouldn't be today. Sixty years later, about one in every ten Americans takes an antidepressant. At least that's what I read online. And those are only the ones who take meds. I don't know why something must be widespread to make it more pardonable, but it does, so please appreciate this fact.

I am only now beginning to understand how truly ill you believed Mom to be. It wasn't some convenient excuse to leave her and marry Barbara. You knew Mom better and longer than I did. She may not have been as ill as some, but to you, she was in neither her right, nor her original mind. And here is my newest epiphany—you believed

Barbara would be a strong, positive influence, a better role model for your own daughters. I *know* this now. You were *worried* for us.

It's not the reason you left us and married her, of course. Your passion for Barb was a force all its own. Still, as you were convincing yourself, looking for advantages in this messy situation, you logically thought if we joined you in your big happy, healthy family where people behaved as they ought to, we would be healthy and happy, too. I never consciously understood this before; now I do. And I can tell you now, Dad—though I never expected to say so—you were right. Not in all ways, but in some big ways, Barb was an asset.

But Mom was, too. I learned to navigate past her quirks. I learned how to listen to her calmly and not blow my top when she veered off in frustrating tangents. I learned to dismiss what confused me and wait for her point, hear what she needed to express. I loved her just the way she was.

You can call her crazy or demented or deranged or whatever you want. For me, it did not detract one iota from her excellence. Being her daughter, living in her house, I can promise you that, where it counts—honesty, intelligence, kindness, self-discipline—Mom was the finest of role models. Whatever her illness, her goodness was greater.

A Typically Human Haunting

Now let's focus on you a little more. In one of her letters to you, Mom wrote that you were "*just plain wonderful.*" It's true. It is also true that you became horrible. Only that was not the real you, was it? It was the desperately unhappy you.

I'll hand you back a little *Hamlet* and propose that there was "a method to your madness." You had to leave us. But how? Consciously or subconsciously, maybe this Shakespearean thought propelled you: "*I must be cruel only to be kind; thus bad begins, and worse remains behind.*" That would explain a lot.

And this too explains a lot: You were no stranger to a father turning horrible and leaving. *You'd been through it all before.*

I've got to tell you, Dad, when you called Mom a "son of a bitch" it confused me. *Did he forget she's a woman?* Today, I believe the booze conjured up other demons in our kitchen, namely your own dead father.

I never met this grandfather. You never once spoke of him to me. We had not one picture of him in our huge box of family photos. When I asked Mom about him, she told me that when she first met you in 1941, you said your dad was dead. But in 1943 you flew to New York for his funeral.

Edward Eugene Kuhn, born in 1892, was *persona non-grata* to his sons, you and your brother, Gene, who never spoke to his children about our granddad, either. You two brothers had a pact of silence. But your sister, Kathie, wasn't in on it, so I pumped her for information.

I found out he was a pharmacist. Also, a bigamist.

She described a family like ours—secure and carefree when the children were small. Then, during the Depression, he lost his pharmacy and turned to gambling. And liquor. She remembers drunken tirades directed at your own mother, our good Grandma Kuhn. Uncle Gene remembered getting between your parents to protect her from blows.

"As his drinking increased, and we kids got older, we lived in constant fear of what he would do to Mammy, and also in a state of shame and disgrace, and tried to hide it."

So, when I asked her if you children were shocked when your father left home, she said, "No. We weren't at all surprised. He was addicted to liquor and gambling. He had become vicious and cruel to our mother. Cursing at her, saying terrible things."

Hm.

Eventually your dad left his family, moved in with another woman, married her, and raised other children. Dad! *You knew exactly how it felt!*

You were a teenager like me who watched your father walk out the door to go live with another family. And not before he turned, as Aunt Kathie described it, *"vile-like, demon possessed."* Did you understand this connection when you were living it? How could you not? Why has it taken me so long to finally understand—you already know what I am trying to describe to you. It happened to you, too!

There was more than one son-of-a-bitch in our kitchen. More than one "louse."

*

Dad, the reason we even know your father married this other woman is a story in itself. In 1968 Uncle Gene attended a New York State educators' convention in Albany. He found himself in the elevator with another man and both were startled to read

"KUHN" on the other's name tag. Naturally, they began a conversation. By the time they wrapped it up, Uncle Gene had met his—and your—half-brother.

As it turned out, Grandpa Eugene—unbeknownst to anyone—raised two Kuhn families at the same time. What did this revelation do to you, Dad? It was only months after Uncle Gene discovered this other secret son that you left us. And here I thought America's mayhem was a catalyst. What about this shock of a lifetime?

You fared so much better than your dad. Your drinking only harmed your family, not your career. Still, like your own father, you left your family, married another woman, and brought up other children. None were your biological children, to my knowledge, but you did adopt and raise them.

As I hit middle age and became more curious about our family health history, I asked Aunt Kathie when and how your dad died. "Oh," she said. "He was about fifty, and it was some irregular heart issue." This made sense because both you and your brother died of heart trouble. But recently I learned the truth.

On another Chicago trip, Brent, Audrey, and I did something new; we met our cousin, Uncle Gene's son, Hans Kuhn, and his wife, Nancy, for dinner. Forty-one years had passed since I'd last seen Hans, a seventeen-year-old boy sitting on a dock in Vermont. Now he sat at the Berghoff on Adams Street, with a handsome head of thick white hair. We swapped stories, and of course, Grandpa Kuhn bore mentioning. I had to be sure I had not imagined the story of Uncle Gene meeting his half-brother for the first time as a middle-aged man in an elevator.

"No," Hans said, "That is precisely what happened. Not only that, this guy wasn't the only half-sibling. There were more. And the reason Grandpa Kuhn came to be a bigamist is that Grandma Kuhn wouldn't give him a divorce. She believed if they stayed married, he would be legally required to support her and their children. So— there you have it—two wives."

All quite surprising, but not the real shocker.

"What happened to him, Hans?" I wanted to know. "Aunt Kathie said he died young of a heart problem."

"No," Hans replied evenly. "He was murdered."

Having long been privy to this information, Hans remained nonchalant. We three were struck dumb.

"By the mob," Hans added.

"No!"

"Yes. He owed too much money to the wrong people. Well, one night some guy came to collect. Or scare him. Or hurt him. He was clubbed over the head and died that night in his room."

Hans took a bite of his sauerbraten, shrugged, and smiled at us. I couldn't speak through the lump in my throat. All I could think of was you, Dad. You *knew* this. You walked around all the time *knowing this! How unspeakably painful for you.*

The conversation resumed and moved on to children and business and vacations. But the horrible knowledge that your father died like that devastated me, as did the fact that you carried that knowledge with you as you lived out your life.

That night in the Berghoff, over the family banter, I called to you silently. *Oh, Dad! I am so sorry. You had pain we never suspected. He was your dad. You must have loved him the way we loved you. Aunt Kathie said that before he was a bad father, he was a terrific father. You must have been so hurt and so outraged about so much. The gin helped you forget, but it made you remember, too. Oh, Dad.*

*

Your sister Kathie turned 100 last week. I got myself to Richmond to attend her birthday party. The day before the party, Uncle Gene's daughter, my cousin Rayer, and I visited with her and fished for more details about your dad. And we got some. She said that after he left your home, no one knew where he lived. It was she who finally located him.

"I was 15 or 16 and I'd have to take a trolley car, walk about eight blocks, get a bus, ride to Great Neck, walk about eight more blocks to the dirty beer joint he shared with that adulterous woman and ask for money due mother and us. I put on a suit and looked like a lady. I can still feel the bitter cold on my legs as I stood in the dark waiting for the trolley in Flushing."

"How did you know how to find him?" Rayer asked.

"I talked to people. I asked around. I walked into that filthy tavern and a man said, 'What are you doing in here?' and I pointed to the bar and said, 'that man is my father.' When he saw me, my father ran out the back door and up the stairs to the apartment he shared with that woman. I followed him up there and said, 'Daddy, we don't have any money. We can't buy food or clothes. We need money.' He'd been ordered by the court to support us, but he constantly lied and didn't. He went down and opened the cash register and took out a few dollars, and I said, 'Daddy, we need more than that.' He frowned and grumbled but he went back to the drawer for a little more. I had to do this a lot. And that dirty husband stealer would always be sitting there, ruling the place."

She said you had to do this, too, Dad—meet your father, hat in hand, to ask for money, not at his tavern, but on windy street corners.

"His was the most wasted life I have ever known. He had brains, talent, personality, good looks but let them all go down the drain with drinking, cheating, lying, and evil women."

"How did he die, Auntie Kathie?" Rayer asked.

"A heart attack."

Rayer and I exchanged a glance. We're glad she still thinks that.

"Did you go to his funeral?"

"No, my mother and I did not go. The boys went. In their uniforms. Mother and I went to his grave afterwards. We wanted to be sure he was dead and buried."

"Auntie Kathie, did you ever see the children he had with that other woman?"

"No, I didn't want to."

"Why not?"

"I would have wanted to spit on them."

*

So that word "louse." How come, Dad? Why was Mom a louse? I can't believe it was a random slur. You used it with too much conviction.

I think hard on this, and something takes shape. Knowing what I now know about your father, I presume you got it from him. That he called his wife, your mother, a louse. He was the drunken, angry name-caller, right? Or … OR… *was it what your mother called your father? Called him one, because he was one?*

A louse, we know, is a cad. A heel. Your dad was that, wasn't he? A louse is contemptible. A louse damages others, often by violating implicit pacts of decency. A louse does damage that cannot be undone. Damage that defiles what was once pure. Your father did that.

So now I think about you and Mom. We've discussed her prodigious ability to push your buttons. Did that feel contemptible? Like tactics only a louse would engage in? Maybe. But still, not quite the answer.

So, I think some more. I think about damage. Damage you don't return from. Damage that defiles. *What damage did Mom ever do?*

She put a lock on our door.

She thought she was protecting her daughters. I don't doubt that for one moment and I am awed by her guts. Still, it caused damage. That lock permanently erased a piece of our purity. It could not be returned, nor undone. I'll never be sure, but it is possible that you never forgave her that lock on the door, that you held her responsible for defiling our relationship. This could still be the wrong answer, only it feels tragically right to me.

But I know another reason. Mom told on you, didn't she?

Of course, she did. She had to tell someone. I know she told Reverend Engle, who, I am sure, would have preferred she hadn't. Still worse, she told your sister. And your mother. And that, would cause serious damage. Those two women revered you. Even a whisper of reproach would not be received well. I doubt they'd even believe it. What did Mom tell them you did? Well, everything they abhorred in a man. Everything ascribed to your father. He got dead drunk, he swore profanely, he called names, said vicious things, didn't come home. They would say, "Impossible for Edwin. Never, never for Edwin." And Mom would have told them about Audrey's conception. She may even have called it rape. Mom was honest like that. Dear God, the tumult that would have caused. More than for the anguish it caused you, you would have hated Mom for the anguish it caused them. One way to protect those poor women, was to remind them she was stark raving mad. Regardless, this crime, this betrayal of you by Mom, would cut you to the quick and seal her fate as a contemptible louse.

But I guess we can both agree—whatever Mom's crimes, she was more than sufficiently punished for them.

Today I think about you and your father and even myself, and the way we relive the dramas we grew up watching. Maybe I'm giving the word "louse" too much power and it was nothing more than the popular insult of your era, the word you heard hurled in your own angry household. I hear myself echo the words and expressions you and Mom used, (though never will you get a "louse" out of me) not as a deliberate choice, but as mindless imitation. Maybe that is precisely what makes us repeat history, our simple human tendency to mimic.

But I think there's more. I think we all feel some drive, conscious or not, to reenact our ancestral dramas, to follow some ancient script, hopefully refining the action and dialogue until somebody, somewhere, finally gets it right. Someone finally lifts the curse.

Or maybe we are all simply haunted.

At the mercy of ghosts.

Two Letters

Something that haunts me, Dad, are two letters I wrote to you. One I sent, the other I didn't. It should have been the other way around.

A lot of time and effort went into the first letter. I didn't dash it off in a fit of anger and send it to you in a huff. I wrote it in one fell swoop, then I revised it over a few weeks. I even shared it with my pastor, to confirm that I had not gone overboard, that it sounded forceful but not irrational.

I was thirty when I wrote this letter and sent it to you. Mom had died a year earlier, and I was angry at you and the raw deal I thought you gave her at the end of her life. After paying her alimony religiously for more than ten years, you stopped payments abruptly while she was at death's door. She died with you owing her money. I found this inexcusable, and I wrote to tell you so.

"You might wonder why I don't call or write much anymore. It's because I am angry. I am angry at you for not paying Mom her alimony." That's how my letter opened. I went on to say, "I see public service announcements on TV saying that even people who file bankruptcy still have to pay court-ordered alimony and child support." I also mentioned how pitiful and unthinkable I found it that at the end of her life, when none of us knew she was terminally ill, she stood in the all-night rest stop kitchen on the turnpike, making donuts at three in the morning. I remember writing, "When you knew that she had only months to live, couldn't you find it in your heart to pay her? With the end of your financial burden so near, couldn't you just pay her till she died?"

I laid into you. Still, I ended the letter by saying I had already lost one parent and I didn't want to lose the other. Life was too short to spend any more time angry. I had wanted to get it off my chest and move on while we still had each other. I guess, it was an okay letter. It was my truth, and it did help me. But I think it hurt you more than I expected.

You didn't call me about it, Barbara did. She said, "Your father received your letter and it upset him greatly. He doesn't know how to respond." I don't think you even got on the phone. I'm sorry about that, Dad. My whole life, it broke my heart to picture you heartbroken, and I never wanted to be the cause.

For all these years, I was left with an impression that you had responded to me, because I am left with your words that you had been going through hard times yourself. And yes, you had been. Maybe a year or two before Mom died is when you landed in the Nantucket hospital with alcohol abuse complications. I know, Dad. You had your own serious health issues. Perhaps I was too tough on you. You were also experiencing a reversal of fortune financially. And although I cannot prove it, I will swear Barbara was behind the end to the alimony. I am sure that after a certain point, she begrudged every cent you gave us. Lord, it must have been rough on you.

And now—only now after 40 years—I found your actual response, your words came from a letter dated two weeks after my 30th birthday, September 26, 1983.

"*Dear Val, A few weeks ago, I received your letter and have taken time to think about it. First, congratulations on birthday number 30! I'm sorry I didn't send a card, but I'll tell you about that, too ....*

Val, as you know, I spent about five weeks in a hospital where I learned a lot and had a lot of time to think. One of the things I learned was to think out responses and examine my own reactions before reacting. In fact, "react" is really not a very good word at all. "Act" is the right word for all of us, particularly me....

I could have reacted to your letter with all kinds of denials because there are lots of suppositions and inaccuracies. I'll mention that many years ago I increased payments on my own to meet "cost of living." One day when we sit down together, we can discuss some of the concerns you have. I hope we can.

One of the reasons I didn't get to send cards off to you and Audrey was that I'm just getting back to work full time and I'm pushing like crazy to make a living, so is Barbara. I feel good now, and I don't drink anything stronger than tea or coffee now.

Frankly, Val, I've never been poorer. But am very optimistic about how well things are going to be… feeling better than I have for a long time…

Val, if I have been the kind of individual you believe, I ask your forgiveness. I'm in the process of changing my life, and AA is a truly great experience.

I've loved you children greatly, I still do."

Oh, Dad.

I wrote that angry letter to you, but I sure wish I hadn't sent it.

My other letter I did need to send but I never did, and when I found it in my stationery box shortly after you died, I could've punched the walls down. I had written it only weeks before, when you were still alive. It was a letter telling you how much I loved you.

Four months previously, in June of 1989, I'd driven with my little children from Maine to Atlanta to visit you. I sat in your hospital room in silence, longing to tell you then, but afraid. I was afraid you'd think I was baring my soul because I knew you were dying, and I thought that might scare you. So, I said nothing. Such a common and foolish mistake.

Back home again, one early October morning, I sat down and wrote what I hadn't said. I didn't complete the letter, that's why I hadn't sent it. But I wrote that I remembered everything— every day of love and happiness you gave me as a child—and how no matter what had gone wrong, it could not diminish what had been right. I told you that I loved you, that I'd always loved you, and thanked you for being such a wonderful father.

And then I didn't send it.

I guess I thought I had time to complete it. No one knew you were going to die when you did. And there it sat, in my stationery box.

Back in the Present
with Answers

Pretend we are back on the ferry, Dad, heading to Nantucket. After we leave the mainland and steam past Martha's Vineyard, there's nothing to look at but sea and sky. Then, after a couple of hours of ocean, a most marvelous magic occurs. Away in the distance, something materializes. In the night, it's twinkling lights. *"Did you see that?"* we say. *A falling star?* No, there's another. And another. There're hundreds—getting bigger, brighter, closer. Why, it's a town! A complete little town out here in the Atlantic!

Approaching by day, it's a vague gray mirage we spy, flickering above the horizon. We squint to make sense of it, until the glimmering vapors burst into houses and stores and buildings, docks and wharves and sailboats, a gleaming gold church dome high on a hill.

The same thing has happened in my brain. I have travelled all the mental miles it took for so many blurry mysteries to emerge from their foggy shrouds and assume form and meaning.

I see so much.

I see the big house of my childhood daydreams. I thought if we could only find it and move into it, our family would be happy again. We would be *us* again. I see now that it's the house you bought for Barbara and her children.

In December of 2018, Brent and I drove up to Kenilworth. I hadn't been there since Christmas of 1978. We parked at the train station and walked the block and a half to Cumnor Road, as you would have walked home every night after work. We stood there on the sidewalk in front of your old house and my teenage self returned. I saw and felt with the eyes and heart of myself today AND the girl I'd been then. I was back— inside that house, inside me.

Dear God, I remember now. This was supposed to be our house. I must have been sick with envy, but I couldn't admit it. I stuffed it all so Dad would be proud of his magnanimous daughter, proud of the strong, mature girl I turned out to be. I feel so sorry for that girl. She worked so hard to hide her feelings.

We stood there a while longer, then walked back to the car and sat there, thinking.

Finally, I said, "Brent, it's great we came here today. I have fresh empathy for the girl I was back then. I needed that badly."

Looking at that big house of yours, Dad, remembering you and Barb and all those happy youngsters in it, visiting you there, then, returning to Mom—so alone, and living so meagerly by comparison—made me think, "Oh, *child, no wonder you were sad.*"

*

Scales are falling from my eyes, as though I've been mainlining some magic memory medicine. I see now that Mom tried with all her might to be superhuman. I want you to see that, too, Dad, and appreciate her valiant mission, considering her obstacles. Like running a marathon with tuberculosis, she pushed through each day and never gave up. Despite the weight in her heart, she was determined to raise us right, make us sound in body and mind.

"Don't stomp so when you walk, you'll hurt your feet. Turn on a light, you'll ruin your eyes. Don't chew your ice or you'll break your teeth. Don't frown like that, you'll get deep furrows." She was right about it all, and she was right to hound us.

She would never tell us what a word meant. She'd say, *"Look it up in the dictionary." She ordered us to: Speak the truth. Live and let live. Try, try again. Follow the Golden Rule. Obey the Ten Commandments.* And think straight. Always, always—*think straight!*

When I told her that I loved her more than anything in the world she told me I must love God more. Oh, how that answer irked me! But it was the right one for her. When I asked her what mattered most in the world, she said, "Health." I didn't like that either, but it was her truth and a wise one. I'd ask her, "What do you want for Christmas, Mom?" hoping for a hint, and she would say, "For my children to be happy and healthy." To my own children I say, "Red gloves, Lily of the Valley Perfume, a book by Elizabeth Berg." Even depressed, Mom was a better adult than I am; better than most, in so many ways.

And here's something else, Dad. It's something you've known for years, but I only found out recently and it sheds abundant new light on Mom's fear of doctors and aspirin, and demands she get some long over-due respect. (I mean, if finding herself locked up and given shock treatments at the hands of doctors isn't enough.)

In 1964, Mom's nephew, her brother's child, was diagnosed with rheumatoid arthritis at the age of eleven. His extremities were

270

turning white, then blue. Doctors prescribed aspirin to relieve his pain and increase circulation. How many aspirins a day? TWELVE TO SIXTEEN! Side-effects included nosebleeds and profuse bleeding whenever he got a cut or scrape. His parents set up heat lamps and massaged him for hours a day, months on end. At age thirteen, he went to the Mayo Clinic in Rochester, Minnesota, where it was determined that he had a very low platelet count *as a result of the aspirin therapy.* Some of the damage was irreversible. That sweet boy remained immunocompromised for the rest of his life. Knowing all this, who wouldn't be leery of aspirin and doctors? Someone not as smart as Mom, I guess.

*

I realize now that my fierce childhood love for you must have hurt Mom. It's not that she didn't want me to love you. It's that I so obviously loved you more than her. And I loved you more than her because you appeared to love me more than she did! At least that is how it looked and felt to me, so I responded accordingly. I was much too young to think of hiding it.

*

Dad, I see your face again and the hatred I perceived in it. You looked nonstop angry, and I took that look personally. Now I see that angry people look at everything angry. It's the only look they have. Even in the mirror.

And I wonder too if what I considered hatred in your eyes, may have been a reflection of what you saw in my own. The more you saw of that in my eyes, the more I saw of it in yours. I withdrew from you, recoiled from your fuming face and your reprehensible behavior, it's true. But in addition, I was a teenager, weathering the assault of adolescence. It was hard on us both.

Plus, now I know—teenagers can bring us to our knees.

*

But Audrey wasn't a teenager when you left. My God, she was eight years old. How could you leave her, Dad? I think of my own children at eight, and I cannot imagine what it would take to make me go. And therein lies the answer, I suppose—it was *that bad* for you in our house, that impossible. Otherwise, you would never have left her.

*

Dad, I see that you did all you could to keep me in your life after you left. I see that you tried in every way to show me that you left my mother, not me. I found my old calendar from the year you left—1969. It shows that you did more than take Audrey and me to dinner once a week. Sometimes you drove out to attend church with me on Sunday mornings. You called to check on me, or just to talk. You were always there, offering me whatever support I needed—financial, emotional, physical. Like driving to Urbana that dark night, to bring me home. *You did everything you could.*

*

Now that I've returned to the present with answers, I'd like to go back to Nantucket. As a child, the trip took three days. Today, from Maine, it's three hours to Cape Cod, and then two hours by ferry to the island. Yet I treat it like Camelot or Brigadoon—a magical place from another life, no longer accessible to me. As if it sits on some cloud rolled past forever. But it's there, five hours away, and I see myself sitting with my stepsister, Meg, the adopted daughter of the father I loved, then lost, then found again. I want to talk with her as women, as mothers, as grandmothers.

I want to tell Meg how sorry I am that she has had to suffer the heartbreak of her husband's sudden death, and more recently her youngest son. Someone so good and kind as she is should somehow be spared.

But I also want to talk about mental illness and say, "Our father said he left my mother because she was crazy, at least that's how the story goes, and what he told your family. But Meg, what if you had left your husband? What if the dark days finally outnumbered the bright ones and you met another man who did not suffer as David did? What if you needed to be with this new man, no matter how it hurt David, or your children? What if living with this new man meant you must leave David, leave your own children, to become a mother to this new man's children? How would they feel, David and your kids? I say all this to help you to see my own mother, after all these years, as a person. To help you understand why I pitied her so, even while I tried to be happy for our father. Why I just couldn't drop the "step" part off of "sister" no matter how much your mother insisted. I owed it to my mom.

Still, I love you, Meg, and I admire you more than you can know. You were only a little girl when your mom met my dad. Only a little girl when they scooped you up and moved you from your home and friends in Connecticut, to a new life in Illinois. You left your own Dad! No one talked much about him, except to call him bad. Did you love him? Did you miss him? You all acted so happy. But maybe you were hurting, too. Like us, you were along for the ride.

Meg, you grew into one of the best women I know. You are the "gutsy broad," Meg—you stood by David in sickness and in health. You didn't have to. Yet you did. Your children will always know that and thank you for it."

But if another man had come along and promised Meg a better life, I will admit it here and now, Dad, she had every right to go with him.

Some stay, some leave. That's life.

Mom

Mom got better. She laughed again, deep and hearty, doubled over, usually watching the Carol Burnett Show. It was a sound and sight so rare that it filled me with grateful wonder. She lived alone for the short time she had left to live, but she planted her flowers and tended her gardens and sewed clothing including my simple white wedding dress when I eloped to Nantucket and stylish maternity clothes. You couldn't prove it by the world, but she lived an artist's life of her own making. Actually, she always had. The war in the kitchen was over. She lost, but she found peace in the silent aftermath.

In one of her old love letters to you, she wrote, "*I love you, Ed, and always will.*" I believe she always did.

In the days before her death, Mom said some inscrutable things. One that still haunts me is this statement: "I hear Ed is coming to Chicago."

You and Barbara lived in Atlanta. Audrey and I cared for Mom in Maine. She made this prediction as if she'd received an oracle.

A week later, right before Christmas, we carried her shiny urn of ashes to Chicago for her memorial service. You could easily have been there, Dad. You asked me if you should come. Had I said yes, you would have come to Chicago as she prophesied. But I said no. Believe it or not, I was thinking of you. Her memorial service consisted of a pathetically tiny gathering of less than a dozen old friends of Mom's and yours. But they had been Mom's friends first, since childhood. I shuddered at the idea of subjecting you to their judgement. I thought they might hate you. Now I know I wasn't giving these adults enough credit. Still, I try to believe you may have been relieved.

Mom was bedridden for the last five months of her life. We sold our house in Clarendon Hills and rented a home by the sea in Kennebunk, where I now lived. My little boys, your grandsons, were both still little toddlers then, so Audrey and Mom moved to me, not the other way around. We set up Mom's hospital bed in the large den where a big stone fireplace and a glimpse of the Atlantic Ocean soothed us all.

If Hospice was available in Maine in 1982, we didn't know about it. Instead, we hired a few kind women to spell Audrey and me several times a week. What a hard time. Mom needed a bed pan at all hours of the day and night and couldn't sit up by herself. Worst of all, she suffered severe and relentless pain. The doctor explained it as "pleural effusion." That's when the smooth elastic coverings of the lungs and chest cavity fuse to the organs. She screamed and cried in pain, but even then, true to her nature, she refused even the mildest of medication. If I urged or coaxed her to please try, she would cry harder. It was agonizing for all of us. Eventually, we slipped small amounts of morphine into her feeding tube. Still, she howled, "*It hurts! It hurts! It hurts!*" I think it was her only way of fighting back. We kept a log as we ministered to Mom, and one of the entries left by a woman named Gladys, reads: "*She has holler all night long.*"

Yes, Gladys, she sure did. It was God-awful, wasn't it?

On her last night on earth, Mom slid into a coma and lay peaceful for a change. We didn't know it was her last day; Audrey and I were still in our twenties; we'd no prior exposure to the dying. We didn't even know it was a coma until we described it to the doctor over the phone. Mom's eyes were still open and by morning, an eerie white veil blotted all color from her left eye. That beautiful pale blue eye.

A snowstorm rolled in from the sea as we decorated the house and sang Christmas carols. Brent was in London on business and called around noon. Mom could no longer speak. But we'd been told that hearing is the last sense to go, so we held the phone to her ear and Brent spoke to her. From her one good eye, tears rolled down her cheek.

Around 3:00, my little boys napping upstairs, Audrey and I moved into the living room to hang fresh evergreen garlands in the windows, leaving Mom alone. In the midst of singing "Angels We Have Heard on High," I stopped. An unearthly knowledge washed over me, and I ran down the hall to Mom's room. I reached her bed just as she took her last breath, followed by a deafening explosion of silence. She died with her eyes wide open, astonished.

*

A few months ago, digging in one of my files, I came upon her medical records from her initial tests with the oncologist, six months before her death. Besides listing the other organs already conquered by her cancer, it also contained a psychological diagnosis. All those years ago, it disturbed me so much I had covered the lines with masking tape, making the words unreadable. Steeling myself, I peeled the tape away and read the words, "Possible paranoid schizophrenic."

So now, Dad, I will give you something. I will admit to you that I know that diagnosis was not completely out of left field. I concede that your crass comments about Mom's sanity were not all merely cruel and baseless remarks. Over time, fears and suspicions the average person would not entertain, plagued her mind. Things went missing. People were listening. (But, by God—*what if they were?*)

That's another reason Mom's old love letters tear me up. There exists no hint in a single letter that a day would come when such a thing could be said about her. To the contrary, as she writes about college and sorority life, she leaps off the page as the quintessential co-ed: brainy, spirited, and extremely popular. A leader destined for success—well-bred, well-spoken, and well-adjusted.

So, I stand by my assertion that whatever altered my mother, sprang from those three weeks in August, when Grandma died, Audrey was born, and grief and depression moved in. Surely propensities existed. Still, nothing could have prepared either of you for her response to what the future flung at you. It was unpredictable and unpreventable. So much of everything is pure dumb luck.

"Possible paranoid schizophrenic."

Well, possibly. But that was only a small portion of her. The rest of her was so much gloriously more.

Verna Marie Fogelsong Kuhn—my mother and your wife of 27 years, Dad— was a medley of superb qualities: She embodied the Golden Rule. She practiced what she preached. She was sanctified by nature. She helped us make May baskets from doilies and violets to leave on neighbors' doorsteps. She spoke sweetly to animals. She drove Audrey and me to Northern Wisconsin to flee the heat and sleep under the stars, she on a picnic table so we could sleep in the car. She brought me a ten-piece set of ceramic dishware that she collected one piece at a time from Jewel-Osco, lugged it on the train from Chicago to Maine, sitting up all night in Coach. She saw angels. She saw the future. She handled her troubles with nothing but a cup of coffee, a cigarette, and her Bible. Even in her worst, most forlorn days, she found beauty wherever she looked. Through it all, she carried herself with grace. She could have been almost anything she wanted, but all she became was your wife and our mother. So, we could be whatever we wanted.

When it came to integrity, Mom was as true to herself, as you were, Dad. It just didn't pan out as well. Except, I take heart when I read the Beatitudes in the book of Matthew—Jesus's "Sermon on the Mount"— particularly when He says, "*Blessed are the pure in heart, for they will see God.*" I have never known a heart so pure.

You

Dad, I know you loved my mother. Months before your wedding in 1943, you wrote to her, "*I want to go to sleep with my lips on yours.*" And she wrote back "*I want that, too,*" and "*every night,*" and "*let's go to bed early so we can stay that way longer.*"

God only knows where that goes. But even when it goes, its existence cannot be erased.

You loved my mother, just not forever. I believe you stayed loyal and positive in the face of her struggles, but when you saw no improvement, you lost hope and built resentment. You drank to numb your frustration, but your drinking got out of control, and both of your altered states—hers and yours— desecrated your once-sacred common ground. I can see how work and pressure, liquor and age, misery in your marriage, and the prospect of a new life with a strong, young woman, were all too much to withstand. Honestly, I give you credit for staying as long as you did.

I understand who you were to Barbara and how differently she treated you than Mom did by that point. You were Barbara's knight in shining armor. She was grateful for every good thing you brought to her life and the lives of her children. Through all the battling, Mom had lost sight of your good qualities, just as you had of hers. Barb saw nothing *but* the good. How splendid that must have felt to you. How could you walk away from it? You couldn't. I told you earlier I needed to believe you had no choice but to leave Mom and now I do. In your one precious life, you went to the love. Love changes everything.

You got a new lease on life with Barbara. You lived the vibrant, productive life you wouldn't have had with my restructured mother. But even you and Barb had your ups and downs. She had her own faults, and your drinking troubled that marriage, too, landing you in the hospital shortly after you retired to Nantucket in 1978, your dream (and mine) come true. What an unfortunate turn of events, that you should live in your house on Cisco Beach only a few brief years before erosion forced you to sell, and the ocean swallowed it up.

You moved to Atlanta, right down the street from Brent. You worked a bit in his ad agency and went to AA. You sponsored many men who needed help—husbands, fathers, sons—the help you needed years ago. You were in your sixties when you got sober, and although I wish it had happened at 206 Grant, it makes me prouder of you than anything you ever did. You and Barb lived a fine life, which, though from a distance, thankfully included me and for a short while, my three little children. You became a champion for the homeless and spent a large part of each day delivering food all over Atlanta. That's who you were. Poor Mom had maybe a dozen mourners at her memorial service. For you, it was standing room only at the largest Lutheran cathedral in Atlanta.

*

Back in 1969, after you left home, you wrote me a letter. You wrote from your heart in your own elegant handwriting and sent it to me through the mail. You tried to explain your side of things, how sorry you were to leave us, how you nevertheless had to go. It was a long letter. Within it you asked me to "*take care of Audrey.*" You told me you loved us. But the one sentence that meant the most to me, the one sentence that sustains me to this day is this, "*I loved your mother dearly for many years.*"

From those other years, those years of discord, it was only your anger, I remember. Then last night I found a photograph of a scene

I've carried in my mind's eye for decades. It's Christmas Eve, 1967. Just over a year before you left. I would have sworn it captured your ever-present ire as you sat like a prisoner at the head of the table. But I just looked at it again, at your face, and it hit me like a gut punch—*it is not anger; it is heartache.* It is so obvious it hacks my heart in two. For ages, I felt sorry for Mom. Never, ever did I feel sorry for you. *Because I didn't know you were sad.* Today I do. I am so sorry.

That radiant twenty-one-year-old sorority girl was your sweetheart, your wife. Whether through grief, depression, postpartum psychosis, or some lasting damage from shock treatment, the woman you once loved had changed. It was the hand Life dealt you both. Before you were mad, you were sad. Oh, Dad, I wish I could put my arms around you this very moment, and console you for your own anguish. Still, although seeing you sad pains me, I must confess it brings me a sliver of comfort. I have always needed to believe it wasn't as easy for you to leave as it looked. Now I can.

You didn't have an easy time of it, Dad. Not in your childhood home, nor in mine. But you were also blessed. You were blessed with two great loves in your life. Barbara brought the sunshine just in time. But Verna was your first love and, for many years, the greatest. That is a truth nothing can change.

*

Life handed me one last blessing regarding you. Our family spoke the phrase "I love you" truthfully, but sparingly. We did not attach it to the end of every conversation like many families do. On a brilliant October afternoon in my 36th year, you and I talked for a spell on the phone. Before I hung up, I impulsively said, "I love you, Dad." You in return said, slowly and emphatically, "And I love you."

Our last words to each other. How lucky could we get?

It Has No End

Who wrecked our home? Everyone. I thought maybe you did. Or at least Barbara. The truth is it was you, Mom, Barb, her kids, us kids, your fathers and mothers, the people around you, Society—everyone. Which boils down to no one.

Mom's mind or your drinking? Both. The scales tip towards her mind, but as a coping mechanism, we both know the alcohol backfired. I don't blame you for drinking, Dad. I know all about drinking to escape unhappiness. Still, you crossed into the land of diminishing returns. More harm than good, for sure.

Did you give up on Mom, before or after you met Barbara? That's messier, but my money is on after. I think you were walking the line, then Barbara pushed you over it. When? The summer before my eighth-grade year, 1966. The summer we vacationed on Lake Cayuga. You may have met her earlier, when I was in sixth grade and too happy to notice. You sure did act like a man on top of the world. New love can do that, right? Audrey and I have even wondered if loving Barbara gave you a fresh perspective and you felt like you could juggle both households. Maybe your newfound joy allowed you to minimize your conflicts with Mom, regard them as aggravations rather than ruination. As long as you had Barbara to return to, you thought you could handle anything. My eighth-grade year. That's when you decided you couldn't.

When did you decide we could live without you? I've settled on December of 1967. And that's okay, I can take it now. Because I used to believe it had been easy, but now I know it wasn't. Now I even think you decided we *should* live without you, *had to* live without you, because the real you knew we were all in agony. There was no easy way out. No tidy solution existed.

Dad, talking to you has handed me some true epiphanies. One of the best was discovering the source of my greatest sorrow. It wasn't the divorce. Or Mom's illness. Or even the horrendous endless fighting, although that is a close second. It was loving you so much, Dad. It was loving you so much then losing you. It was watching you change before my eyes, into a father I thought I had to stop loving, a father who I thought stopped loving me. And it was losing you to all those children, Dad. Losing you in plain sight. Like I became an organ donor against my will. Like I woke up one morning missing a lung, and I'm told, "Someone else needed a lung. So, we took yours. You'll manage."

And I did manage, because I needed you to be proud of me, and if I could hide my heartache—*act strong, understanding, and mature*—maybe you would be. I figured I had lost my place in your heart and with a stiff upper lift, I accepted it. Now that you had Barbara and her kids, I bowed out. I relinquished you. I didn't think I had a choice.

When I started this conversation with you, I wanted to stop feeling angry. I figured that to do that, I finally had to admit to you, that I *was* angry in the first place, that I wasn't as strong and understanding as I pretended to be. Maybe I hadn't fooled you entirely—my shrunken body and whatever Mr. Jones revealed to you about my mental state provided colossal clues—but I still needed to say it. I needed to say it *to you*. And now you know.

When I originally told Audrey that I had embarked on this journey with you, this "Coming Clean" conversation, she said it made her cringe. Her first thought was, *"No! Don't tell him! He'll be disappointed in us."* (God forbid we disappoint you, dead or alive.) I told her it's quite the opposite. You've been cheering me on.

I know now that you and Barb were two of the most fortunate people on earth to find each other, to have each other, in this lifetime. Your good fortune was not good for everyone. Still, while I lament the emptiness it left, I can, and I do rejoice in the fullness it brought. Remember how you told me that all a parent wants is for his child to be happy? Children want that for their parents, too, and Dad, I am *so glad you chose to be happy.*

What is good for some may not be good for all, but what's good for some can sure be magnificent. You were needed, Dad. By more people than us. We might say it was God's plan concerning you. Pastor Engel taught our confirmation class that the way to make a tough decision in accordance with God's will is to ask yourself: *Where is the greatest love shown?* I guess the greatest love was shown by you giving six more children a wonderful father. And I guess the greatest love I can show is to be glad you did.

Here is the truth about our family— it was no one's fault. The fearsome foes in my kitchen were just people. Good people, outstanding even, but bad things happen even when good people are doing their best. That's who raises most of us: good people doing their best, while wrestling their own inner demons.

Assigning blame is futile. You and Mom were products of your genes, your eras, your upbringing, circumstances, experiences, baggage and luck. You brought it all to your marriage, the way everyone does. Add to this Life's skulking secrets, its slings and arrows. Who knows what will result? We cannot predict a thing.

I know now that bad memories eclipse good ones. And the truth is that you and Mom gave us infinitely more good than bad. And that good—*that imperishable good*— cancels out every last sin. And if I could choose my parents all over again, I would ask for Verna and Ed. You hurt us, yes, but we all hurt our children no matter how hard we try not to, including me. Despite everything, Dad, through it all, you have remained my hero. You are both my heroes.

*

In every house, that's what we are, just people, doing what we think will make us happy, hoping it will make others happy, or at least not too sad. We face choices, make decisions, and do our best to live with them. We hurt. We get depressed. The gloom that invades us invades those who love us. We drink to ease our pain, then turn around and cause more. We renounce the past, then go out and repeat it. If we're lucky, we look for help. If we're luckier, we find it.

Our mistakes carry consequences, even when the error is unavoidable and unintentional. Often it is not a mistake at all, just a choice—a simple choice—good for some, not for all.

You were right all along, Dad. It will be okay.
It is all okay.

We hold on.

Epilogue

I've told you everything now. But what would you tell me back? Though I don't expect to hear your voice, Dad, I do hope to perceive it. So, I look out the window at the branches in the breeze. I fasten my eyes to the newborn leaves, open my mind, and feel you say: *You think you acted strong, Val, but understand this: that was no act. You were strong. All along. I am proud of you still.*

And as if that's not enough, the most incredible thing happened a few days ago. Guess what came to me in the mail! Well, I think you know—the big card I made you for Father's Day with all those pictures of me! Almost fifty years later, out of the blue, here comes a package and there inside is that card! Unbelievable! You'd kept it. Even more surprising, *Barbara kept it.* Long after you died.

When Barbara died in 2018, at the of age 83 (on December 10th, the same day as Mom, by the way, 36 years earlier), she had been living on Nantucket again, but some of her belongings remained with her two oldest children in Oklahoma. It was Katie who sent it to me, along with a few other remarkable items, including the program from *Annie Get Your Gun,* my Hinsdale High School triumph from 1971. The timing was purely uncanny. No sooner do I pronounce our conversation complete, than look what I get!

I look at that card and all those photos and—clear as day— I hear my nineteen-year-old heart shouting: *Please, Dad! Please! Remember who I was to you!*

There was also a small white envelope. containing something I could never have guessed at. A note from Barb: *Val, enclosed is a photo your dad kept in his wallet for many years...* And there it is, a snapshot. From 1958. Worn and creased. I am five; you are 41. It's you and me. Me and my dad. *"Amen,"* it tells me.

One last thing …

Some years after you died, I had a most comforting dream.

I am asleep on a cot in a cabin in the woods. The kind of square-frame cabin you find in children's summer camps—screened walls, a wooden door, and enough space for six cots or bunk beds. I am alone in this cabin, asleep in the cot closest to the door on the left. In the deep of night, I awake to find you sitting on the cot across from mine, on the right. It is dark, but you sit in a pool of moonlight, looking peaceful.

I sit up. "Dad? Is that you?"

You smile. "Yes. It's me."

"Are you all right, Dad? Are you okay?"

"Yes, I am, I'm fine."

"Are you in Heaven, Dad?"

"Yes, I'm in Heaven … It's all true." Then you chuckle, "But there's no candy in Heaven so eat up while you can."

We laugh.

"Can you stay, Dad?"

"No, I just came to visit for a moment, to check on you, and let you know all's well."

You stand up to go, relaxed, unrushed. "Lay down now, dearest, and get some sleep."

"Okay," I say. "Thanks, Dad. Thanks for stopping by. And Dad…?"

"Yes?"

"Keep the door open, okay?"

And you say, "Always."

THE END

ACKNOWLEDGMENTS

My road from first manuscript to final book was long and winding. At least three different iterations existed before I settled on the one you hold in your hands. Along the way, friends and family stepped in to read at least one of those versions. Some read professionally, supplying critiques. Others read for pleasure, giving me the much-needed thumbs up. All were deeply appreciated.

First, I must thank Susan Richards, the New York Times bestselling author, who—after meeting me at a dinner—graciously offered to read my original (way longer) manuscript, and then side by side, led me page by page to new writing epiphanies that launched me firmly on my course. Her generosity and expertise were invaluable, and I am forever grateful.

Next, I thank Rich Kent and Kate Kennedy, my two brilliant mentors from the Maine Writing Project at UMaine, Orono, where I tackled my master's at age 59. Both excellent authors and gifted instructors, I am indebted to Rich and Kate for their wise counsel and sincere encouragement.

Thank you to professional editor and long-time friend, the incomparable Suze Allen of Manuscript Mentors for her gifted creative contributions. Thanks also to Deb McKew, editor and writing group leader, for her detailed focus on the nitty-gritty. The early feedback that both Suze and Deb provided propelled me through the thick of the process.

Many thanks to Tricia Weyand, steadfast friend, original writing partner, and one of my earliest readers. Tricia's close study of my first (oh-so long) manuscript, and her years of solid support have meant the world to me.

Thank you to Lisa Stathoplos, long-time friend (teacher, actor and author) for her remarkable artist's eye, her passionate emotional response, and her ardent and continuous encouragement.

Thank you to my other early readers for their bolstering endorsements: Pam Thompson, Ren Drews (RIP), my sister-in-law, Leslie Kay Kuhn, Michael Crockett, and Nancy Frazier. Please forgive any accidental omissions. The road, as I say, was long.

Thank you to the "Real Janet" in Illinois, for her enthusiastic support from the beginning, and 57 years of abiding friendship, through thick and thin; and to the "Real Paul" who gave the green light to every word I wrote about him.

Thank you to the "Real Meg" in Nantucket, for giving me her blessing. I am profoundly grateful.

Thank you to my dear pal and champion, Karen Stathoplos (singer, actor, wordsmith extraordinaire), my absolute final editor. I am ever grateful for her impeccably keen eyes, and her unwavering, whole-hearted devotion to my story.

Thank you to my loving children for a lifetime of support. To sons Matthew and Lance, who read and weighed in with thoughtful observations, and daughter Laura Mariah, who, with pencil in hand, brought perceptive input to every page.

Thank you to my talented, singer-songwriter husband, Bob Danzilo, for his unflagging belief in my role as a writer, and his wholehearted faith in this book from its inception.

And to Brent and Audrey, my brother and sister, who not only allowed me to tell my side of our story to the wide world but cheered me on every step of the way. Thank you from the bottom of my heart.

We are indelible.

RESOURCES

Bruch, Hilda *(1973)*. *Eating disorders, Obesity, anorexia nervosa, and the person within.* Basic Books Publishers.

Public Conceptions of Mental Illness in 1950 and 1996: What is Mental Illness and Is It to be Feared? * JO C. PHELAN Columbia University BRUCE G. LINK Columbia University and New York State Psychiatric Institute ANN STUEVE Columbia University BERNICE A. PESCOSOLIDO Indiana University Journal of Health and Social Behavior Vol41 (June) 188-202.

ABOUT THE AUTHOR

 Valerie Kuhn Reid is a life-long reader, writer, educator, director, and performer. She was born and raised in Clarendon Hills, Illinois, a Chicago suburb, one train stop west of Hinsdale. Valerie left the University of Minnesota in Minneapolis in 1976 with a BS in Theatre and Education and headed to the seacoast town of Kennebunkport, Maine, where she has lived, raised a family, and taught school (most recently 20 years as Kennebunk High School's Theatre teacher and play director) ever since.

At the age of 63, Valerie completed her MS in Writing and the Teaching of Writing, from the University of Maine at Orono, in conjunction with the Maine Writing Project. Although her short story "Moving On" appeared in *Woman's World Magazine*, and two others received honorable mentions in *Writer's Digest* Annual Competitions, this is Valerie's debut book. The mother of adult children—Matthew, Lance, and Laura—she resides in Arundel, Maine, with her husband, Bob Danzilo, and dog Minka, around the corner from her grandsons, Brooks and Boden.

www.valeriekuhnreid.com

Printed in the USA
CPSIA information can be obtained
at www.ICGtesting.com
LVHW090933171024
793757LV00002B/10